MIRACLES
OF
RECOVERY

DAILY MEDITATIONS
OF HOPE, COURAGE,
AND FAITH

HARRIET HUNTER

To Linda & Justin,

Don't ever forget
your miracles
waiting for
you!

Published by: Harriet E. Hunter Publishing

Cover Design by: Babski Creative Studios

ISBN: 978-1-7327736-1-5

This is a work of non-fiction.

The content and opinions expressed in this book are those of the author and do not necessarily reflect the views and opinions, of Alcoholic Anonymous, Narcotics Anonymous or Al-Anon Family Groups

Note: For the purposes of this book, God is mentioned as "Higher Power" except in Today's Meditations. The 12-Steps are cited as: The Steps, the program, the rooms of recovery, are cited as recovery. Alcoholics Anonymous is referred to as A. A. Narcotics Anonymous as N.A.

Introduction
from the Author

I bought a small Toyota Dolphin RV, and with my two big dogs left for a seven-week cross-country trek just shy of the one-year anniversary of my daughter's passing. It was under the trees of some of Wyoming and North Dakota's most breathtaking state parks that my tears began to transform into the heartfelt idea for *Miracles of Recovery*. I had remained sober and clean through my daughter's passing and the death of her dad many years before. Having weathered the worst, I needed to do something more with my feelings. And so my spiritual awakening began.

As I prayed, cried, and opened my heart, God gave me the words to write. His benevolence engulfed me and I saw that, regardless of the situation, a drink could never make things better. The truth shot through me, the hard-core reality of this disease: *to drink is to die.* That thought must never leave me, even when life delivers the unthinkable.

Recovery *is* the life-saving, life-changing solution. If this transformation in recovery happened for me, it will happen for you, if improving your life is what you want *above all else* and you are willing to work for it. Your personal success, along with your personal Miracles, are waiting for you.

My prayer is that you will recognize yourself in these daily and month-by-month inspirations. My hope for you is that this book opens your heart and with courage, you walk into recovery where you will discover your *own* miracles! It may be the first day of your life forever filled with hope. You see, it was for me.

Please, take what you need and leave the rest. Like me, you have the power to choose.

There is a solution.

ACCEPTANCE

JANUARY 1

This New Year's Day morning, I wake wondering if this day will feel different, although nothing outward has changed. The day itself is the same as any other. The rain comes down. I still cook dinner, eat alone, and give thanks. What is different is the fact that I have reconnected to my Higher Power.

In quiet solitude, a gentle peace settles over me. I realize I am breathing slowly in the moment—but not without help. What started out as an ordinary day has become a spiritual awakening.

We no longer have to struggle. Our feet are planted firmly in the here and now with our Higher Power. In complete acceptance, I seize the day and accept what is in these moments.

TODAY'S MEDITATION
I am comforted and worthy of accepting the quiet grace of my God.

"Acceptance looks like a passive state, but in reality, it brings something entirely new into this world. That peace, a subtle energy vibration, is consciousness."
— Eckhart Tolle

MIRACLES OF RECOVERY
JANUARY 2

"Don't leave before your miracle happens!" Most of us new to recovery hear this and think to ourselves, *Yeah, right, but it won't happen for me.*

Overcoming fear and self-doubt, while making the decision to seek help is the greatest and **first** miracle. Our **second** miracle is finding our way to the rooms of recovery. We didn't just fall upon recovery nor was it a roll of the dice. Our **third** miracle is that, regardless of *how* we felt, we sought help, and we followed suggestions. Our **fourth** miracle is the choice we made to remain clean and sober just for the rest of the day.

Those not in recovery ask, "So, what's the big deal?" They do not understand that we have a disease of perception, and that our inability to stop the thoughts brought on by our stinking-thinking seeks to kill us. They will never get it, because they don't *have* it. And until we seek recovery, we don't get it either. We must come to understand how our disease drives us to insanity, or death. This acceptance is our **fifth** miracle.

From here, miracles drop like shooting stars.

We hit our knees at night and thank a power greater than ourselves for doing what we were powerless to do, no matter how hard we tried. Each morning we begin again and ask throughout the day we ask in silent prayer, "Please Help Me!" We invoke divine energy of our Higher Power as our minds open to suggestions from others. Each time we choose to do something different, we *are* the miracle that could not occur without our Higher Power.

We become part of a fellowship as we move closer to passing through the doorway of our deliverance, co-creators of miracles that transform us, one day at a time.

TODAY'S MEDITATION

We don't have to leave before our miracle happens. We don't ever have to leave. Each day we remain clean and sober, *we are the miracle* we once thought impossible.

"There are only two ways to live your life. One is as though nothing is a miracle. The other is as though everything is a miracle." — Albert Einstein

TODAY IS A PERFECT DAY
JANUARY 3

Feeling gratitude in prayer and meditation is grounding. Oftentimes, the feeling that comes before any thought is contentment. We are thankful to be alive in this moment, thankful we are able to draw these pure breaths of peace and find satisfaction in being right here, right now.

As contentment grows, thoughts rise to meet pen and paper. They connect across a spiritual gulf, confirming that we are not alone.

And so, we stand for a moment, stretching upward, celebrating the goodness that we are. Our eyes close. With arms extended, I tease your fingers as yours reach out to touch mine. Together, we feel the warm rush of air push out of our lungs to mix with the breath of billions of other living organisms. It is a signal of a connectedness that assures us we are all part of one, choosing to have a perfect day.

TODAY'S MEDITATION

In this perfect time of now, God, I thank you for allowing me to share the breath of life with others. I feel the embrace of your Great Spirit in a Universe that connects us all.

"Just because you are happy it does not mean that the day is perfect but that you have looked beyond its imperfections." — Bob Marley

RE-CREATING OUR LIVES
JANUARY 4

Recovery is about co-creating with our Higher Power. The process involves accepting different perspectives of ourselves and others. Most of all, we come to trust a spiritual practice, assured that by doing the work, the results we need will come.

A physical, emotional, mental, and spiritual transformation is the actualization of re-creating ourselves. The change begins when we walk into the rooms of recovery and ask for help. The growth continues as we stay the course, follow a few simple suggestions, and work The Steps. We are the miracles of change, the essence of a spiritual transformation that takes place as a result of our sacred program of recovery. We become comfortable in our own skin as, finally, our insides match our outsides. With deliberation, and in orchestration with our Higher Power's divine timing, we are recreated.

We love the person we've always dreamt we could be: strong, intentional, trustworthy, a person of integrity. As we continue our journey through The Steps, we walk hand-in-hand with the Spirit of the Universe. Love and tolerance become our code of conduct.

We see now, the potential for us to become, and to do, so much more. As we work The Steps in all our affairs, we advance toward emotional maturity and peace.

TODAY'S MEDITATION

Each Step comes with its own miracle, which becomes ours if we embrace our capacity to change. With you God, I practice the rituals learned in early sobriety, because I continue to get results.

"Process transforms any journey into a series of small steps, taken one by one, to reach any goal. Process transcends time, teaches patience, rests on a solid foundation of careful preparation, and embodies trust in our unfolding potential." — Dan Millman

COURAGE
JANUARY 5

Courage is faith in action. Courage is what we exhibit as we walk into the rooms of recovery.

For the alcoholic/addict, the broken, the hungover and half-dead, this single act of courage is our defining, most humbling moment.

Mustering the courage needed to enter those rooms is our first challenge. The second is finding the courage to come back, again and again.

Hope and courage grow roots of unimagined strength, one day at a time. Terrifying and uncomfortable, this work for our recovery becomes the foundation for all our decisions. We hear our intuitive *knowing* whisper *if we stay the course* a new boldness of thought will rise. As we return again and again to the rooms of recovery, we see results in the leveling of pride and a birth of hope we never believed possible. In our own desperation, we accept that we are led, no longer in charge, and begin to accept the hard fact that we never were. With courage, we come to believe we never have to return to that place called fear and despair.

Hope—is our courage to live for.

TODAY'S MEDITATION
Only by walking through darkness do we see who we really are. I'm so grateful for the courage that found me.

"I learned that courage was not the absence of fear, but the triumph over it. The brave man is not he who does not feel afraid, but he who conquers that fear."
— *Nelson Mandela*

We often hear in recovery, "If we do what we always did, we'll get what we always got." Still, there remain hundreds of thousands of individuals experimenting with addictions who continue to defy that adage. They could be those our literature refers to as mentally or emotionally unable to recall, from even a week or a few days earlier, the insanity of that first drink or drug. Some are incapable of honesty. They prefer to stay in denial and accept their plight as normal, until death or institutionalization becomes their last slip.

Some are defiant and see themselves through the invincible eyes of a twenty-year-old while making the same claims as those who have failed before them. "It's going to be different this time." And, so the story goes. Those who survive tell us that, without fail, relapse is *always* worse, never better. Those who relapse return in shame, claiming that the sweet-spot of sobriety is impossible to grasp, even as they recognize that their back-sliding demands attention.

Back-to-basics is how we let go of that incomprehensible and demoralized failure. We act as if our survival depends upon what comes next, because it does, as our next move could be our last. We call this *going to any lengths*. If we close our eyes and become honest with ourselves, we remember the extremes we took to maintain our addiction—we never claimed that was too hard for us to do.

Back-to-basics is the walk we take to stay alive and free in sobriety. We do this with our Higher Power and a sponsor, boldly determined to not pick up a drink or drug, if only for this day. We commit for this day alone to do life differently. No matter what, we do not drink or drug. And, if our tomorrow comes, we begin again, convinced that if we want to be different, we must *do* life differently. We must concede that our way did not work. Together with our Higher Power, we renew our efforts and stay sober *just for today*.

TODAY'S MEDITATION

I am grateful this is a program I don't have to practice for a lifetime, but just for the rest of today. If my tomorrow comes, I will hit my knees in prayer, and ask my God to help me.

"A friend said: 'Today the Devil whispered, "You have no strength to withstand the storm." My friend responded, "I AM the storm." — *Author Unknown*

A DISEASE OF PERCEPTION
JANUARY 7

A point driven home for many in recovery is how different we are from "normal" people. We have what is known as a *disease of perception*, one based on contradictions and false assumptions. Some, not addicted, consider addiction nothing more than weakness, something curable with a little self-control. This couldn't be further from the truth.

Alcoholism *is* an all-encompassing *disease*, progressive and deadly. Alcoholism affects its victims spiritually, emotionally, and physically. In the throes of our disease, we are spiritually bankrupt, and have a psychological illness: a thinking-obsession combined with a physical compulsion to drink. We are sure that one drink is too many and a hundred is never enough.

Most of us thought we never fit in anywhere. We perceived ourselves as different long before we picked up that first drink. On the outside, we looked normal. Although respected and accepted by many, we saw ourselves as the odd-man-out. We were never comfortable in our own skins. We boasted an exaggerated ego that masked a deep lack of confidence and self-esteem. We drank to escape, but our disease of perception was accentuated tenfold when we drank.

The addiction cycle is predictable. First comes delusional thinking, followed by a change in personality and accompanied by a soul-sickness. Alcohol is seen as the solution—our confidante, lover, and friend. Stinking-thinking insists we deserve a drink, that we are normal and can stop at will, which is the greatest delusion of all. "If only they would just quit," people say.

If only.

If arresting our disease were as simple as keeping the plug in the jug, there wouldn't be any alcoholism!

Under the light of truth, we accept the effects and repercussions of our distorted perceptions, and we quit drinking, if just for today.

TODAY'S MEDITATION

Today as I come to grips with the truth about my disease, I will work to change my attitude, beliefs, and strengthen my outlook.

"...Even nature becomes your enemy and your perceptions and interpretations are governed by fear. The mental disease that we call paranoia is only a slightly more acute form of this normal but dysfunctional state of consciousness..."
— *Eckhart Tolle*

Taking that Leap of Faith

January 8

It's hell in the hallways. Trapped between my heart and my head, I am under-nourished spiritually, mentally–deluded by sick perceptions. My life is on the line, and I know it.

We arrive at the door of sobriety sick and tired but we're not dead yet, although our risky behavior predicts that outcome. We need to leave the hallway of indecision and open the door to recovery. We don't know what's behind that door. How can we know recovery is right for us? If we're stuck in the hallway, fear of the unknown may be holding us back. Afraid of what we can't conceive, we hold on to fearful thinking.

We are being led by a force we cannot see, one that has *never* left us, or we wouldn't *be* here. By entering that unknown room, we move closer to our miracle, our restoration to sanity. We already *know* we belong in recovery. The time has come to trust the process, to trust our voice.

What can be worse than remaining indecisive until we slip or die in that lonely hallway? By taking that leap of faith and pushing the door open, serenity, peace, and a magnificent comfort become available to us, as they have to all the others who have cowered in the hallway before us, and then found their courage.

TODAY'S MEDITATION
Today I put fear and uncertainty behind me and I open the door to recovery.

"If we never had the courage to take a leap of faith, we'd be cheating God out of a chance to mount us up with wings like eagles and watch us soar." — Jen Stephens

KEEP IT SIMPLE

JANUARY 9

How can there possibly be anything simple about putting a life back together? One so shattered, it stands bare as a tree in winter with nothing but shame and self-loathing for support? Gone are the roots, rotted from our disease. Abused, battered, and too insane, we think, to be worth saving, we are near death.

That we found our way here was not by chance. *Keep it simple* is one of our first messages of hope. What could that mean to anyone broken and without faith?

Keep it simple means we keep coming back into the loving rooms of recovery and stop complicating our lives. There, we're told we can let go of having to know the answers, let go of the lies we tell ourselves about who we are because we really have no idea. We let go of our thinking, because our best thinking got us a seat in recovery, and because we are delusional. We close our eyes and we listen.

To *Keep it Simple* does not require us to respond, smile, or shake anyone's hand. We can mind our own business and simply keep coming back. Nothing more is required. No one needs to know our name, statistics, or address. No one cares what car we drive, or whether we took the bus or were driven by a chauffeur. The fact that we are here, cared about, and safe is all that matters. Coming back is the acknowledgement that we must return again and again to recovery, if we are to maintain our precious sobriety.

To *Keep it Simple* is to live clean and sober, if just for the rest of today. This way of living begins as we learn to relax, to trust, to wake up, and to come to. As we keep coming back, our lives begin to change. Miracles unfold before us. Trusting the process keeps our life simple.

TODAY'S MEDITATION
Dear God, they tell me if I don't drink and I keep coming back, I am a miracle, one day at a time.

"... Don't worry if your presentation isn't perfect; ask from your heart. Keep it simple, and people will open up to you." — Jack Canfield

SAYING GOODBYE TO ADDICTION
JANUARY 10

I always knew I was on a slippery slope. The seductive lure of addiction no longer held excitement. The monster turned its back on me more than once. This time, I felt in my bones a deadening cold betrayal.

Filled with hate and anger, a suffocating fear consumed me like a virus. I infected everything and everyone in my path. Addiction had rejected *me*! No longer could I touch that ease and comfort-place on the mountain top where I reigned strong, omnipotent—untouchable. I could no longer get there, feel the thrill, or hide behind the fraud that was my sickness. My mind pulsed with confusion and twisted thoughts of insanity. I couldn't drink, but I couldn't *not* drink! I stood at the jumping off place called a living hell. Alone, insane, I wanted to die. My best thinking held me, trapped in a downward spiral of death.

I gave up. I quit. A. A. was my last hope, and I dissolved into sobs of surrender. A calming force drew me deep into the group, and for the first time in my life I belonged. I had hope. I cannot explain the miracle of hope that found me that day, but each day, sometimes one hour at a time, I wanted to live just a little more than I wanted to die. The fellowship loved me until I could love myself. The place in my soul where death called my name receded as I began to trust the process that is recovery.

Sobriety through The Steps, its fellowship, and a Higher Power I call God sustains my thinking today. Just for today, I remain clean, sober—and free.

TODAY'S MEDITATION
Thank you, God, for my life.

"Saying good-bye to the things that cause you pain sometimes means saying good-bye to the things and the people—the addictions—who once brought you pleasure." — Cassia Leo

FALLING BACK INTO OLD BEHAVIORS
JANUARY 11

Recently, I was reminded of how easily we can fall back into old habits. A friend, who had managed for years to avoid insulin-dependence through diet and exercise, watched her health deteriorate as she resumed her old patterns of eating. Like the disease of diabetes, the disease of addiction can never be excised. It is arrested only through stubborn abstinence. Once we cross that invisible line to insanity, turning back is not an option.

In recovery, we rely upon the continued grace of a "24-hour reprieve, based upon the maintenance of our spiritual condition." Without this reprieve, we risk losing the recovery we have made.

Just as falling back into her old, bad eating habits endangered my friend's health, cutting back on meetings and isolating create a path that returns us to addiction. We become too busy. Meetings become inconvenient! But moving our recovery to the back seat invites old behaviors to take the wheel, steering us closer to a relapse. We have better odds playing Russian roulette.

We're either moving closer to the light of recovery, or further away, into the darkness of behaviors and thinking that precede a slip.

TODAY'S MEDITATION

Just for today God, let me remember that I deserve to keep the focus of my recovery on me. I will do what I must to ensure another day sober.

"Day by day, your choices, your thoughts, your actions fashion the person you become. Your integrity determines your destiny." — *Heraclitus*

THINK THE DISEASE THROUGH
JANUARY 12

Those of us newly sober struggle to stay away from our drug of choice. Without some power greater than ourselves to replace the incessant chatter between our ears, we pick up a drink or drug. It's the most natural thing for us to do. We must find a solution to get rid of that raw, physical ache in the pit of our stomach. If we do not, we are doomed to repeat what we've always done.

Recovery implores us to think the disease through.

We're asked to see ourselves as we are: half dead, devoid of love of self, and filled with pitiful incomprehensible demoralization. Some of us have physically harmed others and ourselves. Many have damaged property, stolen, cheated and lied to the point of disassociation. Still others have abandoned families and loved ones, harming everyone and everything in their path.

We haven't walked through The Steps yet. We haven't even learned how to crawl. With irrational expectations and exaggerated self-images, we are barely functional! If we are to stay clean and sober for the rest of today, we must *think our disease through* and remember what brought us here. The day we conveniently forget, is the day we stand on the edge of the cliff called oblivion.

Recovery provides a safe-haven for body and mind. We sit with others like us and, together, discover truths about ourselves. We begin to feel safe if just for this hour, as the clamor in our head gives way to calm. Experience shows that without the support of recovery and others in our rooms, most of us repeat our failures because we're still trying to do it our way.

When we gather, hope is available for the taking. In every city, in every state and country around the world, people just like us make the hardest walk of their lives into the sacred rooms of recovery.

TODAY'S MEDITATION
I must never forget the nauseating self-deprecation and destruction that brought me to my knees. The miracles of recovery keep my disease at a safe distance. The process always works when I work it.

"With every step we take we have a choice to make. Our choices determine our actions. Our actions determine who we are." — Randall Marr

LET GO AND LET GOD
JANUARY 13

Let go. Let Go. **LET GO**? How do I let go of opinions, beliefs, and the ever-present stinking-thinking that are normal for me? If I let go of *my* way of thinking, what would be left? Will I still exist, or will my brain shrink from so much letting go?

This process of letting go begins the day we walk into the safety of our rooms of recovery and let go of stinking-thinking long enough to embrace open-mindedness. We suspend our ego and replace it with a humility strong enough to listen, observe, and be open to the miracles of recovery before us.

We begin to let go without knowing we are letting go, as though we are being led by a power greater than ourselves, because we are. Each day sober proves to us that letting go is safe. We get a glimpse of serenity and begin to trust the process of our unfolding. We let go of old ideas, and for the first time, find that hope feels possible. We rely on our Higher Power instead of our flawed and imperfect thinking. We take responsibility for our actions and decisions. We grow up.

Let go and Let God is a measure of our growing maturity. This is the tool we use to separate what is within our control, and what can only be changed by our Higher Power. *Let go and Let God* marks the beginning of establishing healthy boundaries for us as we embrace trust and surrender.

TODAY'S MEDITATION

I'm grateful that, with practice, I receive the wisdom to know the difference between what my business is and what is not.

"The best way to say, "Thank you, God," is by letting go of the past and living in the present moment, right here and now. Whatever life takes away from you, let it go..." — Miguel Ruiz

H. A. L. T.

JANUARY 14

Like any good carpenter, we strive to use the right tool for the job at hand. In this way we avoid frustration and fear. One such spiritual tool is H.A.L.T., the acronym for hungry, angry, lonely, and tired.

Hungry: When we're hungry we must stop and eat. Listening for signals from our body is so important. In recovery, self-care with proper nourishment helps to repair our depleted bodies.

Angry: Anger is an indicator that trouble is not far away. A resentment, we're reminded, is often a drink waiting to happen. When angry, we must pause and prevent harm to ourselves and others. We must ask to be forgiven and talk with a sponsor or close friend.

Lonely: A lonely mind riddles us with questions. What is it about me that is causing me to be lonely? What would make loneliness better? Why am I lonely? Remember *This too, Shall Pass* and don't give in to the need to act out. Redirection through service work, and helping others, lifts us up and out of ourselves. Staying alone in our heads makes for bad company.

Tired: This is a comfortable excuse to slide back into addiction oblivion. Getting sufficient sleep, especially when new in recovery, is important for healing and helping our bodies and minds return to a strong physical and psychological state.

TODAY'S MEDITATION

What wonderful support in the fellowship I have today. I am thankful for the tools of the program that support me.

"You, yourself, as much as anybody in the entire universe, deserve your love and affection." — Buddha

TRUSTING THE PROCESS
JANUARY 15

As I look back over my life with the help of several fourth steps and insightful sponsors, a single observation becomes apparent. I have serious trust issues. I have them with everyone. Afraid I could never measure up, I had to control you because I couldn't trust you. Drinking alleviated the pain that came with the unmanageability of trying to control the pieces of the puzzle that was my world.

The words I first heard in recovery were, *Trust the Process.* It means we walk blindly and relinquish everything we think we know for something we can do nothing more than put faith in. Those three powerful words imply action on our part, trust. We trust that we are safe in changing our life completely through the process of recovery. We trust that when we take a chance and do the next right thing, the next right thing will happen. We trust that if we keep coming back and level our pride enough to take direction, miracles of recovery will transform us from the inside-out. Once transformed, our quality of life improves dramatically.

We are transformed with humility, grateful to continue to trust this process of faith in action. And as we trust the process, change infiltrates our being and, unless we turn back toward the darkness and death of addiction, that change remains.

By continuing to come back, continuing to trust the process, we are confident we will find ourselves where we're supposed to be. Walking in a faith we cannot see.

TODAY'S MEDITATION
Without you, God, I have *no* ability to change me. I am comforted knowing you continue to do for me what I cannot do alone.

"In choosing to practice unconditional gratitude you are choosing to trust the process, to honor your feelings and to place your faith in an outcome of inevitable grace." — William Holden

"We admitted we were powerless over alcohol—that our lives had become unmanageable."

Those of us who admit we are powerless over our addictions understand that Step One is our jumping off place. Committing to Step One means complete surrender. On the surface, surrender sounds easy to do, but it isn't. Our inability to surrender lies between our ears, in our minds.

The disease of alcoholism insists that drinking is okay and asserts that alone, we can manage and control our drinking. This is the insanity of alcoholism. The mental obsession comes first, often days or weeks before the actual drink itself. With excitement, we see ourselves preparing for a holiday or dinner with friends or family. The first sip starts a physical compulsion followed by a mental obsession that prevents us from walking away from a second one and more.

The mind says, "Of course you can walk away!" but go ahead and try walking away if you want to know your truth.

We take a drink, and then the drink takes us. In no time, our lives become unmanageable. This process is referred to as the "phenomenon of craving" whereby, together with our disease of perception, a mental obsession ensures with certainty, our inability to stop once and for all.

In recovery we're told that this is the only step that must be taken with complete perfection. The solidity of this step must be able to survive the next eleven steps. Step One is the problem. When we drink, not only are we powerless over alcohol and find it difficult if not impossible to stop, but the rest of our life is unmanageable. We're told that drinking is just a symptom of a disease that promises death for many chronic drinkers. An alcoholic without a resolution to stop drinking is the equivalent of someone jumping out of a plane without a parachute. We must surrender to the certainty that this will *never* work, and so it is with alcohol. Our drinking will *never* be the parachute that saves us. Sooner or later, it will be the leap to oblivion that ends in our death, jail or institutions. Many continue to believe in the insanity that *this time it will be different*, but the results are, without exception, the same or worse, than before.

Step One is completed with hope that says just for the rest of today, we cannot drink. This is how we stay sober.

Acceptance that we cannot stay sober without help must follow us always. The God of our understanding, and the fellowship give birth to a transformed life. The miracles of sobriety come true for us as we stay the course, one day at a time.

TODAY'S MEDITATION

Please help to keep me sober, God, just for the rest of today. As I lean on you, I trust that I never have to be alone again.

"At times it is strangely sedative to know the extent of your own powerlessness."
— *Erica Jong*

ADDICTION, A DISEASE OF MORE
JANUARY 17

In one of our meetings, a woman raised her hand to speak. "My name is Michelle and I have the *disease of more.*"

The phrase, the disease of more, is so fitting because that's exactly what addiction is. One cookie, one pull of the slot machine, one drink or drug always spells more for those of us with addictive tendencies or personalities. Addictions are born out of a disease of perception. The perception that we can never get enough is just one illusion that keeps us stuck. This notion tells us that more is always better. The complications and long-term effects of our disease never enter our mind.

People with addictions do not think like normal people. This sickness affects our emotional and spiritual self, along with our physical and psychological disposition. We believe that only the getting of "more" can quell our insatiable hunger, until sheer desperation causes us to fill the endless void with faith in our Higher Power and the fellowship of recovery.

TODAY'S MEDITATION
The rest of today is all I need to think about. When tomorrow comes, I begin again, and pray for help to keep my motives pure.

* * *

"We are addicted to our thoughts. We cannot change anything if we cannot change our thinking." — Santosh Kalwar

STAYING CLEAN AND SOBER
JANUARY 18

If overcoming addictions meant nothing more than to not pick up the first drink, we would not have alcoholism. The problem that comes with picking up the first drink is staying-stopped.

Those of us who cross that imaginary line of no return understand in a way only we can, the indisputable, undeniable *trance* of addiction. We have embarked upon a journey that affects the totality of our existence. Brain cells are destroyed, some never to return. Yet, many of us find perpetual comfort in the abyss of insanity, preferring the suffering we know.

Addictions are vultures of the soul that strip away every semblance of the person we once were, until we become unrecognizable, even to ourselves. How can we ever recover? Recovery begins when the addicted person says they are ready to change. Attending that first A. A. meeting is a sure sign we are willing to begin a life-change, but real sobriety takes root in the coming back. Step meetings are found in telephone directories, the internet and hospitals. They occur on the hour in many cities. Today, treatment facilities, detox centers and halfway houses, whose function is to help the alcoholic or addict begin reintegration to sobriety and self-sufficiency, are available in most major cities.

The Steps are simple programs for complicated people. Recovery shows how we remain clean and sober *just for the rest of today*. We practice with a sponsor or the fellowship, staying sober sometimes fifteen minutes, continuing again for another fifteen minutes, and so forth. We postpone engaging our addiction until we reach 24-hours. Then we begin again. Meetings help shield us from temptation and together we stay sober.

The Steps are programs designed to avert deadly consequences for people with the cancer-like progression of a disease that grows worse, never better. Still, around the world, people achieve sobriety every single day through abstinence. Maintaining sobriety, however, requires a steadfast willingness and absolute commitment to go to *any* lengths to achieve long-term sobriety. Alcoholics Anonymous remains for many the most successful, reliable method to maintain sobriety. The Steps, fellowship and meetings, together with the guidance of a trusted friend or sponsor, provide support principles and tools for daily living.

Miracles happen in our rooms every single day. Never, ever, do we have to walk this walk alone —if we don't want to.

TODAY'S MEDITATION
Just for today I know that if I don't pick up that first drink or drug, I am safe. I pray for your Grace, God, to maintain my sobriety one day at a time.

"We can think about the drink all we want but we just don't get it wet."
— *Dick M.*

HALF MEASURES
JANUARY 19

Have you ever tried to bake a cake without eggs? Or take a shower without soap? In recovery we call these *half measures*. Something essential is missing. This cannot be our best effort. We live in a world where time dictates that we hurry up, don't take long, don't be late. We perform as if some effort is better than nothing. We spend our lives dancing to a half-measured beat.

The Big Book of *Alcoholics Anonymous* states that, "Half measures availed us nothing…" The status-quo, insofar as our drinking is concerned, has the power to kill us. If we want to live a happy and healthy life, our disease cannot be treated with half-measures.

So we dig in, resolved to go to any lengths to stay the course, just for the remainder of the day. When tomorrow comes, we say a prayer of gratitude for another day of sobriety and ask the universe, or Higher Power, for help. We do again what we did yesterday. Living in the moment helps to protect our resolve from half-measures and assures long-term success one minute, one hour, one day at a time. Many of us do this with great results. Experience shows if we build on our successes, regardless of how small, we'll achieve another day of sobriety.

TODAY'S MEDITATION
Dear God, I know that half-measures continue to avail me nothing no matter what I do. Please help me to keep my sobriety close to my heart each day.

"The era of procrastination, of half-measures, of soothing and baffling expedients, of delays is coming to its close. In its place we are entering a period of consequences." — Winston S. Churchill

THE GRACE IN THE GIFT OF CHANGE
JANUARY 20

The mere thought of change was my shortcut to fear. I loathed any kind of change. That word alone was all that was needed to make me pick up a drink. *Why change anything?* was my attitude. My addictions, steeped so deeply in denial, could not tolerate the thought of change.

Recovery presents change as a life or death proposition. It screams, "Change or Die!" If nothing changes, we continue the madness. Recovery requires a constant willingness to go to any lengths to sustain grace by making the needed changes in our lives.

One of our first miracles of change was to wake up clean and sober. We knew no human power could maintain the grace it would take day-in and day-out to hold on to that sobriety.

Most of us in active addiction tried every conceivable way to be better, to act stronger, to be fearless and face everything. Not until we traded drugs and alcohol for the miracle of a nameless faceless grace could we find the courage to change.

That courage appeared when we came to believe we were not alone.

Each day, with heartfelt gratitude, we welcome another 24-hours and release who we used to be for the stronger and more competent person we are now.

We have become warriors on a personal crusade for change. The greater our spiritual distance is from the next drink or drug, the easier it is to honor who we've become because of the grace in the gift of change.

TODAY'S MEDITATION

I remember, God, I can do nothing without you. Thank you for the encouragement that keeps me moving toward the light of universal love and acceptance in all things, including change.

"Desperation is the raw material of drastic change. Only those who can leave behind everything they have ever believed in can hope to escape."
— William S. Burroughs

SOUL-SICKNESS
JANUARY 21

Supplied by an abundance of family dysfunction and black or white perfectionistic thinking, I was a product of prejudices and emotional intensity. I was convinced I was doomed to a life in purgatory. I knew no amount of Hail Mary's on the rosary would save me.

Soul-sickness is a key aspect of addiction. Its origin can be traced to internal wounds from emotional, physical, or sexual abuse. These unhealed wounds may rob us of the coping skills necessary to handle problems and typical life issues. Soul-sickness becomes a checking out of life. Soul-sickness has been defined as a state of dejection and depression. Recovery considers this condition an affliction of the mind, self-will, and the soul.

For some of us, soul-sickness showed up as we believed we sat the right hand of the Father. We needed no one as we saw ourselves in complete control of everyone and everything. Recovery, through The Steps, is a program with great success through its spiritual approach to humility and to a healing on all levels. There is no religious affiliation, and none is necessary to maintain sobriety.

Healing soul-sickness begins with a willingness to seek and accept some power, or something greater than ourselves. Our way didn't work. Soul-sickness, exchanged for a loving Higher Power designed by each of us, becomes the hope we cling to that one day at a time we can be happy, joyous and free.

TODAY'S MEDITATION
Dear God, you fill my darkest hours of dread and desperate thinking. I seek you in daily prayer and meditation for the strength and courage I need in all things.

"Problems are solved from the inside out not the other way around."
— *Vivian Amis*

JUST FOR THIS DAY
JANUARY 22

We focus on our breathing. That's how close we stay to ourselves, protecting and nurturing the little child within. As our arms embrace us in a loving hug, we're reminded that we are lovable. We remember we are only breathing in this moment. Because we're alive in the here and now, we don't have to concern ourselves with tomorrow, last week, or the *what-if's* of the future.

Just for today we focus our attention on what is in front of us and do what we must without concern for the outcome. We remember that we are accountable only for doing the next right thing. Our Higher Power is in control of the results, whatever they might be.

For the remainder of our 24-hours, we consider doing something for someone else no matter how small. As we do for others, we become closer to the sunlight of the Spirit and feel content where we are. We look for examples of gratitude in all things and open our heart to a humbleness that resonates as we connect with our Higher Power in prayer throughout the day.

Just for today, we look for acceptance of what is, without expectations. As we breathe in serenity, we are fulfilled and at peace in the moment. Our heart embraces its truth with conviction; we are enough.

TODAY'S MEDITATION
Dear God, just for this day I will work on allowing you to be you, so that I can take care of who I am.

"How is a person supposed to prepare for what happens tomorrow when there's just no figuring out today?" — Jenny Han

THE GIFT OF DESPERATION
JANUARY 23

Walking my dogs in the fresh air, I thank Higher Power for a life recreated in serenity and peace. My contentment in the moment is like being wrapped in a lover's arms: safe, secure, and sheltered, light years away from the life I once led.

Before recovery, I knew only dread and hopelessness. I spent each day cloaked in debilitating fear with a conviction that my world would end at any moment so, what was the point of living? The smaller and darker my world appeared, the more desperate I became.

It is counter-intuitive, but we should remain grateful for the gift of desperation. This desperation forces our cries of surrender to accept the miracles of recovery. It is in turning away from desperation that we find the courage to become willing to believe there is life after our death from addiction.

Our gift of desperation is a constant reminder of what our life can be in an instant if we revert back to old ways of doing. As we *think-the-drink-through*, we feel the hopelessness of months, even years earlier, and the complete desperation that brought us into the rooms. We pray that reminder will never leave us.

Each day is the day we stop where we are and give thanks to our Higher Power who carries us when we cannot walk, and reminds that just for today, life is wonderful!

TODAY'S MEDITATION
I am grateful for the gift of desperation. It brought me to a truth that cannot be denied. Miracles allow me to find a way out of the self-induced stupor of addiction and into the light.

"The gift of willingness is the only thing that stands between the quiet desperation of a disingenuous life and the actualization of unexpressed potential."
— James Patrick McDonald

LOOK FOR THE SIMILARITIES
JANUARY 24

Our first walk into recovery is intimidating. We enter a place completely unknown where people speak a different language, the language of the heart.

Our first suggestion is to listen to, and look for, our similarities with others. The similarities are always there, although it is easier at first to see our differences. In silence, some of us say to ourselves, "I never drank or drugged like *that*. I hurt no one, was not divorced, never lost children or a job. I've never been in jail."

But in time we become comfortable enough to see that while we are all different, the ism's, *I, Self, Me* of our disease, are the same for us all. As we take turns in conversation relating how alcohol or drugs affect our lives and that of our families, a common thread of likeness appears. We soon find ourselves an equal among brothers and sisters. How we arrived and what happened may be marked by difference, but the deadening pain and shame we feel is dramatically the same.

As people took turns sharing their experience, strength and hope, we hear snippets of our own story, each of us becoming part of a shared narrative. This identification with others is a miracle of healing for many. The miracle of hope gives birth to a recognition that this could happen for us too, as we identify with others who are further along in the journey.

This is how the process of becoming honest begins.

As we become honest with others, we offer them ourselves, becoming more open-minded each time. For many of us, this is the first time we are no longer alone. Those who have the guts to keep coming back, become stronger, knowing that together we cannot fail.

TODAY'S MEDITATION
God, help me remember that in the rooms of recovery, I am an example for others to see. In our pain and similarities, we are all connected.

"Understanding languages and other cultures builds bridges…Through understanding, people will be able to see their similarities before differences."
— *Suzy Kassem*

WHAT IS YOUR HIGHER POWER?
JANUARY 25

Approaching Step Two, many of us are apprehensive. Can anything restore us to sanity, even a power greater than ourselves? In active addiction, we gave up a God for our drug of choice, but even that wasn't enough. Now we want restoration without strings. Sick and tired of being sick and tired, we are unconvinced that some power can restore peace and serenity. In active addiction, we wrongly thought we controlled life. Realizing how wrong our thinking is, we become willing to concede that a power exists, and we that are not it.

So, we design a Higher Power we can live with. Some make the rooms of recovery that power. Others find their Higher Power in nature; still others see it in a Great Spirit of the Universe. It matters little what our Higher Power is. What *does* matter is the recognition that this entity is more powerful than ourselves, as our own best thinking failed us.

Once convinced that lack of power is our chief dilemma, we allow a Higher Power to be the force that drives our recovery as we work The Steps, empowered by the assurance that we are no longer alone.

TODAY'S MEDITATION
With the help of The Steps and the fellowship, I believe that something greater restores me to sanity. I can't. He can. I'll let Him.

"For those who believe, no proof is necessary. For those who don't believe, no proof is possible." — Stuart Chase

BLESSED RECOVERY
JANUARY 26

Staying clean and sober, just for today, is the single most important thing I can do. I have given up the insane idea that one drink will be different from the last time.

There can be no illusions that a drink can make anything better. When I drank, shame and guilt transformed me. I blamed *everyone* for my self-loathing and drank self-pity and hate with every glass. Stuck in the sludge of soul-sickness, my thoughts suffocated me. Without hope, death seemed a welcome retreat.

My life flourishes today because of recovery. As miracles continue to astound me, I change beyond anyone's wildest dreams. My purpose now, is to help others by contributing in meaningful ways. For once, my insides match my outsides.

Just for today, I never have to drink again. If tomorrow comes, I ask for the courage and strength to abstain again, and to do those things that will change and enhance my life.

Grace and the life-saving gift of recovery remind me of where I've been, and the changes I've had to make to get me where I am today. Happy! Joyous! And Free!

TODAY'S MEDITATION
Thank you, God, for my life today. I am responsible for my thoughts, my intentions, but most of all, for my actions.

"Learn how to bless others around you without reservation, be generous with the kindness of your blessings to others. A generous gesture may reach and heal a wound." — Kemmy Nola

LEARNING TO LAUGH AGAIN
JANUARY 27

Laughter was no laughing matter to me. This emotion was tucked down so deep, I was only remotely aware of its existence. There was nothing funny about my life.

Our precious room of recovery offers a place of protected acceptance. In that safe place, we are encouraged to laugh and lighten up. As we grow closer to forgiving ourselves, we experience a lightheartedness within looking to find its way out.

Thanks to the fellowship, we begin to trust that life itself is not so serious, but rather, it was the negative way we perceived life that was off. After all, our stories are just that —our *stories*. What was once pathetic doom and gloom can now be looked at as an historical series of events that transpired between people who, had they known better, would have done better.

The fellowship taught me how to laugh lovingly at myself and others not in a way that demeans, but one that demonstrates with compassionate understanding.

TODAY'S MEDITATION

Laughter is the balance necessary to accept all of me. I can be a silly, even funny, participant in my life.

"I never would have made it if I could not have laughed. It lifted me momentarily out of this horrible situation, just enough to make it livable." — Viktor Frankl

RESPONSIBILITY TO OURSELVES
JANUARY 28

I came to recovery broken, my life shattered. By the time I became willing to do whatever it took, I was desperate for relief and if relief didn't come, ready for death to take me. Recovery was the last option, the last house on the block whose door I could knock on for help.

Many people come to recovery to escape the consequences of past actions. The judge, the boss, the spouse, the police; everyone knew long before we did, that something was dreadfully wrong with us.

As the fog of denial lifts, The Steps were the vehicle that moved us toward acceptance of the devastation we inflicted on others while in our addictions. We see now we are hurt people who hurt people, and realize we must be responsible for those wounds or nothing changes.

Miracles of recovery become our hope for a new recreation. For those of us who want all the promises recovery offers, we can never go backwards, for to do so is to surely die. We know too much now. For the first time in our lives, personal integrity and a sincere desire to give back to others has become the mainstay of our existence. We have access to miracles founded in faith no one could possibly be privy to unless they too, have experienced recovery.

We are responsible to ourselves today. We align ourselves with our Higher Power to grow along spiritual lines. Moving forward, we see that our mission is to do the next right thing and help others. We are blessed with the gift of humility, because in faith, we realize we are responsible.

TODAY'S MEDITATION
Gratitude is the beginning of my complete joy in recognizing what needs to be changed in me.

"Our awesome responsibility to ourselves, to our children, and to the future is to create ourselves in the image of goodness, because the future depends on the nobility of our imaginings." — Barbara Grizzuti Harrison

EMBRACING THE GREY
JANUARY 29

I grew up in a family of hard-core extremists. Life events were either black or white. All or nothing. Not until recovery did a willingness to compromise and accept possibilities instead of absolutes become possible. We call this place where absolutes do not exist *embracing the grey*.

This changed perspective makes us aware of our unlimited possibilities. The more we invite change, the closer we come to approaching that middle we call grey. In the grey where open-mindedness dwells there are no absolutes. Only a lack of willingness hinders our transformation. In the grey, we understand, with certainty, that although we cannot see, we are secure. Faith leads us to the unknown where all things are possible.

We realize in the grey that our thinking and judgment are dependable, we find a balance in most things. We come to trust our intuitive thinking. We share with others our successes and our unimaginable growth. Embracing the grey allows us to discard our nevers and replace them with *anything is possible* as we seek the middle.

TODAY'S MEDITATION

Thank you, God, for the capacity to transcend extremes for the middle. I never have to say *never* again.

"In reality, situations are almost always shades of gray, not black or white. Falling victim to black-and-white thinking tends to exacerbate problems, including depression, anxiety, and conflict in relationships." — Jake Van Der Borne

STAYING THE COURSE THROUGH GRIEF

I shared with friends how I maintained my sobriety when my husband suc-
cumbed to cancer many years ago. My thoughts were not about drinking,
but rather how I was going to live without him. When my only child passed,
the question became not how I would live but rather, what was the *point* of
living? I was swathed in survivor's guilt. I was the home-wrecker, addicted
wife, and absent mother. Why I wondered, am I here? Am I being punished?

Miracles of sobriety bring new challenges. We learn the hard way. In order to
live a serene and loving life and provide meaningful help to others, we must
first become an unwavering warrior for ourselves.

Some of us find the gift of grief-absorption. Neither minimizing nor wal-
lowing in our pain, we allow tears to fall in honor of those gone before us.
Recovery teaches us to walk through life's most horrific losses with a dignity
and integrity we never knew we possessed. As we give ourselves permission
to grieve with the same intensity we bring to laughter, we see no difference
now in our emotions. No longer do we deny celebrating them equally. We are
entitled to both tears and laughter.

Many are comforted by the acceptance that unanswered questions belong to
our Higher Power and are none of our business. Our business is to embrace
acceptance and ask, "What is Your Will for me just for today?" As warriors
in recovery, our only choice must always be to stay the course no matter
the cost. We honor those we have lost and we honor our vulnerability as we
remain in the middle of our fellowship and welcome the gentle nurturing
of others with healing hope. As we remember to pray, *thy will be done*, we
accept what is, right here right now. We look down at our feet, acknowledge
our presence, and become a newcomer to recovery all over again. In our
grief, we do everything for our recovery we've always done—and more as our
disease nudges our thinking closer to the hallway of indecision.

We grieve and let go, and repeat this process until the light of acceptance
heals our woundedness. Continued practice brings a gentleness and a loving compassion for ourselves and for others. We remember that everything

passes. Grief becomes a constant lesson to love ourselves with tender, gentle care, as we stay the course and help others.

TODAY'S MEDITATION

Today, God, help me to remember that my emotions belong to me without the judgment of good or bad. This Too, Shall Pass.

"There is a sacredness in tears. They are not the mark of weakness, but of power... They are the messengers of overwhelming grief, of deep contrition, and of unspeakable love." — Washington Irving

STEP TWO

JANUARY 31

"Came to believe that a power greater than ourselves could restore us to sanity."

A beautiful stanza in *Amazing Grace* reflects Step Two in a profound way. The lyrics read in part, *"I once was lost, but now I'm found..."* Step Two opens our hearts to the solution. Step Two is the step of *hope*. For many of us, we are relieved to accept that an all-encompassing Higher Power exists, and the knowing that we are not it!

We accept that our recovery is spiritual in nature. No longer must we aspire to religious ideologies that have deterred many from seeking any recovery at all. Our spiritual beliefs are a personal matter.

That power greater than ourselves can manifest in many ways. A friend shared her spiritual epiphany. Looking outside her kitchen window, she saw the brilliance of the sun streaming through the leaves on the trees. This simple yet profound image represented that power greater than herself. Others find their deity as described in the Big Book of *Alcoholics Anonymous* as the "Spirit of the Universe," or a "Great Reality Deep Within." Still others commit to their fellowship or their G.O.D. *Good Orderly Direction*, while some find a *Group Of Drunks* as their power. Neither right answers nor wrong answers exist, only our *individual* answer.

TODAY'S MEDITATION
Freedom in Step Two allows me to design my God with the qualities that I need. Trusting this process is my door to a spiritual intimacy necessary to move forward to Step Three.

"Prayer is not asking. It is a longing of the soul. It is daily admission of one's weakness. It is better in prayer to have a heart without words than words without a heart."— Mahatma Gandhi

RE-CREATING OUR LIVES
FEBRUARY 1

Chapter 5 of "How It Works" in the Big Book of *Alcoholics Anonymous*, tells us that "Half-measures availed us nothing..."

A. A. 's 12-step program, so divinely written, explains the importance of our changing everything one day at a time. Most people familiar with recovery understand that just changing jobs is stressful enough, but the thought of changing everything is overwhelming!

Prior to recovery we lived a well-orchestrated lie at every turn with denial as our shield from the truth. Many of us chose, as if at a buffet, what we thought was enough to ease the pain of addiction. Some believe meetings are enough to maintain sobriety but the *substance*, the strength of fortitude to support changes necessary for the long drought ahead wasn't there.

Re-creating our lives requires a spiritual awakening and action without negotiation if we are to sustain sobriety. Such change shows that having worked The Steps in all of our affairs, we have been transformed. We are reminded that progress is essential as we grow along spiritual lines. For those who want everything the miracles of recovery have to offer, there can be no short-cuts whatsoever. We lived our lives before recovery one shortcut after another.

Today, our life depends upon what we do differently every single day to re-create the life that we deserve.

TODAY'S MEDITATION
I'm grateful to know none of this must be done perfectly. Each day I will always be a work in progress.

"It is not in the stars to hold our destiny but in ourselves."
—*William Shakespeare*

TRUSTING OUR HIGHER POWER
FEBRUARY 2

Trusting a Higher Power while in our addiction insanity was impossible. So much dysfunction and hate prevented faith for some of us from being actualized.

It takes the miraculous gift of sobriety to gently open hearts to a trusting awareness that a Higher Power, something all-powerful and all-encompassing exists. Only then can we let go of our control and our need to know the unknowable. In this surrender to a higher power we find our miracles.

As we trust the process of recovery, we surrender. Sheltered in a comfort that proves we have no need to know the constitution of faith, we accept what is.

As we awaken, we trust we are still breathing. We detach from our need to understand and accept a humble walk into the unknown. Our place in the universe is purposeful, and our Higher Power is all that we are not.

TODAY'S MEDITATION
Dear God, I am comforted to accept you as you are. Just for today I will not question or look for answers that are none of my business.

"Basically, there are two paths you can walk: faith or fear. It's impossible to simultaneously trust God and not trust God."
— Dr. Charles Stanley

ACT AS-IF

FEBRUARY 3

What joy there is to know we can begin our day over again, right where we are! Maybe we need to pause and become centered again or just have time alone to reflect where we've been and where we are now. Whatever the reason, if restarting our day is important, we need to act as-if.

Act as-if differs from *fake it till we make it*. In recovery, we're done with pretending or faking anything anymore. We demonstrate new positive behaviors and embrace new emotions while *acting as-if* this new mindset is already a part of us, until it becomes automatic. And with repetition, it does!

We *act as-if* we're open and honest. We *act as-if* people are being who they are without harboring an expectation to the contrary. We *act as-if* in a hundred ways because we're practicing a new way of living.

One day we wake up to see we've become the person we've always wanted to be and embrace our authentic self. Acting as-if becomes real.

TODAY'S MEDITATION
Today I practice being perfectly connected to you, God. I will act *as-if* until my actions become my new behavior.

"Stop acting as if life is a rehearsal. Live this day as if it were your last. The past is over and gone. The future is not guaranteed."
— *Wayne Dyer*

AWARENESS, HERE AND NOW
FEBRUARY 4

Some days we wake already ahead of ourselves, thinking about what we will be doing, or should be doing six months from now. Other days we see nothing at all, blinded by obsessive thoughts that lock us into compulsive fear and dread of what is around the corner.

We who have addictive personalities know our thinking never sleeps. Our minds expect we will drift off into our *what if* or, *maybe I should…* We've entered a place of daydreams and watch them morph into a cloud of fear that takes us out of control. We're unable to stop that incessant, squirrel-caged thinking unless we are first aware that it has taken us over.

Acceptance gives us the awareness that if we can spot that cage in our brain, we can *stop* right there. We are rocketed back into our 24-hours of living where we belong. Staying in the moment of today is the *only* place where our thinking is safe.

We're only living right now. There is nothing else. We keep trying to reach for tomorrow but it never works without compulsive thoughts and fears of the unknown.

We're convinced we are functional and efficient as we keep our focus on what needs to be done before us right here, right now. Here we allow ourselves one step forward in our thoughts as we keep the parameters of our thinking small, within the confines of our 24-hours. In the *awareness of here and now*, our convictions and actions make for history in our todays, and nothing more.

TODAY'S MEDITATION
I'm grateful to stop where I am and begin my day again with a simple prayer of, *God, please direct my thinking.*

"*In yourself right now is all the place you've got.*"
— *Flannery O'Connor*

BE RIGHT OR BE HAPPY
FEBRUARY 5

I grew up in a tumultuous home where alcohol abuse elicited yelling, plead-ing, and nasty threats of retaliation from one parent to the other. We children tried to hide or ignore the fighting but could never get far enough away.

As we grew older, Mom became more protective, controlling, even stifling in her effort to hold on to a sense of normalcy. One dirty dish in the sink would trigger a barrage of name-calling and tears.

After lots of encouragement Mom went to an Al-Anon meeting. Feeling a victim, she listened as a member spoke, "My sponsor asked me do I want to be right, or do I want to be happy? It is impossible to be both at the same time." With tears in her eyes, the member told of how she had decided to be happy. She described how she slowly took back her self-esteem and power by putting her attention where it had belonged all along — on herself.

After hearing that, when our dad came home, Mom didn't argue, whine, or try to convince him of anything. She changed her perspective and let go of his behaviors. Then the miracle happened! Mom detached with love from Dad's actions. Over time, in the space created through mom's detachment, *Dad* recognized that he had a problem. As they took part in their separate programs and worked The Steps, their lives together improved. Both discov-ered they preferred to be happy more than they needed to be right.

TODAY'S MEDITATION

Dear God, as I practice minding my own business, I see how having to be right has little to do with my being happy, which is what I want most of all.

"Happiness is a risk. If you're not a little scared,
then you're not doing it right." — Sarah Addison Allen

THE MAGIC OF STEP TWO
FEBRUARY 6

"Came to believe that a power greater than us could restore us to sanity."

Step Two is where we *came-to*. Some of us came-to reluctantly, while others rejected the idea altogether. They refused to consider the possibility that there was anything that could be bigger or more powerful than themselves.

As if by divine intervention, authors of our literature were quick to interject that no one cares if we come to believe or not. Recovery is designed with each of us in mind regardless of religious affiliation. Whatever our declaration or walk of faith is, we trust it because we helped to create it.

We design a Higher Power based on a set of ideals personal to us that encourage us to live with humility and honor. This co-creation of our destiny makes passage through Step Two acceptable in a way unique to each of us. No judgment is allowed, or is any given.

We finally came to realize that our job is to be responsible for what *we* do. Our Higher Power is responsible for the results of what we do.

TODAY'S MEDITATION
In this realm of the spirit, I am free to believe however I please.

"It was a great relief to me to learn that I simply didn't have to understand. After all, you don't have to know how a tree grows to make a fence out of wood."
— A.A. World Services Inc.

FEAR OF TOMORROW
FEBRUARY 7

As a child I lived in perpetual fear, expecting the other shoe of disaster to drop. Life was bleak and without hope. As an adult I asked my husband to not dream because I was convinced dreams would never come to pass.

Fear of tomorrow is our reminder we're taking today for granted. When we focus on negativity instead of gratitude and allow anxiety to dominate our thoughts, we become bankrupt spiritually. Our literature asks that we think only about our present 24-hours, or whatever part of our day we have left.

Fear of tomorrow is called projecting, and it is a waste of precious energy. With imaginary blinders on that hold us here, we look down at our feet, returning to the security of now.

Working in small increments of time helps to keep us efficient and our thoughts where our Higher Power is.

Prayer and Meditation give us comfort.

Doing the next right thing, or sharing with a friend, pulls us back into the safety of today.

Practicing positive thinking by changing our perspective helps to alleviate our fear of tomorrow by accepting what is right here and right now.

TODAY'S MEDITATION
I'm grateful, God, that day-by-day, hour-by-hour, moment-by-moment, I overcome fear when I remember to keep my world small and focus on what is right in front of me.

"The regrets of yesterday and the fear of tomorrow can kill you."
— Liza Minnelli

PRINCIPLES BEFORE PERSONALITIES
FEBRUARY 8

Principles before personalities is a frequent topic of discussion in recovery. Without principles, any hope of a spiritual grace is gone. We still walk and talk in old behaviors because this is all we know to do.

Some of us speak of spiritual principles being referred to as "contrary virtues," seen as the opposite of the *Seven Deadly Sins*. These contrary virtues we strive for are humility vs. pride; kindness vs. envy; abstinence vs. gluttony; chastity vs. lust; patience vs. anger; liberality vs. greed; and diligence vs. sloth.

These are among the core principles that help to ground us as we focus on transforming our lives through The Steps. They become our laws of truth, enabling us to achieve a life of emotional and spiritual peace. For the first time in our lives we cease fighting others as we subscribe to principles before personalities.

How comforting it is that the process of recovery gives us principles to aspire to. By living the principles we've practiced, we find a way of life that serves as an empowering foundation for change. The miracles that unfold before us forge our new reality. Sometimes quickly, sometimes slowly, the principles will always materialize if we work for them.

TODAY'S MEDITATION
We are the lucky ones. We have spiritual tools laid at our feet that guide our thinking each day. All we need is the willingness to pick them up.

"A people that values its privileges above its principles soon loses both." — Dwight D. Eisenhower

Detaching

February 9

The art of communicating is a delicate dance. As the act of detachment is introduced, one partner sometimes fears incorrectly that this means divorce, while another might become wary of new behaviors from the partner who is in recovery.

People who know and love us lack information about the recovery process because they are not actively learning this new way of life. Ultimately, recovery belongs to us. There are times when the partner of someone in recovery is fearful or full of skepticism. When this is the case it is okay to detach with love, to take a step back and move away from being responsible for the behaviors of others who threaten or try to deter us from our recovery. Loving the person, but not owning responsibility for their behaviors or expectations is what detaching with love is about.

Many of us never knew we had the right to our own opinion concerning what behaviors were healthy and safe for us personally. We often accepted inappropriate conduct and outcomes regardless of how they affected us. Recovery teaches us to trust and rely upon our own certainty. Detaching and defining new boundaries gives us the permission we need to accept our motives and actions, regardless of whether others understand. We can still accept differing viewpoints and behaviors, but detach when we feel uncomfortable or threatened or when those differing opinions jeopardize our recovery. How do we do this with finesse? Some of us can change the subject or not engage, defend, or explain ourselves. After all, others just like us, have a right to their opinion. Al-Anon Family Groups is the forum for the families of the alcoholic to recover.

No one understands what we need or don't need better than we do. The more we tap into what we know, the stronger the confidence in our decisions become. We can, and should, trust our instincts when it comes to what is safe and appropriate for us. By practicing detaching with love, we protect our serenity and happiness and assume authority over that which we know we must change. At the same time, we treat those around us with love, compassion, and kindness.

"Some people believe holding on and hanging in there are signs of great strength. However, there are times when it takes much more strength to know when to let go and then do it" — Ann Landers

COMBATING FEAR

FEBRUARY 10

So much of what we do as a newcomer in sobriety makes us feel as though we're fighting a war with ourselves. And to some extent we are. In this war we engage our emotional, mental, spiritual, and physical self.

This war is personal.

For those of us in recovery or active addiction, fear is the adversary engrained in our psyche, the one hardest to combat. We fear everyone and everything, real or imagined. We can't distinguish fact from fiction, and we don't know how to live with the fear.

To get rid of fear, we must face it head on where it lives, in our hearts and in our imaginations. This distressing and volatile emotion can only be overcome by walking *through* it. Tiptoeing around fear, ignoring it, or wishing it away does not help. Isolating, minimizing, or refusing to discuss what we are afraid of only makes matters worse.

Working The Steps is the pedal that propels us to the other side of fear to freedom. There is no middle ground, but with practice, The Steps make it achievable for all of us.

TODAY'S MEDITATION
I'm so grateful today for the willingness to face my fears and *do it anyway.*

"You gain strength, courage, and confidence by every experience in which you really stop to look fear in the face. I can take the next thing that comes along."
— *Eleanor Roosevelt*

CONVINCING OTHERS
FEBRUARY 11

Visualize yourself on trial, having to plead your case, coercing, and manipulating the truth enough to convince others. Before recovery, we were unrelenting, convinced that whatever we contrived had merit. Being self-serving, we cared for nothing more than getting what we wanted when we wanted it.

As our sobriety becomes reliable one day at a time, the desperation in our desire to be heard and understood lessens. We let go of the need to convince others. We quit justifying our point of view and we stop fighting to be right.

Those who are not addicted cannot grasp the enormity of our long-term commitment to recovery. They say, "You don't have an addiction, you just need to cut back," or "It's been long enough now, can't you stop these silly meetings?"

We honor our course, grateful for the knowledge that *we* are the ones who must grasp the gravity of our recovery, no one else.

As lucidity smashes our repeated arguments and denials, the significance of our journey in sobriety becomes clear. With restored integrity and new resolve, we align ourselves with our Higher Power and our sobriety. These two ideals are the foundation for making peace with ourselves.

At peace with ourselves, we allow others the space to discern their own paths as we *Live and Let Live.*

TODAY'S MEDITATION

Dear God, as I awaken to peace, I embrace all that I am. Together, we are one on our road to recovery.

"What other people may think of the rightness or wrongness is nothing in comparison to my own deep knowledge, my innate conviction that it was wrong."
— Elizabeth Gaskell

EGO DEFLATION

FEBRUARY 12

Early in recovery, shreds of insanity give way to clarity. We see the complexities of our disease and how addictions take root in a soul-sickness that obscures our defects. One example is an over-inflated ego. We are consumed by desires, convinced we need no one and nothing other than our drug of choice.

Many of us were ready for a complete overhaul, including an overhaul of our ego. Our sobriety cannot endure long-term without it. Still, our ego fights recovery whispering, "There's nothing wrong with you." As we lie in the gutter, our ego proclaims, "I don't have a problem!"

The Steps are the taproot of a growing humility that admits how displaced our idea of our own omnipotence is. An image of who we really are appears as we stumble down from the throne. As EGO (Edging God Out) nudges us to climb back up, humility reminds us that all our best thinking got us was a seat in recovery.

We must get out of our own way and recalibrate our ego. When we experience *EGO deflation,* we become right-sized. Humility allows the restoration of our sense of our true importance and placement in the Universe. We accept there is a Higher Power, and that it is not us. Humility begins to replace grandiosity as tolerance and acceptance smother self-righteous indignation.

We're reminded that life is a daily lesson in powerlessness and letting go.

TODAY'S MEDITATION

Daily prayer helps me to keep my ego right-sized. I surrender to all I don't know and leave the unanswerable to my God.

"Every normal person, in fact, is only normal on the average. His ego approximates to that of the psychotic in some part or other and to a greater or lesser extent. "— Sigmund Freud

CHANGING PERSPECTIVES
FEBRUARY 13

At a party, an artist admitted that some found it difficult to see the beauty in her work. She then whispered, "It's easy to do when you change your perspective. Look closely at the abstract. Now, with eyes closed, what emotions come into play? What images become clear? Where do the colors take you?"

I felt my heart beat faster as a change in perspective brought an awareness, invisible until now into view.

In recovery an ability to change how we interpret our world becomes an important part of our daily lives. As we listen to others share without judgment, we notice our own compassion growing within. We begin to question everything we thought we knew as though viewing it from a higher plain.

Adjusting our perspective is the beginning of accepting that there are many ways to interpret what we see, and that judgment without a *change in perspective* only clouds our vision.

As clarity dissipates the haze in judgment, we recognize, with humility that the more we think we know, the less we know.

TODAY'S MEDITATION
I'm grateful that as my truth grows, so does my ability to change my perspective.

"Your perspective is always limited by how much you know. Expand your knowledge and you will transform your mind." — Bruce H. Lipton

Faith in the Fellowship
February 14

Getting together with a group of strangers was never comfortable for me. I felt insecure and out-of-place. The thought of walking into the crowded rooms of recovery scared me to death. Fear, the hallmark of my disease, preferred that I fail: isolated, afraid, and alone—hopeless and trapped inside my own head.

Joining the fellowship of recovery was life changing. I became part of a herd gathered from every walk of life and was accepted as an equal. Their laughter, which came without judgment, proved that if they were happy I could be too. Laughter became contagious. I relaxed, and laughed knowing that together we could all stay clean and sober.

Fellowship, faith, and sobriety happen in our spiritual rooms of recovery. Hope is there in abundance. Sacred trust generates a respect for each other on our mutual journey. Together, we are safe.

Although experiences differ, we recognize that our common pain brought us into our rooms. Faith flourishes as we watch our miracles multiply. While many of us stay sober in sobriety, others slip, but keep coming back. We begin to *live and let live* without judgment or reservations. Within our village of recovery, we grow into the responsible people we have always wanted to be.

TODAY'S MEDITATION
I am grateful for the loving arms of the fellowship where I trust myself and others, and become a responsible member of society.

"For where there are two or three gathered together in my name, there am I in the midst of them..." — *Matthew 18. verse 20.*

FEAR OF BEING ME

FEBRUARY 15

One of the biggest consequences of my addiction is the length of time it has taken for me to get over my *fear of being me*. I never knew where or how to begin to accept and understand who I am.

My bingeing and embarrassing behaviors were coupled with claims that I was fine, that I needed no one, yet I couldn't balance a checkbook, or remember the events of two minutes earlier. I cared more for a quick and permanent escape than I did about living; I hated who I had become.

Slowly as we recover, we begin to accept ourselves, warts and all. As faith replaces the fear of not being good enough, we grasp the light that shines hope on the possibility that we are worthy of giving ourselves the love and kindness we so deserve.

Release of secrets whether imagined or real, sets us free from self-centered fear. Images of perfection leave us. Recovery proves we don't ever have to return to that dark demoralized place where death beckons us. Instead, we choose faith, humility, and acceptance.

TODAY'S MEDITATION
Dear God, the miracles of recovery allow me to let go of the *fear of being me* because I know you love me, and so do I.

"Just being ourselves is the biggest fear of humans. We have learned to live by other people's points of view because of the fear of not being accepted and of not being good enough for someone else.." — Miguel Angel Ruiz

GLUTTONY, HOW MUCH IS ENOUGH?
FEBRUARY 16

Those in recovery often tell stories of gluttony. The phenomenon of craving that is the mental obsession, the physical compulsion to drink combined with a soul-sickness tells us we need nothing at all but our drug of choice to make us enough.

The question of how-much is not what baffles us, but rather the motives behind the obsession itself. What is our payoff that comes from indulging or bingeing? What are the emotions that inflame gluttony? Why is it that no amount is ever enough? Although we know we are never satisfied, what then, makes us demand more?

When we care enough to ask the questions surrounding what is enough, the answers begin to appear, and speak to a different frame of thinking and doing. We are not all-or-nothing people, but with gluttony, we apply all-or-nothing thinking. This mindset of all or nothing is the hallmark of our addictions.

Recovery helps us *to be* enough, to *have* enough, and to find truth in the realization that our thinking and actions must rest somewhere in the middle. The middle is the balance we need to become content. We have enough. We *are* enough.

TODAY'S MEDITATION
I have a choice today. With your help, God, I can let go of obsessive cravings that mask my self-loathing. Today, I am enough!

"We only dislike the glutton when he becomes a gourmet-that is, we only dislike him when he not only wants the best for himself, but knows what is best for other people." — *Gilbert K. Chesterton*

Rising out of Darkness
February 17

All of us are on a journey that is spiritual in nature, but how we move through life's caverns of darkness and despair is unique to each of us.

Falling to my knees in desperation, I awake enough to see the light. I begin to write, *I am worthy of life, I am deserving.* I don't stop writing until I've written every single truth I know about myself but could not see until this moment.

In the hours that follow, I experience the wide-eyed awareness of a toddler as these life-affirming truths empower me. Thoughts begin to reshape and redefine all I ever imagined I was, as I abide with complete and unabashed bliss.

We were all born with purity and innate goodness but now have to dredge through the darkness of our caves to find it again. That same cave of darkness will still call our name from time to time. Life on life's terms still happens. What changes are our actions and reactions.

This profound shift in our psyche is the absolute knowing that with our Higher Power we can reach the light of His compassion. Regardless of what life presents, we seek gratitude for this transformation and rest in acceptance of all that we are. Because of the miracles of recovery, our lives have changed.

TODAY'S MEDITATION
Dear God, I trust the pure essence of my existence because you allowed this transformation to happen to me. I present myself to you, resiliently courageous in the face of doubt.

"... I know that when we die and it comes time for God to judge us, he will not ask, 'How many good things have you done in your life?' rather he will ask, 'How much love did you put into what you did?" — Mother Teresa

HANDLING CRITICISM FROM FAMILY
FEBRUARY 18

Within addiction recovery, our home is where many of us feel the most vulnerable, most closely scrutinized. Family members are fearful and desperate to know if we are done with those meetings. What are they for? Why are we going to so many? Everyone expects a new normal. They want a new normal without the addictions, without the leaving behavior, the lying, the stealing, the missing work and the not coming home behaviors. And they want it now. They've had enough. They don't understand the nature of our disease and are afraid of what they don't know. But trust is not reinstated overnight. Page 83 of the Big Book of *Alcoholics Anonymous* reminds, "Yes, there is a long reconstruction period ahead."

In recovery, we accept handling criticism from family members as our responsibility because we made the situation what it is. We know we must rely upon our Higher Power and the village that is recovery to redirect our thinking process and regain a foothold in sobriety.

We must not be in denial of the role we once played in our family's disposition. We have an obligation now to allow them to feel their feelings. Just like us, they are entitled to their emotions and opinions. Our responsibility today, regardless how anyone else feels, is to find a balance of open communication and loving kindness as we stay in recovery and meet family needs.

Our family does not fully understand our journey of recovery because they've not experienced it, but they have watched us fall again and again. We need to show them love and tolerance, and forgive ourselves as we stay the course, one day at a time.

TODAY'S MEDITATION
God, help me forgive myself enough to let go of what others don't understand. Today I ask only to be helpful, useful and kind.

"Let no one ever come to you without leaving better and happier. Be the living expression of God's kindness: kindness in your face, kindness in your eyes, kindness in your smile." — Mother Teresa

Jealousy in any intimate relationship is a combination of anger, sexual arousal, fear, and love. Sometimes jealousy has to do with loss and is the basis of some of our most distorted thinking. Experiencing these feelings, we say, "If I can't have you, no one can." Or, "You're mine!"

On the surface, jealousy looks like love, but, seen through the lens of jealousy relationships become distorted. Is that what love is?

Jealousy is a demonstration of control, not love. It manifests a lack of trust and confidence. Manipulative and self-serving, this deranged mindset has the power to destroy relationships. Jealousy doesn't work and is never healthy. This emotional disturbance is destructive and often results in tragic consequences to those we love and to ourselves.

Although knowing and enforcing our boundaries is essential, (jealousy does sometimes point out undesirable behaviors in our partner) being open, honest, and loving in intimate communication is the healthy way to go.

Sometimes a third-party professional with a background in domestic violence in a neutral place will provide much needed clarity and support with or without the significant other.

It is okay to seek help.

TODAY'S MEDITATION

Dear God, thank you for the awareness of my perceptions, relationships, thoughts and actions. As the great arbiter who sits before me, I ask that Thy will, not mine be done.

"A competent and self-confident person is incapable of jealousy in anything. Jealousy is invariably a symptom of neurotic insecurity." — *Robert A. Heinlein*

LEARNING TO LIVE IN PEACE
FEBRUARY 20

My ability to live in peace a day at a time in recovery continues to be a work in progress.

Some of us think peace means the chatter between our ears will calm to a whisper. Others hope that once in recovery, the world will immediately love and embrace us. We expect relationships to return to that fun-loving place where they began.

But none of this happens. There is no peace.

We wonder, *what is the point of staying sober?* We feel ignored, unappreciated. Doesn't everyone see we have changed?

We came to recovery expecting to receive sustained peace. We didn't believe those who told us peace must first be earned. Gradually we have come to accept the fact that we experience sustained peace only with diligence and hard work as we move through The Steps. Why is finding peace so difficult to obtain? Because the peace we seek comes from the inside-out, as we learn lessons about ourselves one day at a time.

With a steadfast focus on our own life instead of the lives of others, we experience this transformation of peace each time we let others be who they are. Like a gentle wave flowing back to its origin, we *Let Go and Let God*.

Peace engulfs us as we walk along spiritual lines, guided by our Higher Power.

TODAY'S MEDITATION

God, help me to remember that each day clean and sober brings me closer to the peace I seek.

"You find peace not by rearranging the circumstances of your life, but by realizing who you are at the deepest level." — Eckhart Tolle

ACHIEVEMENTS IN SOBRIETY
FEBRUARY 21

As a newbie in sobriety, everyone remarked how much I had changed. I couldn't see the changes they did and felt disappointed. I expected a newer, better version of me.

I remember asking, "Why am I not further along?" A sponsor suggested I write down everything I have done different since recovery, so I did.

As the list grew, I saw where I had set boundaries saying, *No* I saw the fact that I put my sobriety first. I had written gratitude lists and picked up the telephone to call new friends. I had become responsible at home and had quit blaming others. As I wrote everything down, a new image of me appeared.

My list includes examples of the many changes we make each day but take for granted that confirm what others already know: we are being transformed. We accomplish much, day-in and day-out, but forget how far we have come. Writing what we have done different each day gives a new appreciation and understanding to see the fears we've walked through.

For those who make these changes, they are baby steps, easy to write off as insignificant. However, each change we make is the harbinger of our miracles yet to come. We are gaining a warrior's strength in a way we might not see otherwise.

No matter how small, each achievement in sobriety serves as the confidence necessary for us to persevere and become the rock of a deep and abiding trust we can stand on when life gets tough.

TODAY'S MEDITATION
I am grateful I am on the right path. Sometimes quickly, sometimes slowly, change comes.

"Change your behaviors and your feelings will follow." — Susan McManhon

LETTING GO OF OLD IDEAS
FEBRUARY 22

For some of us, letting go of old ideas continues to be one of our most difficult obstacles. After all, these ideas were *our* ideas, right? Why would we get rid of them if we created them?

Insistence on *letting go of old ideas* is grounded in the realization that our ego clings to past behaviors and ideas, regardless of their benefit or harm. Old-thinking results in our old-way of doing things which often spells a return to active addiction.

The Big Book of *Alcoholics Anonymous* tells us on page 58 how *letting go of old ideas*, although difficult, is necessary, saying "… the result was nil until we let go absolutely."

Old ideas keep us stuck where we are, while we expect different results.

In recovery we learn to let go and change everything, one day at a time. These changes are central to our sobriety as we work in concert with our Higher Power. Just for today we seek to exchange self-centered, ego-centric thinking for a God-centered, universal higher-thinking that embraces moral-driven motives and principles.

Every day is a day to uncover, discover, and discard old ideas as we come closer to self-actualization.

TODAY'S MEDITATION
Today I remember that old ideas avail me nothing and ask God for the willingness to carry out changes in all that I do.

"A man's mind is stretched by a new idea or sensation, and never shrinks back to its former dimensions." — *Oliver Wendell Holmes Sr.,*

MANIPULATION IN THE WORK PLACE
FEBRUARY 23

One of the first things told to me on the job was that I wasn't being paid to make friends while at work. Sounds harsh, I know, but those in management are there to manage, which can make forming friendships difficult.

Recovery reminds us to be wary of taking on management positions. They are not a sweet spot for us, as our overinflated ego, combined with control issues and a need to prove ourselves, seem to come naturally. These traits are only exacerbated when we are put in charge. The corporate playing field can be more treacherous than the corner bar, and many have paid a price for decisions made out of self-righteous indignation, jealousy, or greed.

Our responsibility is to show up on time and do the work we were hired to do. We may resent superiors, especially when their behavior becomes personal. We may feel intimidated, or even angry when asked to do more work, or when a job well done has gone unnoticed.

Recovery reminds us that showing up is growing up. We remember when we are disturbed, regardless of the situation, there is something within us we need to learn. Above all, we want to be trustworthy. So, we take steps to keep the focus on our job, our responsibility, and allow others to do their part without judgment or interference. *Manipulation in the workplace* is best left to others.

We wear imaginary blinders to help us stay where our feet are planted. If others blame us or fall short on their obligations, we trust management to do their part as we focus on the job in front of us. We don't get in the middle of anything unless we are requested to do so by those above us. As we mind our own business we come to trust that, just like us, everyone will do their jobs to the best of their ability.

TODAY'S MEDITATION
Today I will allow others to be who they are and keep the focus and attention on the job I'm entrusted to do.

"Controllers, abusers and manipulative people don't question themselves. They don't ask themselves if the problem is them. They always say the problem is someone else." — Darlene Ouimet

Releasing Resentments

February 24

Resentment is a damaging emotion some of us harbor day-in and day-out without letting go. This tragic emotion begins innocently. Someone does something, says something, and we take offense. We file this event away in memory. That is how the emotional disturbance starts. The perceived offense repeats and resentment, like an emotional virus, grows insidiously. It feeds on our pride and arrogance gaining strength with each occurrence.

We don't think we are keeping track of these insults; however, until the same behavior occurs over and over. This repeated affront to our ego demands attention. Add to this many other actual or perceived irritations from other sources. Before the day is half-over we have accumulated enough negativity to put us in the middle of a mental and emotional whirlwind.

Anger builds and, like a volcanic eruption, can explode into rage and violence.

Before this happens, we must speak with a sponsor or trusted friend and move the resentment into the light. Resentments are the number one destroyer of our hard-fought sobriety. Daily serenity depends upon our ability to find compassion for ourselves, but also for the other guy, sufficient to keep us free from this toxic scorekeeping.

TODAY'S MEDITATION

Dear God, I am responsible for my emotions, reactions and the choices I make. With your help in prayer, I ask questions and pause to avoid the trap of resentment.

"... thoughts of resentment, anger, and hatred represent slow, debilitating energies that will disempower you. If you could release them, you would know more peace."— Wayne W. Dyer

SELF-CARE

FEBRUARY 25

It took years for me to understand that self-care was acceptable. Any time I stood up for what I wanted or needed, I felt selfish. How could I ask for things for myself? Guilt and a sense of shame followed. It was easier to tuck away my wants and needs. Addiction says we do not deserve self-care.

Recovery teaches us fundamental differences between self-care and being selfish. The true measure of selfishness was our devotion to our addictions and neglect of everyone and everything else.

Self-care begins the day we decide we've had enough pain and can no longer squelch our sick feelings of remorse and shame.

Our life becomes a self-focused quest for change when we put the drink down for good. We give ourselves permission to feel, to cry, and to grieve emotions which open the door to self-care.

From that single decision to honor our need for self-care, we begin the shift to wanting to live. Priorities change as the healing powers of hope and faith grow. As we learn to trust the process and connect with our newfound fellowship we embrace self-care. We take pride in our appearance and develop a belief that we deserve, as a child of the universe, to be happy, joyous, and free. Because we do.

TODAY'S MEDITATION
By keeping the focus on me instead of blaming others, I become aware of my needs. As I make my list of what I deserve, I am amazed.

"You are not responsible for fixing everything that is broken. You do not have to try and make everyone happy. For now, take time for you. It's time to replenish."
— Pam Belding

MORE WILL BE REVEALED
FEBRUARY 26

There are times when events defy our understanding. A friend's baby is born prematurely, a relative loses their job. We can't understand what's happening, or why.

We often push, demand, and force our way to answers not yet available to us. They come not in our time, but always in the time chosen by our Higher Power. We forget we are but a tiny part of something beyond our comprehension.

How do we know the right thing to do? We're directed to have faith, and to let the Divine force of the universe use us right where we are until more is revealed. Our job is simply to be useful in the now. We take comfort in the fact that while we have no answers our Higher Power does, and these answers are none of our business because it's not our time to receive them. The truth is it may never be our time.

We think we cannot live without knowing, but we will, and we do. If more is to be revealed, it will appear in the order of all things as we become open and mature enough to receive the answers.

We embrace the unknown and trust our Higher Power's perfect timing. We may not get what we want, but we will always receive what we need.

TODAY'S MEDITATION

Dear God, I wait for your sign. How will I know? The answer is always unmistakable. It rises from deep within.

"And now, Lord, for what do I wait? My hope is in You." — Psalm 39:7

Relief from the Bondage of Self
February 27

These words are a source of discomfort for those of us in recovery. Who understands better than we do how burdened we are within ourselves in our addictions? Living within our island of self and chained to childlike emotions, we wanted what we wanted without regard for anyone. If getting what we wanted meant barging to the head of the line or stepping on someone's toes, we cared little who was in our way.

We remained a slave to our disease. Stuck in a drug-induced trance, drawn to a single thought of more, we ruined our lives and the lives of others. Many lose jobs, reputations, and families; yet, these tragic losses could free us from the bondage of self. No limit could explain what we would do to have enough of what we thought we needed. Enough was never enough. We are sick people trying to get well from a disease that never sleeps.

The solution to all our problems is found in the rooms of recovery. Twelve-step programs give us a way out of our tortured and delusional thinking so that the bondage of self can be broken. But if we are to relinquish this extreme exhibition of selfishness and self-centeredness, hope and faith must take its place. The Steps makes this possible. How fortunate we are to have the precious gifts of sobriety to use when we need help. New ways of responding to life promote freedom from the bondage of self, one of our treasured miracles.

TODAY'S MEDITATION
Dear God, please use me as a channel of your peace so I might be set free of the things preventing me from reaching you.

"Freedom, then, lies only in our innate human capacity to choose between different sorts of bondage, bondage to desire or self-esteem, or bondage to the light that lightens all our lives."—Sri Madhava

NON-NEGOTIABLE SOBRIETY
FEBRUARY 28

Our lives are filled with absolutes, things that are non-negotiable. Among them are death and taxes.

What about our sobriety?

What about our personal, long-term commitment to ourselves? Shouldn't these be non-negotiable?

Our addiction is a disease unlike any other. One slip reveals how fast our disease progresses, like a cancer, suddenly out of remission. Like any fatal illness, the progression is predictable and comes with guaranteed consequences of jail, institution or death. We know because we watch what happens to those who are still experimenting. Without sobriety, our condition never gets better, only worse.

Only complete and total abstinence guarantees sobriety. Our conviction that absolutely nothing is made better with a drink or drug must be non-negotiable.

We come to believe that we must stand on our truth. For we know, nothing is greater than our priceless gift of sobriety.

TODAY'S MEDITATION
Thank you, God, for a sustaining truth that tells me I deserve the miracle of uncompromised, non-negotiable sobriety, without which—I stand for nothing.

"The wise treat self-respect as non-negotiable and will not trade it for health or wealth or anything else." — *Thomas Szasz*

SELF-KNOWLEDGE
FEBRUARY 29

A friend of mine is brilliant in every way. She has a six-figure job, two master's degrees, three children, and a loving, doting husband. On the surface, she is the epitome of success.

She refuses to concede that she is a chronic drinker and has issues with several prescription drugs. Alcohol soothes her soul when nothing, not even her family, can. Everyone around her sees the ruse she is enacting. Her family has tried intervention, taking her keys away and more. But my friend has too much self-knowledge. Living in denial, she fights with everything she has to maintain her addictions. Self-knowledge whispers *let's face it, you have never been this successful. It's clear you don't have a problem.* She feels sure she's not hurting anyone. Denial defends her. She's been to a few recovery meetings, but self-knowledge insists she's is not like any of them. She can take it or leave it.

At a recent dinner party, my friend's husband said he would order her one drink quota for the night. Convinced she could drink just one, she brought the drink back and settled into the conversation. Within minutes, she motioned the waiter for another. Immediately her husband reminded of their agreement. She stood up angrily slammed her chair back, spewing threats of divorce, demanding her husband stop putting restraints on her. "After all," she said, "With my education, I can handle anything."

TODAY'S MEDITATION
Thank you, God, for the humility that allows me to see that self-knowledge avails me nothing, and for the willingness to remember that I am the problem. Today, I will not drink.

"My failures may be my greatest successes. It is in failure that I have often drawn closer to God, learn to depend more on Him than myself, gained self-knowledge, and seen things in their right perspective." — Mother Angelica

PAUSE

MARCH 1

Many of recovery's watchwords are simple, but have a profound meaning. Take the word, "pause."

This non-threatening word was so completely foreign to me early in recovery. I was perfectly comfortable with knee-jerk responses before letting whatever was on my mind spew out without thinking. Before recovery I thought I had all the answers for you, for everyone whether you asked for them or not. I thought my job was to enlighten you!

Recovery teaches us to not speak unless spoken to. We learn that what we think doesn't matter because it was our best thinking that got us a seat in recovery. We are instructed to pause when agitated or doubtful.

The miracle of *pause* begins as we silently count to ten before speaking, which helps to distance ourselves enough to ask, *did someone ask for my input? Is what I am about to say truthful? Necessary? Kind?* If the answer to these questions is yes, then we can speak. Otherwise we have nothing of value to contribute. The time has come to learn humility in the pause. We realize we have no solutions for anyone but ourselves, nor do we have anything to prove. With that pause, we avoid becoming part of the problem, nor do we have anything to prove.

TODAY'S MEDITATION
Dear God, please put your arm over my shoulder and your hand over my mouth. Amen.

"When you feel stress begin simmering within you, pause.
Remember you are the master, not your emotions." — Anonymous

SOBRIETY, A 24-HOUR REPRIEVE
MARCH 2

In recovery, we are told we have a 24-hour reprieve from our disease. That reprieve remains in force based on the maintenance of our spiritual condition. Like a stay of execution, when our spiritual condition is aligned with our Higher Power, we have the assurance of remaining clean and sober for the rest of the day.

How do we maintain our spiritual condition? We stay in prayer many times throughout the day asking to be close to our Higher Power, and we have faith in the moment. We trust courage as we face the unthinkable, the unantici-pated, and the unimagined excitements and ravages life presents, so we don't slip backward into the consuming darkness deep within. We must continually seek to grow along spiritual lines in order to be helpful and useful to those around us. We are reminded too, that *Faith without works is dead.*

We don't have to panic no matter what life or death brings to us. The fellow-ship of recovery has given us the tools to use. Most of all, we have opened our hearts and walked in faith with the God of our understanding.

Facing and surviving our darkest moments ae possible because we maintain continual contact with our Higher Power and keep the focus on our sobriety.

TODAY'S MEDITATION
I'm grateful to know that when I continue to do the next right thing, the next right thing happens. Sobriety is my solution to living.

"We are not cured of alcoholism. What we have is a daily reprieve contingent on the maintenance of our spiritual condition. Every day is a day when we must carry the vision of God's will into all of our daily activities."
— *William Griffith Wilson*

STEP THREE:
MARCH 3

"Made a decision to turn our will and our life
over to the care of God *as we understood him.*"

Prior to recovery I operated with selfish objectives. How will this benefit me? How could my will in a situation prevail successfully so that I win? My question preceding any decision I made was, "What's in it for me?"

Thankfully, the Big Book of *Alcoholics Anonymous* was written with intention and in a precise order. First, we came into the rooms of recovery in Step One. In Step Two we came-to; we awoke enough to experience our miracle of spiritual awakening. We began to have enough faith in *Step Three* to decide to turn our life and will over to the care of God in whatever way we understood God. We were asked to decide to surrender our best thinking to that of our Higher Power. We admitted we are His children and He is the Father. Throughout the day we reminded ourselves we are subordinate.

The vision of the Third Step Prayer prepares us to develop the trust and humility needed to get out of our own way–to surrender and quit playing the Director. We trust that "God could and would if He were sought." As we came to see our own imperfections, "Thy Will not mine be done," became our daily plea.

Without the confidence in our ability to turn our will, and our life, over to the care of God in *Step Three*, how could we possibly be prepared for Step Four? We turn our will over and take it back what seems like a hundred times a day. And that's okay. Doing so is what happens in the Third Step. We practice human progress, not human perfection. We concede to our imperfection and defer to our Higher Power from whom all power comes.

TODAY'S MEDITATION
Today, I know over time my Third Step will become automatic allowing you, God, to be in charge. Only then will I be ready to submit to the fourth step.

"Put your trust in God and move forward with faith and confidence in the future. The Lord will not forsake us… If we will put our trust in Him, if we will pray to Him, if we will live worthy of His blessings, He will hear our prayers."
— *Gordon B. Hinckley*

FEAR OF THE FOURTH STEP
MARCH 4

When I first heard about the *fourth step*, I decided right then to skip that one. I didn't trust you and was terrified of what you would think if you ever found out the truth about me!

That's what we all thought. These and other stinking-thinking thoughts precede a relapse before we ever get close to the fourth step. Trapped in our uniqueness, we feel certain no person alive has ever experienced what we have. We are sure we will die a thousand deaths if we confide in someone sharing our deepest secrets, the ones we promised long ago to take to our grave.

This combination of low self-esteem, exaggerated pride, and ego speaks to us in the dead of night. The power of our disease must never ever be underestimated. It uses our darkest secrets to keep us sick, preserving and growing its hold over us. We are *not* unique and we do not die sharing our truth with someone we trust enough to work The Steps with. However, many people *do* die by missing this vital step to recovery.

We must find the courage to move forward. If we're not there yet, we can revisit a previous step. But sooner or later, through steadfast humility, faith and a swallowing of our pride, we will come back to face the fourth step with the help of others. And in so doing, we come back from the dead.

We work The Steps together, because alone, we're already dead.

TODAY'S MEDITATION

Dear God, thank you for positioning this step to be right where it is. Step Four has given me the time and space needed to trust the process enough to move forward.

"Though our decision was a vital and crucial step, it could have little permanent effect unless at once followed by a strenuous effort to face, and to be rid of, the things in ourselves which had been blocking us. Our liquor was but a symptom. So we had to get down to causes and conditions."— Big Book of Alcoholics Anonymous; Page 64 of Chapter 5, How it Works

SELF-JUSTIFIED ANGER
MARCH 5

We believe *self-justified anger* is fine for normal people, but if we have the disease of addiction, self-justified anything especially anger, gives us permission to escalate to the next level, self-justified indulgence. We say, "Oh yeah? I'll show you," and we do so by falling off the wagon hurting others and ourselves.

Anger, self-justified or not is considered one of the *Seven Deadly Sins*. Our literature tells us anger is best left for those more qualified than us. For us, anger is a sure sign of emotional insecurity. When combined with worry and depression anger blames others for our own wrongdoing and we play the role of the victim. It reminds us that when we harbor grudges and plan revenge for such defeats we beat ourselves with the club of anger we had intended to use on others.

Anger is an invitation to personal disaster. We never handled this emotion well. Our ego hotly engaged, is ready to jump at the chance to retaliate. Thoughts become delusional as we prepare for an assault of emotional and physical harm. When we set ourselves up to get even, we experience a psychological payoff of excitement. This caustic energy induces fight-or-flight adrenaline to flood our bodies and we prepare to retaliate.

Prayer and meditation offer pause that then suggests choices. We can choose grace and dignity as we detach from the behaviors of others. One choice is to walk away. Recovery proves we no longer need to Justify, Argue, Defend or Explain (JADE) our beliefs to others, when to do so would make a delicate situation worse. We allow the other person to feel what they feel because they are as entitled to their emotions as we are to ours.

Detaching with love is a powerful tool. It reminds us *they know not what they do,* and that *we* are the ones whose focus must be on our emotional sobriety.

We take the high road because we have a responsibility to our serenity foremost. To do otherwise is to risk going backward, closer to picking up a drink or drug.

TODAY'S MEDITATION

My miracle is to be able to turn the other cheek and remain a part of the solution. With God's help, I breathe in serene peace and remember to *Live and Let Live*. I no longer have anything to prove.

"Anger is the enemy of non-violence and pride is a monster that swallows it up.
— Mahatma Gandhi

THE GIFT OF SAYING NO
MARCH 6

A friend talked about how hard it is to say the word, *no*. Such a small, inconspicuous two letter word can hold angst and incredible fear for many.

Some of us grew up with strong messages of, "Don't you dare say no!" and that if we did say it we were uncooperative, hurtful, or selfish. So, we stifled ourselves and went along to get along, silently wishing we had just said no and walked away. Obsessed with what others would think, too shy, or too uncomfortable to appear contrary, we often let ourselves down. We found consolation in the fact that we disappointed no one except ourselves with our silence and punished ourselves for the sake of others.

Learning to say no begins when we make a pact promising to be true to ourselves first. If we are honest, imagine how many times we would have said no instead of yes? Saying this assertive word takes practice but as we say no to silly, inconsequential matters, we begin to take our power back. We get to practice when our children ask to sleep overnight at a friend's house, and we prefer they stay home. We practice when our husband says he's ready for us to leave for the game, when what we want is to stay home and do what we want to do.

Saying no moves us *beyond* the mistaken belief that we do not deserve to say what we mean.

Recovery *expects* us to say no as we become stronger and elevate our voice. When we say no because saying yes would have negative life-altering implications for our family, or ourselves, we do so automatically and with conviction, because we've practiced our truth on much smaller situations and have suffered only minor repercussions. We will not be swayed, nor will we change our minds. We're ready to be heard and believed. No *always* means no.

TODAY'S MEDITATION

Thank you, God, for my inner-child who grows stronger when I say no. My voice resonates with strength, foreign but assured, as I protect boundaries for myself, and those I love.

"Trusting your gut is always the best thing - no matter what people around you insist you should be doing or saying or thinking. Only you know and once you live in truth, your heart is completely free." — Liberty Ross

WORRY

MARCH 7

My parents were absorbed in their own emotional trauma, and I assumed the role of the fixer over my other four siblings, trying to soothe fears and insecurities. Here my unmanageability spiraled. I had no control. My worry was born out of an exaggerated sense of responsibility and fear. I fought to be heard in a home where no one listened.

The soothing arms of recovery slowly changed my perceptions. Willingness is instrumental to finding a hope and faith not felt before. Gradually, worry is exchanged for a trust enough to *Let Go and Let God*.

I was instructed that worry is the business of my Higher Power. My business is only to do the next right thing. The Serenity Prayer helps to reinforce that the "wisdom to know the difference," begins and ends with me.

Hearing this, I focused on what was in front of me to do and as I took a deep breath, I let go of the outcome and all of the "what-if's" and the "yeah-but's." Added confidence opened a pathway to trust the process of faith. as practice forged the willingness to concede that my power begins and ends with me in doing the footwork.

It was suggested that I create a *God Box* and label each piece of paper with my worries. One-by-one they went into the Box. As I let go of each one I also let go of the possible outcomes of my worries. My Higher Power took them from me.

TODAY'S MEDITATION

Thank you, God, for this miracle of letting go. I am not responsible for worry. I do the work in front of me and give my worry to you as you already know the outcome. It works when I work it!

"If you believe that feeling bad will change a past event, then you are residing on another planet with a different reality system." — *Wayne Dyer*

ANNIVERSARIES IN SOBRIETY

In sobriety we have celebrations that marks the time we have been clean and sober. Chips signify a one-day-at-a-time hard-fought battle on our anniversary.

But opportunities for celebration such as weddings, holidays, and other exciting get-togethers can promote high anxiety. At these times vigilance may be necessary to protect our precious sobriety.

If new in sobriety, or if we find our sobriety tested, especially at celebrations, we remain close to our sponsor and the fellowship. Some questions we ask ourselves when considering involvement in celebrations of any kind are, "Can I be emotionally safe there by myself?" "Am I going with someone else in recovery?" and "What are my motives for going?"

We trust our intuition and decline from going if doing so is in our best interest. A good sponsor can guide us. We can drive our own car for a quick escape. Just having telephone numbers of other friends in recovery can be reassurance enough to continue in confidence. Everything passes, whether we indulge our addictions or not. Each day we face sober is another miracle achieved. We may pick up the thought, but we resolve not to pick up the drink.

TODAY'S MEDITATION
Just for today I remember that regardless of circumstance, this is just another day. Thank you, God, for leading me as I walk through the excitement of the day. *This Too, Shall Pass.*

"We are not a victim of our emotions or thoughts. We can understand our triggers and use them as tools to help us respond more objectively."
— *Elizabeth Thornton*

BALANCE

MARCH 9

My mother worked hard to make everything perfect. Growing up in a home where perfection ruled I adopted an attitude of why even try? I knew I could never measure up. The stress and tension of trying were too painful. Falling short reminded me I was never good enough, and failure was easier to live up to than perfection. It took a long time to realize perfectionism was my mother's way of making sure no one would see the depth of dysfunction that flourished in our home.

Perfection is not for us. It belongs to a much greater power. Recovery assures us that the middle of the road is where we need to be. Not too far left or too far right of center. We no longer see a black or white world. In all things, we change our thinking and find comfort in balance.

We start by letting go of our *must do today* thinking and the rationalization of *yeah-but's*, by using the mantra, *Easy Does It, but Do It*. The question, "Will it matter 24-hours from now?" is the gauge that measures what must be completed today.

As we become honest with ourselves and our Higher Power about priorities breathing becomes easier, and the allure of martyrdom lessens. We discern the difference between the need to put the dishes away and the need to spend time with family. The grey in the middle is our pivot-point. It motivates us to ask our Higher Power, *how important is it? Will it add, or detract from what I need to achieve?* The more we honor our Higher Power and intuitive self, the closer we are to finding the balance that is our truth.

TODAY'S MEDITATION

I am grateful that the easier, softer way is in the grey. After all, perfection never belonged to me anyway. It belongs to you, God, who is absolute perfection in all things.

"Give, but don't allow yourself to be used. Love, but don't allow your heart to be abused. Trust, but don't be naïve. Listen, but don't lose your own voice."
— Luna Belle

WE ARE BETTER THAN WE THINK WE ARE

MARCH 10

As negative messages found their way into my psyche, my perceived deficiencies and fears cast a constant rain of doubt. My inner-critic and old beliefs sought to undermine the best of me. I forgot that my thoughts alone do not represent who I am and never were my truth.

Just because we *think* something does not elevate it to our reality! We know the negative labels we have worn for years came from somewhere or someone else. They are not who we are today. The mantra *we are better than we think we are*, helps us replace old beliefs with strength and trust in ourselves. Today we know we are intuitive and responsible people doing the best we can with what we know. When we know better, we do better. We strive for a balanced self-esteem and a new way of discernment of who we are.

Sobriety gives us clear mirrors to see our true goodness as we grow in authenticity. We know, too, this goodness deserves to be strengthened, nurtured and embraced. We've neglected our intuitive knowing far too long.

Embracing *we are better than we think we are* helps to return us to our center as a strong reminder of who we are. Believing that adage, we no longer look at the dust of yesterday. Positivity, through right-thinking, continues to convince us of our worthiness today.

TODAY'S MEDITATION

I know whichever wolf I feed the most becomes the strongest. Today I will not feed my negative thoughts or allow them to define me. Instead I will feed my positive thoughts, encouraging them with food called truth.

"Drop the idea of becoming someone, because you are already a masterpiece. You cannot be improved. You have only to come to it, to know it, to realize it."
— *Osho*

INVENTORY AND THE FOURTH STEP
MARCH 11

As we move forward in The Steps, we see how important the fourth step is to our long-term sobriety. We've expected this step for so long, getting close yet dragging our feet at the enormity of the task it presents. The pain, shame, and guilt, buried without reconciliation all those years have locked us in a state of unmanageability. Many of us cut and run or bury our heads back in the sand. We lose courage, weaken, and our addiction wins yet again.

Step Four is not meant to reinforce the enormity of our pain and shame. This thorough moral inventory is a search in every nook and cranny for fear, defects, and the harms we have done to others. Step Four is vital to the freedom from the bondage of self that comes in Step Five.

Walking with our Higher Power, we entrust our past to a professional, a sponsor, or a confidant, without fear of being condemned. We are on a critical fact-facing mission, overturning and casting aside every stone in our path. We have criticized the behavior of others and have hurt them for their perceived misdeeds long enough. Now, we are confident in our ability to be honest about our own behavior, a rigorous assessment so long avoided.

As we struggle to complete our inventory, it is easy to forget that the first three Steps have built the framework of faith. Comforted now, we trust a Higher Power to provide the strength and courage we need to face what we are ready to see. We must remember we no longer walk or face anything alone.

We've come a long way toward acknowledging facts about ourselves, and understanding that no one judges us but ourselves. There is no final score. We are ready to dump the junk we hid in our mind's closet for so long and live without fear of rejection. Step Four cracks open the door to freedom.

With humility, we're ready to admit long forgotten truths about ourselves as we are lifted now in courage and mature acceptance. Like every other step before and after, Step Four is a process. The miracle is that we are preparing ourselves for the humility that comes in Step Five.

TODAY'S MEDITATION

Dear God, as you hold my hand, I trust this process. Through faith, I will be set free.

"Confession of errors is like a broom which sweeps away the dirt and leaves the surface brighter and clearer. I feel stronger for confession."
— *Mahatma Gandhi*

CHANGING OUR MINDS
MARCH 12

In my addictions seldom could I decide what to do and when I did, I would often change my mind forgetting why I said what I did. Having the freedom to change my mind was discouraged by my husband as if doing so would change the course of our marriage. Once a decision was made, it seemed to be etched in stone.

Recovery tells us it is our right to change our minds. After prayer and meditation, we examine our intentions and motives and move forward if we feel confident the change is right for us. Learning to follow our instincts is a new behavior.

We ask, "How important is changing my mind?" If to do so offends, or otherwise hurts someone we want to be sure we are doing so for the right reasons, not just for the sake of making a change.

Practicing listening to our Higher Power allows us to discern our real purpose and intent. No longer do we need to go along to get along.

Today, we accept responsibility for how we feel, and celebrate the opportunity to change our minds with honesty and integrity.

TODAY'S MEDITATION

Changing my mind today comes with clarity and freedom that is tempered with humility. Asking for what I need gives me the wisdom to know the difference and the power to carry it out.

"Change anything about your life that cannot be accepted. Accept everything about your life that cannot be changed and move on with your big dreams!"
— *Israelmore Ayivor*

SELF-COMPASSION
MARCH 13

Self-compassion is a term almost never discussed. We know we extend compassion to the other person. If someone were to ask what does self-compassion look like how would we respond?

In our addictions we had no compassion for ourselves or others. We were stripped of emotions and had stopped feeling much of anything except panic and fear of not having enough of our drug of choice. The more we hid secrets and ourselves from others, the greater was our need to recede from reality. We became the empty shell of our former selves.

Recovery was our refuge, and the way to thaw hearts that barely beat that softened thoughts with the addition of compassion. We grasped hope, listening for an hour to others whose lives were transformed to sanity and believed it would work for us too.

One aspect of self-compassion is the ability to give to ourselves the same loving kindness we try so hard to extend to others. But in recovery, we see that we can't give away what we don't have. Learning to encourage ourselves with positive gentle messages is the beginning of a love of self which then extends to others. We gain acceptance of our imperfections and find a genuine affection for who we are. This is self-compassion.

Now when we look within, we find compassion for ourselves is waiting to surface. This is where emotional healing begins, with our loving arms around ourselves.

TODAY'S MEDITATION

Before I can pass anything on, it must be within me to give. Today, God, help me to let what I say and do begin with me.

"If you do not love yourself, you cannot love others... If you have no compassion for yourself, then you are not able of developing compassion for yourself."
— *Dalai Lama*

LEARNING TO REACH OUT
MARCH 14

It's startling how comfortable we become directing our world all by ourselves. Sometimes, we don't even include loved ones. Sometimes, we stop communicating yet seem surprised when relationships become threatened, even non-existent.

Isolating, keeping others at arm's length, makes for sick and lonely thinking. Victimization and low self-esteem gain strength. We who suffer from addictions already know this slippery slope. We are told that if we want to experience life differently, we *must* do life differently.

Learning to pick up the telephone and call a friend, no matter how hard at first, becomes easy with practice. Each time we speak to someone with compassion, we become a little more caring and a little more compassionate too. We see, as we share with others, we are no longer thinking of just ourselves.

Someone once said if we want to have friends we must first be a friend. So, we do something different and make ourselves useful instead of useless. We do this because we need a real connection with others and as that connection develops; we learn to be there when needed. What a joy it is to comfort and be comforted by others.

TODAY'S MEDITATION
Dear God, thank you for giving me the courage to reach out to others, and for being with me when I need you the most.

"Sometimes, reaching out and taking someone's hand is the beginning of a journey. At other times, it is allowing another to take yours." — *Vera Nazarian*

DOING IT ANYWAY
MARCH 15

Before committing to recovery, lip-service and broken promises were as close as I got to living life with intention. Both kept me from having to do anything uncomfortable.

Recovery teaches us to *do it, anyway.* Feelings have nothing to do with our ability to act. If it is important, we have to do it, regardless of how it makes us feel. We don't have to like it.

Taking the easy way out was normal for us. It was our comfort zone. We preferred to drag our feet like children trying to avoid doing something asked of us hoping to be left off the hook.

The difference between "thinking about," and "doing" is the action we take. Each time we move away from our comfort zone by doing, we grow in courage, self-esteem and confidence.

Without this dedication to *doing it anyway,* we would never have the integrity or the warrior mentality it takes to face life on life's terms, clean and sober no matter what it looks like.

TODAY'S MEDITATION

I'm grateful that, regardless of what I think I know, my self-assurance comes when I get out of my comfort zone and do it anyway.

"Before I knew you, I thought brave was not being afraid. You've taught me that bravery is being terrified and doing it anyway." — Laurel K. Hamilton

EQUALITY IN SOBRIETY
MARCH 16

Our preamble says our singleness of purpose is to stay sober and help others to achieve sobriety. There are no management dues or fees, merely suggestions as all of us have equal merit.

Experience shows one way we keep our side of the street clean is to not engage in gossip, manipulation, or judging others. With lives at stake we learn to focus on the solution. Who are we to talk about others? We are no better than anyone as we are all here for the same reason and all share the same affliction. We all seek asylum from our self-imposed insanity; all of us are sick and suffering. In this we are all the same.

Our shared disease with its hopelessness, pain and absolute desperation, is the common denominator that reminds us we are one. No person is above any other. Our stories disclose similar heartaches, fates, along with the feeling of demoralization that brought us into recovery.

No one can be turned away if they have a desire to stop drinking, which makes us all equal, each with the same right to be here.

TODAY'S MEDITATION
As we share our journey of truth in recovery, we find we have no need for superiority or righteousness, as our common thread is our disease.

"We know that permanent sobriety can be attained only by a most revolutionary change in the life and outlook of the individual..." — Bill W.

FALSE EVIDENCE APPEARING REAL
MARCH 17

As I review my life, I'm embarrassed to admit how much fear consumed me through the years. Even today, I fall back into fear. For years, fear devoured all hope of forward motion; prevented me from coping, from rising above, from taking a chance. I lived as a victim of my delusional thinking, obsessed and paranoid.

Recovery says one definition of fear is *false evidence appearing real*. It reminds us that feelings are not facts. Fear is an emotional reaction to life. It presents skewed messages from a variety of people, memories, experiences, and the darkest corners of our addiction.

Our feelings are neither bad, nor good, they are what they are—and then they dissipate.

We examined our fears and released them, one by one, in the Fourth Step. We made a list and asked ourselves, "Why do I have this?" "Is it helpful to keep it?" and, "Is it real or imagined?" We ask, "Can I let it go?" When we saw how irrational our thinking has been, we let them go.

In time, armed with these questions, we let go of fears that once controlled us. We see what, and how, we think have the power to control us.

As willing students, we realize we never were the person we always thought we were. Today the space where fear lived is filled instead with loving and uplifting affirmations.

Since we know better, we can do better. Room for the sunlight of the Spirit and calming peace guides our decisions as we look at fear for what it is, and what it is not.

TODAY'S MEDITATION

In my treasured rooms of recovery, the truth really is setting me free one day at a time.

"Our enemy is fear. Blinding, reason-killing fear. Fear consumes the truth and poisons all the evidence, leading us to false assumptions and irrational conclusions." — Rick Yancey

FINDING A PEACE WITHIN
MARCH 18

I always imagined self-sacrifice and hard work would bring me the peace I so longed for. I grew tired and restless as I waited for it to come. Edging God Out (EGO), I relied upon my best thinking. Then a friend told me peace is an inside job. Upon hearing this, I doubled my efforts by getting involved helping others at every turn, believing osmosis would transform the emptiness inside me. I had misunderstood the value of an inside job. I was trying to earn peace by doing good works but never looked within myself for what I sought.

When we allow everything and everyone to come before us, we experience emotional burnout. As our physical world becomes more important than our spiritual world, we lose our balance. Instead of peace, what dominates is a growing disappointment. We stay disillusioned until we expand daily rituals to include spiritual awareness and look inside.

How do we get to peace?

First, we must make room for it. Before we accept assignments that involve blocks of time and energy, we ask ourselves questions and examine motives for taking them on: We question our importance: Could someone else do it? How important is it? Is it more important than the precious time we need to pray and meditate or have a relaxing lunch with a friend? How would helping ourselves and others put us closer to the peace and serenity we seek?

The more we understand and honor our motives, the closer to peace we come.

TODAY'S MEDITATION
God, if you asked me for my truth, what would I say? The answer is my need to trust you, to clean house and help others. In these efforts, will I find my peace within.

"First keep the peace within yourself, then you can also bring peace to others."
— *Thomas a Kempis*

THE FIXER

Those of us who take care of others wear many hats: head nurse, mother, spouse, wage earner, go-to person.

There is an imaginary pedestal we *fixers* stand on. We are the on-call detective, the one who solves problems for others with confidence, satisfied to have answers for everyone. We are important, assured someone needs us. If new in recovery we work all the harder to deliver whether or not we were asked.

Others have always found us to be effective, at least until they became healthy and no longer need our help. When that day came, they found their independence. As we saw we were losing control over them we became overwhelmed and struggled even more to keep our authority over those around us.

Sustained recovery brings new accountability and independence to both ourselves and others as we take part in the delicate dance necessary to sustain relationships. Recovery teaches that love and tolerance is our code. We support the independence of others in our homes and friendship circles. When they grow up, no longer needing to our help, we may find the path to loving communication and nurturing a hard one to walk. We are no longer in charge, no longer the fixer. Instead we learn to detach with love and patience.

As our power wanes we strive for equality and stay engaged as a help-mate. Our pedestal is gone. As we rely more upon ourselves, we allow others the pace and responsibility for their own transitioning. We focus on our journey. Acceptance, and *Live and Let Live* become redefined, one day at a time as we work together in our relationships.

TODAY'S MEDITATION

Putting my needs first, I gauge how much is left to give to others and pray for the wisdom to know when the help I have to offer is no longer needed.

"Perhaps there could be no joy on this planet without an equal weight of pain to balance it out on some unknown scale." — *Stephenie Meyer*

LETTING PEOPLE IN
MARCH 20

Many years ago, I lived with a housemate who spent her life alone in her room. She never came out to talk with us, to eat dinner with us, or to just hang out with the rest of us. I knew then I would work to never be like her. But in my addiction, I created an isolation of my own, a story that is told over and over in our rooms of recovery.

It's been a long and lonely journey in the rooms trying to become comfortable with others. One reason we stand by the mantra *Keep Coming Back* is because left to old behaviors, we could slip right back into the arms of isolation and fear. In isolation, our addictions often return with a vengeance.

In the fellowship of recovery, we are reassured by the similarities we share. Finding others like ourselves, we let our guard down and become comfortable. In our rooms we are all sick people trying to get well. Just like me, we are all in this together, sharing our experience strength and hope as we gain personal strength on our individual journeys, one day at a time.

TODAY'S MEDITATION
Thank you, God, for letting me get over my fear of people and showing me that my journey is one I share with so many others.

"The best way to look back at life fondly is to meet it—and those along your journey—warmly, kindly and mindfully." — Rasheed Ogunlaru

GRIEVING IN SOBRIETY
MARCH 21

Grieving and pain can paralyze, leaving us with regrets and unfinished business. Some of us choose not to grieve. We imagine that if we don't give grief power by thinking about it, our grief will dissipate into thin air. Some of us pretend for years we're doing just fine, as others prefer taking grief into their own hands to deal with it once and for all.

Grief and anger, if left unchecked, often hit like a tidal wave crashing over us knocking us sideways without warning. These emotions have the power to inflict damage to ourselves and others, often at the most inopportune times.

In recovery we have a responsibility to ourselves. We must allow our woundedness to heal by facing grief and painful emotions, wearing them like a loose garment.

What does that mean? It means we give ourselves permission to explore and find acceptance with our feelings regardless of the pain. It means we face and walk *through* them until we no longer need to hold on to them; we keep walking until we come out the other side where they no longer control us. We do it, despite how we feel. Although feelings are not facts, the consequence of not finding peace through acceptance or forgiveness can mean continual and long-term discomfort. It can jeopardize our sobriety.

We practice giving love and kindness to ourselves while seeking the spiritual and emotional strength of others. We empower those who honor us in our quest for serenity and acceptance with an equal measure. Some of us do this by asking for, and receiving, the help we need. Some of us journal as we work through our feelings so they don't work us.

By giving ourselves the space and time necessary for introspection, we discover a newfound acceptance deep within. We come to our own rescue and survive some of our darkest, most painful of days and still come out the other side clean and sober.

"While grief is fresh, every attempt to divert only irritates. You must wait till it be digested, and then amusement will dissipate the remains of it."
— *Samuel Johnson*

GUILT
MARCH 22

How many times have we chastised ourselves for something said or left unsaid, done or left undone? Either we did too much or—not enough.

As a child, we ate the lie we heard from family and authority figures and believed that we could and should make a situation right. When we couldn't, we assumed guilt believing it was all our fault. Over time, our sense of guilt became so big it overshadowed everything we thought we were. We couldn't see through to our own goodness.

Imagine the size of our list of, "If only's," "Should have's," and "ought to's." Those phrases begin all the stories we told ourselves about our failures. It wasn't the truth then, and it isn't the truth today. Our guilt became permission to believe we were less than. We did what we needed to be done, no more or no less.

It's time we let go of our old beliefs and the inappropriateness of guilt. Guilt does nothing to elevate inner-confidence or serenity nor does it contribute to the emotional freedom we so desperately seek. In recovery, we replace guilt with an empowering mantra of, "We are doing the best we know how, and so is everyone else."

Inhaling inner courage, we let go of guilt. We find a balance in who we are and find we *are* enough. We let go of hurtful assaults to our psyche, our own past failures, and embrace who we have always been; a spiritual being living an imperfect, human experience.

TODAY'S MEDITATION

Thank you, God, for gifts disguised as lessons and for your forgiveness which is all I need.

"One of life's most difficult lessons is to accept that we are either fighting to hold on, or fighting to let go. Letting go liberates us from thinking we can control what is." — Beth Harrer

HEALTHY RITUALS

I grew up without a purpose and jumped from one problem to another. Without a plan, I lived in a maze of confusion. Being overwhelmed felt normal.

In Al-Anon Family Group meetings, "How Important Is It?" became a sacred chant for me. As I prepared a list that included putting myself first, versus taking care of everyone, I discerned the inconsequential from what is vital to do today. Everything else could wait.

The goal in recovery is to forge new habits and healthy rituals that promote clarity for a serene existence. Maybe we need to stop what we are doing and examine our thinking. Does the whirring and stirring, the rush from one fire to another, make us productive? Are we resentful, wishing we had time for ourselves, but remain unable to disconnect from other self-imposed obligations? Are we confused and going nowhere fast?

If we could reconstruct our day with purpose, giving ourselves priority, what would we tell ourselves to do? We'd tell ourselves we need and deserve to begin new daily habits and implement healthy rituals that give us hope and direction. We'd ask ourselves, what rituals give us joy? Which do we detest, and why do we still engage in them? What actions can we let go, to allow for more time for ourselves?

We deserve to stop long enough to answer these questions. It's how we change, and how we learn what is enough yet bringing us closer to ourselves and to our Higher Power. As we begin our written inventory, we become focused, efficient, and better able to care for ourselves and the people we love.

TODAY'S MEDITATION
Today I deserve to set priorities, choosing what is best for me, creating new rituals.

"A daily ritual is a way of saying I'm voting for myself;
I'm taking care of myself." — Mariel Hemingway

HUMILITY
MARCH 24

One definition of humility is to possess the quality of humility. When we accommodate others from our highest self, we think of others more and ourselves less. Humility should not be confused with humiliation whose object is to make someone ashamed.

How often has our behavior lacked the tempering effect of humility? Each time we went that extra mile for our addictions, humility was never the goal. Self-centered pride and big-shotism was. We sought recognition and adoration from those around us. Our over-inflated ego, blown out of proportion from a lack of healthy self-esteem would not stop. If we did a good deed, we put ourselves on a pedestal, expecting grandiose accolades that never came. Standing on that lonely pedestal we felt resentful and hurt.

Humility is the lesson that will right-size our ego. With humility, we practice quietness in prayer. We do random acts of kindness. Humility reminds us we are not in charge. We come to believe in the eyes of our Higher Power; we are no better, or worse than anyone else. As we seek to keep our ego small through humility, we make room for our Higher Power.

We practice selfless acts hoping we will grow along spiritual lines. In prayer, humility allows us to resonate with vibrations and energy of our higher self. As we breathe as one with our Higher Power, we absorb the sanctity of the moment.

TODAY'S MEDITATION
Today, I ask for the grace of humility and an ego sufficiently small to get out of God's way and allow Him to prevail over each thought and earnest plea.

"Humility is the ability to give up your pride and still retain your dignity."
— *Vanna Bonta*

STEP FOUR – ASSETS
MARCH 25

One aspect of Step Four discussed in AA literature, is the ability to bring to light our goodness in our strengths. Someone refers this goodness to as our assets.

In our years of self-loathing, personal assets never came to mind for many of us. Buried deep underneath our shortcomings, these assets never saw the light. Step Four asks us to identify the things blocking us from the sunlight of the Spirit. With the help of a wise sponsor, we seek to find and list our assets. As we spot them, we discover the goodness that was there all along, although we couldn't recognize that self before recovery.

We list our assets in Step Four to provide the stability of balance, and to counteract our delusional and over-exaggerated negative thinking about ourselves. As we inventory our harms done to others and ourselves, we list our assets too, for we are not born bad. We believe we are redeemable. Deep within us lives the rest of who we are. We face our own goodness, many of us never dreamed was there.

Begin with a clean sheet of paper. List your assets and then ask your sponsor what you have left off the list. Sponsors have the advantage of seeing what we cannot see about ourselves—yet. We are sick people, trying to get better. Faith and hope quiet the barrage of negative messages as we work through harms we have caused others. We trust that more will be revealed in the Fifth Step.

TODAY'S MEDITATION
My assets provide courage for me to believe that I am worth saving. Now that I see my own goodness, I know my truth. Thank you, God.

"Loving ourselves through the process of owning our story is the bravest thing we'll ever do." — Brene Brown

IDENTIFYING FEELINGS
MARCH 26

Each day we receive situations that cause us confusion and frustration. In early sobriety we find that as we become honest we see with frustration, how powerless over everyone and everything we are, that we control nothing except ourselves.

As adults, while comfortable expressing disharmony and dissatisfaction, we cannot find words to express wholeness and satisfaction. Many of us feel too disconnected to do so while others feel only guilt or shame.

Some of us discover that writing gratitudes and answering how they made us feel, is a way to identify feelings. How does it feel to experience contentment? What words do we express to identify how it feels to be loved, validated and understood?

Buried beneath our woundedness is the open, honest, child-like wonder we forgot we are. Recovery affords us the chance to invite those feelings to once again flourish, because until we do, we will always settle for less of ourselves.

Courage provides the permission necessary to honor this part of us so long ignored. We create a list of the feelings we deserve and bask in the power of those positive words.

As we open ourselves on an emotional level, we become better at identifying the emotions we feel. Once we name the emotion, we can claim it. When we allow the word to become real, we replace indifference and negative sentiment that once hurt us. In naming and claiming our emotions, we are sure who we are now.

What a joy it is to know words can't hurt us any longer without our permission. We honor ourselves with the voice of our choosing with the power of the words that identifies how we feel at the moment.

TODAY'S MEDITATION

Today I seek out positive truths about myself and allow them to be my light. I deserve to embrace every positive affirmation that is me.

"Feel the feeling as though the prayer has already been answered, and in that feeling we are speaking to the Forces of Creation, allowing the world to respond to us." — Gregg Braden

JUST ENOUGH

MARCH 27

A friend in recovery shared the emotional toll endured these last months concerning her addicted daughter. Working her program, she prayed to come to terms with acceptance of her own powerlessness.

Exhaling, she told of how she had just enough hope, just enough faith, and just enough self-compassion to stay the course, just for the rest of that day. With courage as she spoke, others saw what it could be like to have just enough of something needed to get through any obstacle.

Some on the journey of recovery experience the total depletion of their reserves. Others fall out of sight, slipping back under the cloak of relapse, rejecting any sustaining faith.

During our own crises, when it seems the universe grows dark with despair, it's deep in prayer with our Higher Power that we breathe an angelic plea; *give me enough strength to trust a little more.*

We either accept the moment's grace, embracing the just enough to survive the trial at hand, or, in denial, we fall to disappointment and relapse.

TODAY'S MEDITATION

I close my eyes, aware I am alive, and embrace with enlightened clarity that I've been given just enough power to achieve anything I choose, just for the rest of today.

"Man must have just enough faith in himself to have adventures,
and just enough doubt of himself to enjoy them." — Gilbert K. Chesterton

OWNING OUR TRUTH
MARCH 28

I came to recovery unable to make decisions and gave everyone around me the power of choice over what was best for me. I had no voice, and I didn't care. So terrified was I of picking the wrong door to walk through, I preferred the safety of being cemented in place.

Recovery shows the miracle of being true to self is not a notion or inspiration. Our truth is uncompromising and absolute, regardless of what anyone else suggests, or what their expectations or opinions are. We know our truth will set us free, and it does.

Our ability to be true to self, heightens personal integrity, something some of us never had. The precious gift of sobriety has taught us that our truths are already within us. Our job is to recognize, accept, and own our truths, no matter how uncomfortable it feels at first. We deserve to discern our truth as it defines who we are while embracing our authenticity. Our truth alone is the thread that connects us to the Sunlight of the Spirit, validating who we believe we are right here, right now. Only through working together with our Higher Power will we find our true selves.

TODAY'S MEDITATION
With eyes open, I accept all of me. Finally, I'm learning to entrust my heart to the goodness that is me.

"As I began to love myself I found that anguish and emotional suffering are only warning signs that I was living against my own truth. Today, I know, this is "AUTHENTICITY". — Charlie Chaplan

I AM RESPONSIBLE
MARCH 29

Looking back on my life, as the oldest of five, I can see my part in our dysfunctional family. I was a juvenile delinquent; wild, obstinate, and defiant to the adults in my world. Then I think of my marriage and the destructive role I played there. Held captive by addictions and lashing out with vindictive and jealous behaviors, I considered myself the victim of that dark and troubled childhood and carried my resentments with me. Anyone in my path, including my husband, assumed ownership for my indiscretions since nothing could ever be my fault.

In recovery, honesty is the one truth we cannot evade if we want a better life. We know if we want to be better, then we must do better.

Working the Steps with a sponsor opens our eyes to the truth about our disease and *our* behaviors. As we admit and claim ownership for both actions and consequences, along with intentional acts of omission, we change and become responsible. Healing begins the day we hold ourselves accountable for our actions and behaviors toward those we love, including those we call family.

TODAY'S MEDITATION
Today I am grateful to be responsible to my family, friends and co-workers, but especially to me, and me alone. If I am not the problem, there can be no solution.

"I am free, no matter what rules surround me. I am free because I know that I alone am morally responsible for everything I do." — Robert A. Heinlein

IT TAKES A VILLAGE
MARCH 30

As a child, I never saw myself as good enough. After all, I couldn't repair my broken family. Dad was often absent or passed-out drunk. Mom was raging, out of control with five young children to care for. Messages of pain, hopelessness, and anger were expressed through dysfunction.

Drugs and alcohol became my solution for escape well into my adult years. My addiction acted as a barrier between you and me. It allowed me to wear the disguise of superiority until it stopped working. I only *thought* it protected me, but it was just the imaginary committee in my head reinforcing what turned out to be a set of mistaken beliefs.

It takes a village of recovery: fellowship, steps, meetings, and a host of sponsors to illuminate the path to hope. Those who want all recovery has to offer in the way of miracles, find we need them all, and always will. Why after all this time? Because it predicates our insidious disease on the belief we deserve nothing, are worth nothing. Our disease that never leaves us is doing pushups, waiting for the opportunity to infiltrate and take over our obsessive thoughts of indulging by making it a reality.

Hard work, a strong trust in the process of recovery, the support of our community, and the lead of our Higher Power prove how deserving of self-worth we are.

Find your village because you are no less deserving than I am.

TODAY'S MEDITATION
What a miracle to not only believe my own goodness, but to share it with others. I owe my life to the village of recovery.

"I'm every woman. It takes a village to make me who I am". — *Katy Perry*

NOT OUR BUSINESS
MARCH 31

I wondered why bad, unspeakable things happened. Was I being punished for the turmoil I'd created, and the pain I inflicted on others? Why did some people die while others lived?

I demanded answers to these questions after my husband, father and my only child died. Why had they died? Why was I left to live, the drunk mom, wife and caretaker? Why not me? I fought with my Higher Power. I needed to understand and have closure but none came. I took off my gloves, stepped out of the ring and gave up the need to know.

Recovery tells us that ninety-nine-point nine percent of what happens in life is none of our business. Life is the business of our Higher Power. Accepting what is, we concede that something out there has the answers. It reminds us; *You be you, I'll be me, and let God be God.* To trust the wisdom of a Higher Power that we are being led is all that is necessary.

What serenity we enjoy when we accept that we are just another cog in the wheel of life, without having to have answers that are none of our business.

TODAY'S MEDITATION
Thank you, God, for allowing me to see my proper place in the world and for comfort in accepting what is.

"It's not my business to try and make God think like me... but to try, in prayer and penitence, to think like God. — Aiden Wilson Tozer

Step Four
April 1

"Made a searching and fearless moral inventory of ourselves"

This is the step that sends fear into the hearts of just about every newcomer who walks into recovery. It's no wonder that this is where many slip away rather than face important but unpleasant facts about themselves

Before recovery we were sure we would die if we faced what we've done. Years of hiding secrets reinforced the notion that no one could have ever suffered shame, humiliation, or harm as we did. But again, we were mistaken.

One fact is certain: we are better than we think we are. Instead of allowing fear to overwhelm us, we are comforted in Steps Two and Three and are no longer walking nor living our lives alone as our Higher Power is guiding our path.

Step Four is nothing more than a *fact-finding mission*, the gateway to the freedom we want more than life. This is our opportunity to clean house. And so, we delve deep to expose what happened in our addiction, how it affected us, who was hurt, and the role we played. This is the first time many of us have looked, clear-eyed and sober, at our flaws without the distorting filter of our drug of choice. It may also be the first time we have acknowledged the assets that confirm we are redeemable.

With help from a sponsor, we throw out everything detrimental to our inner-light, making room for a Higher Power who stands in waiting, ready to work with us.

We ready ourselves with a prayer for the freedom and acceptance sure to come in Step Five. As we take inventory of who we are with honesty, openness, and the willingness to see we are comforted, ready to grow in courage, tenacity and the faith to face all we are.

TODAY'S MEDITATION

I see now this is but a beginning of a new freedom and a new happiness. As I face my own honest inventory, I acknowledge there is a lifetime of work to do, but I walk on faith, no longer afraid.

"Forgive the past. It is over. Learn from it and let go... Do not cling to a limited, disconnected, negative image of a person in the past. See that person now. Your relationship is always alive and changing." — Brian L. Weiss

LONELINESS

APRIL 2

Growing up, I was always lonely. I was lonely in my marriage. Lonely at family gatherings. I was saturated with poor self-esteem and felt empty inside. I had little-to-no faith, and a constant awareness of never fitting in. Anywhere.

This ever-present loneliness seems, for most of us, to be the core of our addictions.

In recovery, we learn the depth of our soul-sickness, our loneliness, and seek a stronger relationship with a Higher Power. As we grow along spiritual lines, the difference between being alone and being lonely become clear.

Dedicated working of The Steps, connection to our higher power, along with the strength of the fellowship, allow for the discovery of a self-esteem sufficient to enable us to stand and live alone or in harmony with others.

Because of this relationship with our Higher Power, we never have to be lonely again.

TODAY'S MEDITATION

Thank you, God, for the ability to see that our alignment with our God works in conjunction with our recovery.

"At the innermost core of all loneliness is a deep and powerful yearning for union with one's lost self." — *Brendan Behan*

MEETING MAKERS, MAKE IT!
APRIL 3

Some people believe all they have to do in recovery, is to show up at meetings. They think walking through those doors suffices to provide the principles and perceptions necessary to change lives. There are those, too, who can achieve long-term recovery without the program.

But for most, the process of recovery begins by taking part in meetings as it is one place where our Higher Power resides. Our literature tells us that God, as we understand God, is standing right in front of us when healing begins.

While meetings are often essential to recovery, they are only a piece of recovery. For those who stay, there are valuable lessons to learn in our sober survival. Here we become a part-of something bigger than ourselves as we listen and work with others. We absorb a multitude of guiding principles in our meetings, with reminders to take what we need and leave the rest.

Most of all, we look for similarities within the group. Our misery—and our recovery—love company. The biggest similarity is that we share is our common malady, our addiction, which is a three-fold disease: physical, spiritual and emotional. We also share a three-fold solution: unity (meetings and fellowship); service (helping others); and recovery (the 12 steps). These three elements represent the whole of recovery. Each work together, when we work it, to bring success in achieving long-term sobriety, no matter how many other methods have failed.

While for most of us it is not enough to just attend meetings to experience all recovery has to offer, meetings are our place to begin, to return to again and again and find acceptance.

TODAY'S MEDITATION

Just for today I will be a meeting maker and earn my seat by participating in my three-fold solution: unity, service, and recovery.

"Courage is the most important of all the virtues because without courage, you can't practice any other virtue consistently." — *Maya Angelou*

PERSONAL INTEGRITY
APRIL 4

Integrity is the holding of strong moral principles and character. In our addiction, we had no morals or character to stand on. No one trusted us, nor were we dependable. We were self-absorbed, egotistical—liars, cheats and thieves.

Recovery helps to develop a personal integrity we can live up to. As we learn to become reliable and trustworthy, as The Steps live in and through us, we embrace the beginnings of personal integrity. Our families see it, friends and employers see it, and most of all, *we* see it.

Our Higher Power plants seeds of integrity and over time, credibility flourishes. It becomes clear to those who know us we have worked for it and deserve it.

With patience and deliberation, we re-create ourselves, becoming a trusted servant and friend to others, someone we can depend upon and respect too.

TODAY'S MEDITATION

Please show me, God, how to exhibit integrity to myself and others. I pray for guidance, and trust your timing, knowing that more will be revealed.

"Integrity gives you real freedom because you have nothing to fear since you have nothing to hide." — Zig Ziglar

POSITIVE AFFIRMATIONS
APRIL 5

As far back as I remember, I was all I thought about. My obsessive/compulsive thinking signaled the start of my addictions. A lack of a moral compass was a part of me long before my addictions were engaged. A lifetime of slow, painful change became necessary to eradicate self-defeating, hurtful thoughts and actions. Recovery was the forum of miracles and positive affirmations that came true for me.

Practicing positive affirmations is a strong emotional healer that destroys destructive thinking. As we recognize the power these encouraging affirmations carry, we feel them at the same time as we see them.

How comforting it is to admit we are that same person when we look in the mirror. We embrace who we've always wanted to be as we grow in self-assurance with the help of positive affirmations.

TODAY'S MEDITATION
I am grateful for the courage to change the things I can, which begins and ends with me. I've found a way to make myself and my thinking whole.

"Affirmations are our mental vitamins, providing the supplementary positive thoughts we need to balance the barrage of negative events and thoughts we experience daily." — Tia Walker

THE QUIETNESS OF CHANGE
APRIL 6

Dawn breaks. As the morning opens its eyes from the silence of my porch, I see robins, the first to hail the start of this new day. I hold my breath as they venture close enough for me to observe their beauty.

As I look around me, spring flowers lift their buds, poised to bloom, while others as yet unseen, prepare to break the earth's surface. With the warmth of spring that encourages new growth, I feel my Higher Power encourage me to change also in the quietness of time, as I yield to forces beyond my control and sight.

In the footwork of prayer and meditation, I'm assured that more will be revealed.

Although, I do nothing more in this moment than inhale, I'm experiencing a miracle in the quietness of change. Like the plants all around me, I am transformed as I stretch, moving closer toward the light.

As I exhale, I thank the Universe for hope and acceptance of what is, and what will be, with *the quietness of change*.

TODAY'S MEDITATION
Dear God, I know you have me exactly where I'm supposed to be in this moment since nothing happens by mistake in your world. I accept that change can come quietly, but always in response to your will.

"When we are no longer able to change a situation,
we are challenged to change ourselves." — Viktor Frankl

Drifting along in our kayaks, I was stunned as I listened to a dear friend share her ever-present feelings of incompetence and of never fitting in. She explained how a lack of self-esteem kept her paranoid. In crowds and at work gatherings, she often stood on the sidelines, afraid to participate, because she was too uncomfortable in her own skin.

Locked in repulsive delusional thinking, she was sure everyone was looking at her, talking about her, judging her. Even though she did her best to be inconspicuous, she remained convinced she was the center of everyone's attention.

The good news is that most of what concerns other people has nothing to do with us. We are all we think about, it's true, but everyone else is concerned with their own personal lives.

Our over-exaggerated ego screams, "It's all about me!" But no, it is not. Recovery teaches that we are not that important.

We are no more or less important than the next person; we are just another cog in the wheel of life, and so is everyone else. Although we thought we were about the center of everyone's attention, that never was the case.

TODAY'S MEDITATION

How secure I am today accepting that life never did revolve around me, it was only my thinking that made it so.

*"You probably wouldn't worry about what people think of you
if you could know how seldom they do." — Olin Miller*

SECRETS

APRIL 8

For many of us the secrets we held close added to our soul sickness. What we knew but couldn't tell because it would reveal who we *really* were, kept us in a prison of terror.

Some of our secrets were about the perfectionistic demands for blind loyalty that dominated our households. To measure up to those expectations, our secrets never had a voice. Unspoken, each secret became another elephant in the room. The more they were ignored, the bigger they grew, becoming more terrifying in our minds. Each was an embodiment of the dreaded D's: don't talk, don't tell, and don't feel.

Other secrets, sometimes so atrocious, kept us in bondage of self for a lifetime. Most of the time, our secrets morphed, growing disproportionately within our warped imaginations.

As the secrets we kept produced negative energy, the path to a drink or drug seemed the easiest way to go. It relieved the enormous pressure needed to ignore that phantom elephant in the room.

Recovery tells us we are as sick as our secrets and no longer afford to have them. As we The Steps, the gift of freedom becomes real. Secrets we once thought would strangle us can be set free.

Free of secrets we become transformed, lifted out of self-loathing, becoming useful to others, and to our Higher Power.

TODAY'S MEDITATION
God, let me always remember that the sunlight of the Spirit is where secrets wither and die. I remain free of secrets when I give them to you.

"There are people so addicted to exaggeration
they can't tell the truth without lying." — Josh Billings

EXPECTATIONS
APRIL 9

Expectations without recovery are not a pretty sight. Our disease exaggerates our expectations and when they go unfulfilled, they are put on the fast-track to resentment. We blame others and before we know it, we're facing a resentment. Without recovery, our disease wants us to believe what we feel is someone else's' fault.

Unmet expectations lead to accusations, arguments, and anger. We blame others seeing no fault in our own behavior. Thwarted expectations say we're not getting what we *think* we deserve; that somehow, *we* are being short-changed. Someone or something is not measuring up to our standards, and we are disappointed. When an expectation fails to materialize, we are hurt, and we are resentful.

With recovery, it is easy to see how unfair, even selfish, expectations are. Wishful thinking, locked in our heads, can have negative and hurtful consequences for ourselves and others.

How do we stop engaging in expectations? We get honest and bring unresolved issues into the light. We examine our own thinking. Where had we been selfish, self-centered, dishonest? Being aware of self-talk, we take deliberate care to not make assumptions about others. We avoid the trap of a more dangerous foe: a resentment just waiting to happen.

TODAY'S MEDITATION
Not having expectations means I must be true to myself. Expectations disappear when I honor my motives and sincerity.

"Never blame people for disappointing you, blame yourself for expecting too much from them. Expectations always lead you to being disappointed."
— Anurag Prakash Ray

PERFECTIONISM
APRIL 10

Perfectionism strives for flawlessness. It sets unreasonably high standards. It demands hypercritical self-evaluation and unrealistic and unfavorable comparisons with others.

In recovery we come to realize that the quest for perfectionism ("I," "She," "Me,") is a self-induced setup for failure. This perfectionistic state is often associated with depression, addictions, and other mental health manifestations.

Imagine someone who believes they can never measure up. Then imagine that they are in a hamster wheel that rolls over and over as they try to get to perfection. It is easy to see they never will because they are going nowhere. As long as we run in the hamster wheel of perfection it will never satisfy us, nor will we ever measure up. We have to stop running and realize that perfection is a myth.

Recovery gives us permission to accept that we are imperfectly alright where we are and we're always enough. The easier, softer way in recovery is to embrace the place that we are, just for today. As we become assured through working The Steps that we are not walking alone and that we are loved just the way we are, the myth of perfection takes a much-needed back seat on our journey. Perfection no longer controls our thinking.

We trust this space and time as being enough because, in this moment, there is no other truth. Our Higher Power is perfect and all knowing. As we come to terms with our imperfections, we release delusions and don't struggle. We come to believe that we are all we need to be.

TODAY'S MEDITATION

What a relief that by Letting Go and Letting God, I reclaim my balance and accept that God has me right where He wants me, just for today.

"Always live up to your standards — by lowering them, if necessary."
— Mignon McLaughlin

STANDING IN THE LIGHT
APRIL 11

Someone once said, "Things would have been different if they had more light." I thought, *what does light have to do with anything?*

Recovery shows if we consider our Higher Power as energy coming from a Spirit God, we know that Spirit is the light of the universe, the light that allows us to see.

"Walking in the sunlight of the Spirit" is a metaphor for growing along spiritual lines. When our spiritual life is well-lit we know better, and we do better. In the realm of the spirit, believing *is* seeing.

Each time we open our hearts, willing to let in the light being emitted by something greater than ourselves, we tap into the light of our own goodness. Here we have the highest knowing that whatever this power is, we are not walking alone.

As we become aware we are not alone, the knowledge of a gentle presence engulfs us and we are led, moving in blissful peace.

Although we walk without seeing what is ahead, we remain steadfast in the warmth and security that comes from the aura of the Great Spirit, our Higher Power as it leads us.

TODAY'S MEDITATION
Thank you, God, for the discernment that enables me to choose light instead of the darkness that comes with the dead-end paths I follow when led by my own self-will.

"Dare to reach out your hand into the darkness to pull another hand into the light." — Amrit DeSoi

*"Admitted to God, to ourselves, and to another human being
the exact nature of our wrongs."*

Faced with *Step Five,* many of us resist, change our minds, or become paralyzed with fear. Others drink or drug or run way from this step. We think that
no one else could understand where we've been. We're convinced too, that
if others knew what we've done, we'd be rejected yet again. But years were
spent absorbing these lies, trusting these irrational beliefs as they played the
message, "You don't deserve to be fixed."

No longer can we afford to disregard the fact that secrets held close, keep us
sick, stuck in the sludge of false beliefs. Like a cancer, these beliefs fester and
we become convinced there really *is* no one worse than us; and, we will never
be forgiven.

Step Five is vital to our survival. Recovery gives us mobility forward. Step
Five opens doors to humility and courage as we confess truths about ourselves with a sponsor, a professional or trusted friend who honors the sanctity
of our secrets.

The good news is that not one person has died from revealing their darkest
secrets, the ones the person had reserved for the grave. To deny ourselves the
healing of Step Five puts us closer to relapse, or worse.

By now, we have taken questions to our sponsor, to meetings, and to our
Higher Power, who is with us on our journey. Having come this far, we are
at peace knowing our Higher Power will reveal nothing more than what we
can handle.

When we hold secrets we are looking, not at the person we are today; but
at the person we *used* to be, the one entrapped in old stories full of blame,
conjecture, and pain.

Step Five is begins a transformation of our story as we become a person
re-created in faith. We've worked too hard and come too far to give up now,
what is for many of us, one of the greatest miracles of The Steps: our freedom
from and acceptance of harms done to ourselves and others.

If we ask, our Higher Power will continue to walk before us toward forgiveness. I know, because He is still in front of me.

TODAY'S MEDITATION

Dear God, I pray for the willingness, honesty and open-mindedness to withhold nothing. The quality of my life depends upon complete honesty.

"The secret to happiness is freedom...
And the secret to freedom is courage."- Thucydides

STRONGHOLD OF UNFORGIVENESS
APRIL 13

One of the most difficult tasks I have ever had in my life is to forgive myself and others. I crucified several people in my head daily for a lifetime of hurts and put myself on that cross of unforgiveness. Full of self-pity, it took years of recovery to accept that I was the one suffering.

As we assemble a bridge of hate against others, we bring internal misery from years of wishing them harm, convinced our life would be better if they passed on. Self-centered pride screamed for revenge, as we enjoyed a sick sense of righteousness over these resentments. We became treacherous and alienated everyone as we reinforced our personal fortress of justification to use against them. We were the victim—stuck in self-righteous indignation.

Working The Steps revealed how to absorb a new forgiveness. With great trepidation, we let go of indignation and looked for compassion for ourselves and others. We saw that our misgivings, justifiable or not, never belonged to us. They belonged to our loving Higher Power to pass judgment. The grace of our Higher Power with the power of The Steps shelters and soothes our woundedness. The light of forgiveness changes *us* as we do the work. With this newfound forgiveness, we become free from the fortress we built of justification, and replace it with an angelic peace never thought possible.

TODAY'S MEDITATION
Dear God, miracles of recovery continue to bring me closer to you. Thank you for the humility of compassion to honor myself so that I may give more to others. I am being set free.

"He who is devoid of the power to forgive is devoid of the power to love... When we discover this, we are less prone to hate our enemies."
— *Martin Luther King, Jr.*

THIS TOO, SHALL PASS
APRIL 14

There are days when our feet first hit the floor and we revert to old ways of thinking. Without taking time for prayer and meditation, our subconscious finds a message that repeats, "Life Sucks" and the habit of negativity picks up where we left off before recovery. Internal messages of, *is this all there is?* or, *what's the point?* fills our minds with despair. Before we know it, thoughts transform our demeanor and expression. It's not pretty. It's not recovery and serves no purpose other than to make real fatalistic thinking. We allow ourselves to become, yet again, victims of our delusional thinking.

It's important to remember that *This Too, Shall Pass*. As we let go of old ways of thinking and embrace hope, we come to believe life is not one big setup to keep us stuck. We remember what we already know–*This Too, Shall Pass*. It always does.

By allowing ourselves to get out of our own way and repeat this loving mantra, we look at our feet and see right here, right now; we are alive and have choices. We can seize the day with a boldness of sober excitement and allow everything to pass. Right where we are!

TODAY'S MEDITATION
I'm so grateful to remember as I get out of the way and open my heart and my mind, everything passes.

"This is the ending. Now not day only shall be beloved, but night too shall be beautiful and blessed and all its fear pass away." — J.R.R. Tolkien

VICTIMIZATION
APRIL 15

As a child, I learned and found comfort playing the role of the victim. I received the attention I craved. Being a victim was a perpetual excuse for self-pity, as hope and emotional growth withered away.

Being the victim allowed us freedom to blame everyone else for our short-comings and aberrant behaviors. We rationalized our lives were messes and absolved ourselves of all responsibility. Blind in self-pity we exclaimed, "If you had my life you'd feel sorry for me too!"

Remaining the victim was necessary for a short-cut to self-destruction.

Our awareness in recovery became the truth necessary to admit victimization is nothing more than a comfortable guise we created to stay emotionally irresponsible. We learn we have choices today because, after all, we were not born a victim.

As we recover and grow on an emotional level, the need to stay victimized diminishes. We get down from the cross and take responsibility for our decisions and actions. We become convinced of our inner-strength and abilities and let go of old messages of victimization.

Another miracle is born.

TODAY'S MEDITATION
Today I am strong and with God I can be free. Today I will not be a victim.

"We must always take sides. Neutrality helps the oppressor, never the victim. Silence encourages the tormentor, never the tormented." — Elie Wiesel

WHEN IN DOUBT
APRIL 16

It feels empowering to have answers to everyday situations. Sometimes we don't even think about our responses. We have this intuitive knowing that tells us we are not living in a bubble but moving in response to a higher vibration where our knowing lives. What about decisions we are not sure of?

I've been struggling, and after putting my house on the market for a year it still has not sold. On paper, reasons for and against selling were equal. After cleaning, fixing and painting, I still didn't know what to do.

There is only one solution. When in doubt, do nothing. Forget it. *Let Go and Let God.* The timing is not right. It feels like we are forcing an outcome to suit ourselves. We are convinced of what we need when we need it, but what we hear is impatience. When we assert control before being ready to see the big picture and what it means to stay or go, we are trying to run the show.

More is always revealed from our Higher Power whose timing is perfect when we're ready to accept it. We find, until then, we become content where we are, going about our business. It will feel right, and it will be right.

How will I know this? There are no mistakes in the world of our Higher Power.

TODAY'S MEDITATION
Dear God. I am reminded that when in doubt, I rest and do nothing at all. I trust more will be revealed when the time is right.

"Our doubts are traitors and make us lose the good
we oft might win by fearing to attempt." — Shakespeare

It's a Family Affair
April 17

The alcoholic and/or drug addicted family provides the perfect arena for dysfunction. *Normal*, for many of us, was often the elephant sitting in the room. Denial ruled the family unit and commanded that no one talk, feel or tell others about what happens behind our closed doors. Although the elephant is imaginary, our dysfunctions were real.

Many of us felt abnormal loyalty to parents we sought validation from. When validation didn't come, we isolated, too afraid of other kids and adults and preferred to be alone. Some of us were troublemakers in school, seeking attention any way we could. Others became teacher's pet, carrying the mask of denial wherever they went.

Under the spell of addiction, many mothers were overachievers or, just the opposite, strung out depressed, neglecting everyone and everything. Anger, domestic violence, child abuse or neglect often dominated the home, producing fear and a pervasive sense of helplessness for everyone involved.

Fathers carried their own burden in active addiction. Oftentimes they were a portrayal of complete disappointment and rigidity, or a master of forgiveness when sober. "If only you…," or, "This is your fault!" filled the room as family members tried to detach from his or her own disappointments.

In a family of addiction, no one wins. Everyone is affected. Sometimes the father admits he doesn't want his wife to sober up because he loses the control he once enjoyed. The mother often wrestles with contempt after the father recovers. His preoccupation shifts to the fellowship of recovery and helping others. He's still not around, and he's still not available.

The family may require months or years to heal. Professional help, sobriety, and a never-ending willingness to succeed together, are requirements necessary to change family dynamics in the home. And it happens every day, all around the world.

TODAY'S MEDITATION

Watching an entire family recover and regain harmony and trust is a miracle beyond measure that can only be granted by the grace of God.

"God can restore what is broken and change it into something amazing. All you need is faith." — Joel 2:25

RESENTMENTS
APRIL 18

A confrontation between my sister and me occurred because I was not invited to a family holiday party.

Our literature tells us that, "We step on the toes of others and they retaliate…" How true this is for those of us in recovery. We reach milestones in recovery as we accept that when we are in disharmony with the universe, *we* are the problem. As we walk this spiritual path, we become aware and welcome responsibility for our part.

We make amends without delay, as to do so is the contrition that reminds us of continual need to keep our side of the street free of resentments. Humbled, we offer forgiveness for our peace of mind, and disregard who threw the first stone. It matters little who was right or wrong. We do it because *we* deserve to be free from the hurtful and often destructive pangs of resentment.

A sister in sobriety reminds me, "They know not what they do." For those without a program of recovery, how could they possibly understand? This is *our* spiritual program, no one else's.

We are responsible for burying the seeds of resentments.

TODAY'S MEDITATION
Thank you, God, for the security of knowing it is with your help that I forgive myself enough to forgive others.

"Without forgiveness life is governed by…
an endless cycle of resentment and retaliation." — Roberto Assagioli

STEP FIVE: WITHHOLDING NOTHING
APRIL 19

I found that being honest is never what it seems. Although my intentions are pure, the truth was never delivered in its real state for fear of rejection or hurt feelings.

We know that honesty is as real as the information we have at the moment. The tentacles of honesty reach out to assess others' mental and emotional reactions and ability to accept the truth. Would our truth hurt someone else? Would it make us look like a failure in your eyes? What would others think about us? These are some fears that come to mind as we prepare for a thorough Fifth Step.

With faith, we approach this step with the assurance of freedom that comes from facing the unthinkable. We're convinced we must stay the course, withholding nothing. Having come this far, confidence tells us for the first time in our lives, we deserve to be rigorously honest with someone if we are to enjoy the freedoms recovery brings.

The Fifth Step is an invitation to courage. The other side of the bridge to freedom promises life-altering rewards as we face our fears and let go of debilitating secrets. For the first time, we are liberated from guilt and shame. Knowing we're being led by a Higher Power, that we possess faith without boundaries, we face our fears and do it, anyway.

The miracle of our truth is waiting to be freed.

TODAY'S MEDITATION
Thank you, God, for walking with me. I shed my cloak of guilt and shame and replace it with my hand in yours as you lead.

"Our past is a story existing only in our minds. Look, analyze, understand and forgive. Then, as quickly as possible, chuck it." — Marianne Williamson

ACCEPTING OUR LIMITATIONS
APRIL 20

Sometimes the invincibility of our youth clouds our reality. Regardless of age, we insist if we do more, move more, we will keep aging at bay. We want to believe we will enjoy into our 80s, the same stamina, strength, and quick-thinking we enjoyed in our youth. Denying the inevitable can often put us in harm's way.

Recovery is much the same way. On many levels, we know the way out of our addictive misery depends upon accepting new boundaries and adjustments in our thinking because addictions have no boundaries. We're taught to create new healthy and life-preserving constraints to assure a serene journey while we develop confidence in ourselves.

Sobriety requires adjustments in friendships. We are no longer safe in the same bars, or the same friends' homes with the same people who still use. We look at visits with family and examine new motives by asking, "Are we still proving how capable we are?" "Will we be doing the same thing, expecting different results from others?" "Will everyone be celebrating in the usual manner?" Recovery requires higher standards as we recreate ourselves with boundaries that have *our* best interests at heart. We must prepare ourselves and accept these limitations and others if we are to succeed in long-term sobriety. Self-preservation asks that we put our interests and emotional safety first.

Others balk and don't understand. What matters is that *we* understand and are comfortable and secure within new boundaries we established for ourselves. We trust recovery is the easier, softer way. This new behavior is *self-care*. For those who never imagined this day would come, discernment is one of our most treasured gifts. We embrace our new limitations.

TODAY'S MEDITATION

I am grateful for gifts I cannot see but protect me from within. I feel courage from the miracle of inner-transformation and the security in acceptance of new limitations.

"The boundary to what we can accept is the boundary to our freedom."
—Tara Brach

FREEDOM FROM SELF-SABOTAGE
APRIL 21

How many times have we heard others put someone down with, "You're not good enough to do that," or, "You'll never be able to…" Do these or similar statements resonate within you?

These are the telltale signs of self-sabotage. We see it in others. Maybe they are comfortable without taking chances. Maybe we settle for less than we deserve in the workplace or home, minimizing our desires to keep the peace. We *become what we think*. We need to stop rehearsing our rejections.

Over time, self-sabotage becomes form fitting, snug in the misidentification of our self-worth. It feels familiar, safe and warm. We know self-sabotage well because we've endured it for a lifetime. Self-sabotage is the mechanism used to denigrate our power, as if we have none at all. Somewhere we heard we should promote others while sacrificing ourselves to gain friends and keep the peace. To do so would be to tell ourselves the greatest lie of all: We deserve nothing, but others do.

Treating ourselves with the same gentleness and loving care we give to family and others is what we need. There is plenty of inner strength and fortitude already deep inside, and we deserve to hear it reflected in our voice. So why *not* let it begin with us? No longer can we allow ourselves to take part in self-deprecating talk.

We are worthy and must expect more from ourselves. *Our* voice is listening, waiting for the echo of words that promise love and kindness for who we are. We hear in the confidence practice brings. When we change the way we see ourselves, we get to change our lives and the way others see us too, with resonating confidence.

TODAY'S MEDITATION

Today I am conscious of how others speak to me and how it makes me feel. I will not accept negative, demeaning talk from anyone, even me, as I recreate with loving care who I want to be.

"Liberation from self-sabotage requires an understanding of how we co-create the life we experience… we participate in the circumstances of our lives by giving consent, consciously or unconsciously, to much of the pleasure or the pain we experience." — Peter Michaelson

Being Humble
April 22

I never understood how working The Steps was an act of humility. Our literature discusses the act of being humble with others, and to our Higher Power. One definition of humility is to reconsider what we think we know. Humility is a state of mind that reminds us when we put faith before all else, we come after our Higher Power, not above, or not before. Humility and humiliation are exact opposites.

In recovery, each Step overhauls our ego. We saw how in Step One; we were an island unto ourselves, needing no one. The solutions of Steps Two and Three gave way to an unmistakable reality of a power greater than us. Steps Four through Nine strengthened humility as we cleaned up the wreckage of our past enough to forgive ourselves and others. If we were to maintain a life free from our unrestrained self-will and addictions, Steps Ten through Twelve must become perpetual action-at-work.

We remind ourselves perfection for us, is not the goal of our Higher Power. Rather, we seek through humility to keep our ego small by growing along spiritual lines. In prayer and meditation, we accept humility each time we remember we are not in charge. With each plea of *Thy will, not mine be done*, we submit once more, to our reliance on our Higher Power.

TODAY'S MEDITATION

Dear God, were it not for you leading my path, I would not have any measure of humility to navigate the minefields of my human failures.

"True humility is intelligent self-respect which keeps us from thinking too highly or too meanly of ourselves. It makes us modest by reminding us how far we have come short of what we can be." — Ralph W. Sockman

STEP SIX

"Were entirely ready to have God remove all these defects of character."

If by now we are still unsure of our defects, having uncovered a good many in Step Five, we review previous steps and pray for a willingness to see deeper. A simple application of willingness is necessary to become entirely ready to have our Higher Power remove every defect of character.

Some of us have been ready for years; others have difficulty in letting go of anything, regardless of harm. We hold on to defects with the same excitement we held on to our addictions, for dear life. We ask why we need them still when our goal is to be free.

Remember the key word in Step Six is *willingness*. Some defects we gave to our Higher Power effortlessly. Others need greater spiritual intervention and more time before we are ready to let go. Nothing happens in our time, regardless of our willingness or resolve, until our Higher Power is ready to do so.

In our desire to have defects removed, we list them on paper in one column. In another column, we ask, "Am I now willing to have God remove these from me?" Our answer is a yes or a no. The point with any step is forward motion. Our only requirement with Step Six is that we continue to pray for willingness.

TODAY'S MEDITATION
I realize, God, that no matter how hard I try to let go of defects, you allow me to keep some of them for my journey.

"...The Holy Spirit can't take from us what we will not release to him. He won't work without our consent. He cannot remove our character defects without our willingness, because that would be violating our free will... asking God to heal us, we're committing to the choice to be healed." — Marianne Williamson

CHANGING EVERYTHING
APRIL 24

I remember someone said recovery is about changing everything, one day at a time.

First, we stop addictive activities that brought us to our knees. Transformation occurs as we show up for our meetings. We become comfortable with ourselves and others in the rooms as hope develops.

Baby steps of confidence soon become visible and hope emerges as our new normal. Life takes on new meaning. We imagine a kinder, gentler world, as angels of faith take our hand, nudging us gently forward on our personal journey toward peace.

Although we do not understand, we have faith and trust we are no longer alone. One day at a time, we welcome life and embrace changes never imagined possible. With a God of our understanding, we become the cocreator of our life and journey. This co-creation happens because we crossed the bridge to faith.

TODAY'S MEDITATION

God, the mustard seed of hope reminds me I am right where I belong. I feel secure in stepping out in faith, so long as you are with me.

"The good news is that you don't know how great you can be! How much you can love! What you can accomplish! And what your potential is!" — Anne Frank

GETTING OUT OF OUR COMFORT ZONE
APRIL 25

I have discovered that the ability to enjoy life and feel excited in my skin is in direct proportion to getting out of my comfort zone. I remained frozen in place in my addiction, wasting a lifetime, as fear ensured my failure. Negative thinking said to stay put, isolate, and trust no one. I relied on my only love and reliable constant of comfort—my drug of choice. I remained stuck at an emotional level and at the same age I began my addictive career. I had no coping skills to live life sober.

The Universe continues to open hearts to the fact that those of us under a sustaining grace of sobriety are absolute miracles because we have grown. Each day sober, we seek opportunities to face our fears by doing life differently. We know that whatever reminds us of ease and comfort is often a guise called "stinking thinking."

Staying outside of our comfort zone is where personal growth thrives. We honor ourselves as we rise above routine situations replete with cunning, baffling, and powerful traps to hold us back. When we're out of our comfort zone, we conquer our fears, taking control and grow in courage by doing it anyway, otherwise we remain stuck in negativity and immature thinking.

We are warriors on a personal quest for spiritual, emotional, physical, and psychological maturity. The more diligent and determined we are in practicing new principles of our program in all of our affairs, the stronger is our conviction, of who we want to become. We reach for faith and tenacity and set aside old ideas of what we thought we knew and we do it anyway, like it or not.

TODAY'S MEDITATION

God, thank you for endless opportunities to seek new strength and courage. My faith is in you.

"We have to be honest about what we want and take risks rather than lie to ourselves and make excuses to stay in our comfort zone." — Roy Bennett

CROSSING-OVER

People with addictive personalities understand the implications of crossing over. We have already crossed over an imaginary line where no human power could change the course of our disease. We hear in our rooms there is no changing a pickle back to a cucumber. And so it is with the alcoholic-addict.

Some of us cross-over into other addictions. Many with an addiction are dual-addicted. Some of us do drugs and alcohol while others are addicted to shopping, gambling, sex, and more. For others, it could be anger or work. This crossing-over can be as dangerous as the original addiction we started with and speaks to the insidiousness of addictions overall. We don't begin and end with just drugs, or just alcohol, or both. It is our *thinking* that spells "more," because of a complex, complicated need to change the way we feel.

We have a *thinking problem*, a disease of perception that tells us more is better. Normal people never wonder if they need more of anything but we do. We, who are in recovery, know whatever keeps us from having to feel works.

Recovery prepares us to short-circuit our delusional thinking. This explains why we must always be on guard. Our addiction never stops because our thinking never stops. A village of recovery combined with an omnipotent Higher Power provides tools, courage and a willingness to change one day at a time.

TODAY'S MEDITATION

Today I am aware of my thoughts and desires, but especially motives. I cannot afford to exchange one addiction for another.

"Carefully watch your thoughts, for they become your words. ...Consider and judge your actions, for they have become your habits. Acknowledge and watch your habits, for they shall become your values. Understand and embrace your values, for they become your destiny." — *Mahatma Gandhi*

SPIRITUAL ALIGNMENT
APRIL 27

Someone mentioned that everything he tried to do either didn't work, came out wrong, or made an already bad situation worse. Friends around him laughed as they had experienced similar situations.

Those of us on a spiritual journey know what it means to "be out of spiritual alignment." Our EGO is Edging God Out. Our literature refers to this as *self-will run riot*. We tried, but could not find serenity by ourselves.

Our Higher Power waits for us to get out of the driver's seat. As we pray for divine intervention, we trust it will be received. The alignment is what we're after. The result that comes from accepting the alignment is the business of our Higher Power.

How do we know when we are aligned with our Higher Power? As we stand in the doorway of His perfect timing, we trust an orchestrated process that unfolds in a time known only to the Universe. Faith and attunement say, "If it were supposed to be different, it would be," regardless of the outcome, or the force we wield to change it.

TODAY'S MEDITATION
When the student is ready, the teacher appears. My God opens minds and hearts of those ready to experience His perfect timing.

"Whatever I 'align' myself with are the very things that will create a 'line' into my future." — Craig D. Lounsbrough

FREEDOM
APRIL 28

Running through open fields and woods, I am six years old and fearless. Aware of my freedom, a penetrating sense of being protected seeps through me as I run alone. Today, I know I ran with my God in complete abandon.

Recovery lets us experience that same freedom. We take suggestions and learn how to let go of addictive behaviors. We let go of self-destructive thoughts and resentments and gain what we long for the most: that little girl's spiritual connection at the moment.

One of our Ninth Step Promises assures that, "We are going to know a new freedom and a new happiness." With help from our Higher Power, character defects become reduced or taken away the more we grow in humility and along spiritual lines. But, we must work for it.

Each Step promotes freedom from a bondage of self that seeks to squash our authenticity and hope. Daily we reaffirm our trust in our process of recovering from a hopeless state of mind and body. Faith and confidence let us walk closer to freedom as we give thanks for our recreated selves.

TODAY'S MEDITATION
God, when I take your hand and pray that Your Will be done, the closer to my own truth I become.

"The only real prison is fear, and the only real freedom is freedom from fear"
— Aung San Suu Kyi

LETTING GO OF OLD BELIEFS
APRIL 29

An alcoholic home provides an abundance of negativity, hopelessness, and rage. With each passing year, I saw more of the depth of my emptiness.

Recovery from a sick bondage of self provides for a new way of living, but what had to come first was a new way of thinking. Steps Four and Five unraveled a lifetime of self-defeating incriminations that perpetuated more lies and shame until we had become the embodiment of guilt and regrets.

If we want to experience inner peace, then we must change our thinking and let go of old tapes. We need to work to replace doubt with hope and each negative inclination, with a positive affirmation. Was this going to be easy? No, it will not. But the consistency of effort and faith, with the power of a newfound self-worth, is the route to the loving, kind, and brave person we always wanted to be.

We see the best of ourselves today, and trust with abiding assurance we deserve all things wonderful, according to our Higher Power. Together we write new and meaningful messages and let go of old beliefs that no longer work for our best interests.

TODAY'S MEDITATION
Thank you, God, for helping me to let go of old, mistaken beliefs that held me hostage for so long. With your help I embrace the authentic person I am today.

"To let go is to release the images and emotions, the grudges and fears, the clingings and disappointments of the past that bind our spirit." — Jack Kornfield

R.I.D. SYNDROME
APRIL 30

In a meeting, someone brought up the topic of having a case of the R.I.D. syndrome: restless, irritable and discontented. We all laughed in recognition.

Often, we are out of sorts and off balance emotionally. We can't pinpoint why, which produces more discontentment. We doubt ourselves and ask, "What is going on with me?"

The act of verbalizing these feelings helps them to dissipate. We who are new to recovery, learn what to do with these feelings as they arise.

One reason why our meetings are vital is we learn, among other things, that feelings are not facts. Often, nothing more is needed than to bring those feelings to light in conversation in a safe space, our meetings.

We take our power back by recognizing when we are restless, irritable and discontented. These feelings are just that and nothing more. The antidote is increased conscious contact with our Higher Power, and often, by the simple act of sharing our feelings with others.

When we are R.I.D., we feel our feelings and remember, *This Too, Shall Pass.* Until then, we practice letting them be what they are without over-reacting or overindulging. Our miracle is we decide to live sober, regardless of how we feel. Today we know that everything passes.

TODAY'S MEDITATION
Dear God, thank you for my spiritual consciousness that helps me to move out of the way of myself quietly, peacefully as I allow this discomfort to pass me by.

"Men and women drink essentially because they like the effect produced by alcohol. The sensation is so elusive that, while they admit it is injurious, they cannot after a time differentiate the true from the false. They are restless, irritable and discontented, unless they can again experience the sense of ease and comfort which comes at once by taking a few drinks—drinks which they see others taking with impunity." — Alcoholic Anonymous, page XXV.

EXPECTATIONS OF SELF
MAY 1

In our addictions, grandiose expectations of ourselves keep us stuck which is the result of our disease of perception. Here, we become our own worst enemy: persistent, inflexible and controlling, convinced that inflated opinions of ourselves and others are accurate. But these inflated images hide what we are responding to, which is the small voice inside that tells us we are defective, not enough, and deserve the insults of others and ourselves. One form self-punishment takes is an excessive-exaggeration of our expectations. Expectations so big they set us up for continual failure.

Some of us knew our expectations were enough while in recovery, but we never got the message. Today, we look at expectations and ask questions to help define a new normal, a new sense of what is enough for us.

We assess, "Am I still reaching to achieve other people's unrealistic expectations or my own?" "Do I even know what they are?" "Do those expectations benefit me, or are they designed to satisfy others?" "What would it take for *me* to be enough right here, right now?"

In recovery we strive to make our expectations reasonable, balanced, and most of all, fair. Working The Steps gives us a new awareness of our limitations and boundaries. We no longer feel the need to live up to unreasonable expectations of others. We are the only ones who can assess what we need from us to feel comfortable in our own skins. The answers are already within us.

We know we are enough when we seek in prayer, and then ask for the answer to the question, what do I expect of me in a situation?

TODAY'S MEDITATION
I am grateful for the relief that comes with knowing my expectations are right-sized today.

"I'm not in this world to live up to your expectations and you're not in this world to live up to mine." — *BRUCE LEE*

FEAR OF FAILURE

I have struggled a lifetime with my fear of failure, often believing I would be better off dead than trying something and failing yet again. So terrified was I of any success, I started and stopped half a dozen careers, preferring the ability to get away from myself as I indulged in illegal activities, I would do anything to not feel the sickening dread that never seemed to leave me. I was scared of change, and afraid of staying the same. I was terrified of living and terrified of dying.

Recovery shows that, while fear protects us when it activates our survival instincts and gets us out of dangerous situations, we don't need fear as a constant companion. Facing our fears and walking through them provides proof that we are better, stronger, and more courageous than we ever imagined.

The more responsibility we take for ourselves and our feelings, the greater is our ability to dissolve the fear of failure. But learning this lesson takes practice.

We must first learn to distinguish the true from the false. Journaling our truth using strong and affirmative language can be a start to visualize our transformation. We change our perspective and appreciate even our failures because they are the lessons necessary to reorder our thinking.

Are there days when we are still afraid? Yes. But those days become less frequent and less intimidating with practice.

Do we face our fears and do it, anyway? Yes, we do. We no longer shrink from fear or obsess. Instead, we look forward to the adventure because when we put down our fear of failure, we can overcome anything.

TODAY'S MEDITATION
Recovery reminds me through my daily walk with God, there is no need to fear failure as I am being led.

"You'll always miss 100% of the shots you don't take." — *Wayne Gretzky*

STEP SEVEN
MAY 3

"Humbly asked Him to remove our shortcomings"

Attitude adjustments allow us to move closer to our Higher Power and to others. Step Seven is all about adjusting our sense of humility.

Humility comes to us in our Higher Power's time. We concede to willingness in Step Three, commit to cleaning house in Step Four, and get a pure taste of humility through confessing our defects to our Higher Power, ourselves, and another human being in Step Five. We came, in Step Six, to believe our Higher Power could remove defects of character, as we prepare to ask Him to do so in Step Seven.

Step Seven is a prayer for help. Some of us pray on our knees. Others plan a thoughtful ritual prior to the Seventh Step Prayer. Some ask their Higher Power for help in the car as they listen to the radio. How we do it matters little. What matters is that the action is a sincere request that our shortcomings and defects of character we identified in Step Six, be removed.

Step Seven challenges us to change dark to light. As that light surrounds us, it exposes the truth about our defects and leaves us assured that our Higher Power will remove them in His own time, not in our time.

We have taken Step Seven when we pray for the release of defects that separate us from our Higher Power and from others, knowing the answer to that prayer will come.

TODAY'S MEDITATION

Please continue to remove those defects, God, which keep me from being of service to you and to those around me.

"We're often ashamed of asking for so much help because it seems selfish or petty or narcissistic, but I think, if there's a God - and I believe there is - that God is there to help. That's what God's job is." — Anne Lamott

How many times have we stuffed feelings down deep, too afraid to feel them? We told ourselves, "Oh no, I don't want to go there, now." Like Scarlett O'Hara in *Gone with the Wind*, we said, "I'll think about that tomorrow."

We prefer to live on auto-pilot. Eventually, those suppressed feelings erupt without control. We lash out, burst into angry tears, or exhibit inappropriate behavior or laughter.

Recovery teaches how to stop denying the compassionate side of ourselves, the part that assures us we deserve to feel our feelings. We are designed for emotional balance. Grieving losses won't kill us. One way we honor ourselves and those who died is to feel grief. Grief allows us to walk through the dark valley and come out the other side. We feel the feelings for what they are without acting out. Feelings are not facts, but they are an emotional response to the loss of what was.

Experiencing grief over what cannot be changed is a necessary part of moving on. The same is true of negative sentiments of all kinds. Anger, hurt, and disappointment deserve attention as soon as possible. The speed with which we acknowledge them is equal to the speed with which we release and let them go.

But what about negative sentiments that linger from the past? We often look back with guilt or remorse over how things that coulda, shoulda, woulda been. Time is our Higher Power's gift to us to accept, to feel, to heal, and to let go. In fact, recovery subscribes that to do otherwise invites a pity-party we cannot afford to have any longer.

As we release the energy emotions generate, we are stronger for having experienced these feelings, and for letting them go.

TODAY'S MEDITATION

Thank you, God, for these lessons of letting go that are vital to my long-term recovery. Today I meet them where they are. Only then as I get out of my way, can I let them pass.

"The most effective way of healing is to feel the pain, then let go, then move on without looking back once in a while. Then a new horizon opens its door right before your eyes." — Ces Peta

GETTING BACK TO CENTER
MAY 5

I've been feeling off balance much too often. Too much thinking and not enough sharing with others makes for sick thinking in no time. This general anxiety tells me it is time to, once again, get back to my center.

Remember as a child, the thrill of a Merry-Go-Round as you fought centrifugal force to hang on, grasping a pole to pull toward the center before you lost your balance? Feeling the thrill while safe, balanced, and, joyous, as the ride zipped around, you felt grounded and secure, even safe, regardless of how fast it spun. That was because you were holding on, leaning toward the safety of the center.

Those who are new to recovery must work to maintain that place of centeredness, that place that keeps us from spinning out of control. Striving to stay centered affects everything we do, and we learned how one lapse, one yield to fear, can be enough to rock our emotional world.

But we let go of our center. It happens to all of us.

What can we do to regain our foothold and get back to center? Prayer and meditation always help. Engaging daily rituals or beginning new ones grounds us where we are. Getting busy, sharing, and helping others gives us true purpose. We find balance through healthy combinations of trusting our Higher Power and attending to our own personal affairs.

Chances are good that when we are off-balance in our thinking, we need to get back to the magic of the Merry-Go-Round, pulling ourselves toward the safety of the center.

TODAY'S MEDITATION

I'm grateful that simple adjustments to my spiritual tool kit of action are all that is required to get me back on track to find my center again.

"...the fact that we need to return to our center lets us know that we will drift away from what matters. This drifting is part of being human, and so, there is an ongoing need to find our way back to what matters..." — Mark Nepo

RULE 62

MAY 6

Growing up, I knew my thinking was flawed, different from others around me. I absorbed the caustic energy generated by two immature parents and made it mine. I interpreted their negativity and anger, real or perceived, as something I must have done. "This is all *your* fault!" remains the greatest lie I ever consumed.

Recovery promotes honest and truthful discovery of ourselves. One way we do this is through Rule 62: *Don't take yourself too seriously.* We must absorb new messages that tell us what other people think of us—belongs to them. Rule 62 speaks from an inferiority complex. Just like me, others are entitled to their opinions. A friend said, "What comes out of *my* mouth is about me." What others feel about us has no effect on how *we* feel about us. No longer are we drenched in drama, over-reacting to every glance or word someone shared, dissecting it for its hidden message.

Today, we recalibrate our ego screaming for attention concede we are no longer the center of the universe. Rule 62 is a reminder that we breathe in peace and ease without the paranoia of being punished and accept with both shock and relief—we *never* were as important as we thought we were.

TODAY'S MEDITATION
I am so grateful for the freedom that comes with Rule 62, and can now accept myself as-is, because my ego has been subdued.

"Don't take anything seriously. Nothing others do is because of you...
When you are immune to the opinion of others, you won't be the
victim of needless suffering." — Miguel Angel Ruiz

IT'S NEVER TOO LATE
MAY 7

Many of us believe life has passed us by. We think we are too old; too entrenched in our thinking; or too stuck in addictive, counter-productive behaviors to change. Self-doubt and fear, along with a hundred old mistaken beliefs, stand ready to sabotage our good intentions.

We already have enough discernment to move beyond where we are now, or we wouldn't be able to see this truth.

And so, we step in front of our thinking, and do it anyway. As we strip away the "What if's" and brave a leap of faith, the Universe softens our landing, as the ground beneath our feet seems to rise to meet us right where we are. Our actions have so much tenacity behind them.

With faith, we fill in the blanks in our thinking, reaffirming ourselves with a Higher Power we already know. Healthy opportunities appear now wherever we go. Although we didn't know it, we have always deserved our goals. We only needed to be convinced that we were ready to face whatever was blocking our paths.

This is the time.

Today is the day.

TODAY'S MEDITATION
Dear God, with you I am capable of achieving anything I believe I can. To do so I must simply begin putting one foot in front of the other.

"Follow your passion. The rest will attend to itself. If I can do it, anybody can do it. It's possible. And it's your turn. So go for it. It's never too late to become what you always wanted to be in the first place." — J. Michael Straczynski

GROWING ALONG SPIRITUAL LINES
MAY 8

As we defeat our demons, we are sure that growth along spiritual lines is vital to our successful recovery. Our primary purpose is a partnership with our Higher Power, and to help others. Everything good, including sustained sobriety, flows from this union.

Prayer and meditation ignite the energy that reconnects us to internal bliss, and we become grounded in this intentional purpose for living. Here, we are ready for enlightenment and inspiration.

Dr. Wayne Dyer speaks of spiritual growth as a oneness. He explains that harmony with our own spirit generates a likeness to our Higher Power. In that state the Universe receives us as divine spirits, conceived out of a oneness, and to a oneness we return.

We seek balance and harmony to ignite our highest self. In that state, we are in concert with our Higher Power's will for us, available to ourselves and others.

In this meditative process, opening the celestial doors to spiritual enlightenment invites our Higher Power to unite our emotional and physical selves.

We are focused, humble but confident in a state experienced as a grace that never exhibits from ourselves alone. We observe a connectedness to inspiration and peace as we transfer this energy into our actions with others. In bliss, we walk in rhythm with the Great Spirit's stride.

TODAY'S MEDITATION
Thank you, God, for the gift of knowing that as I seek you, I cannot be in disharmony at the same time. You exemplify all that I need in my life.

"Let us never forget to pray. God lives. He is near. He is real. He is not only aware of us but cares for us. He is our Father. He is accessible to all who will seek Him."
— Gordon B. Hinckley

HELPING OURSELVES FIRST
MAY 9

With an in-flight emergency, attendants tell us to strap on our own oxygen mask first, and then help others.

In our fast-paced world, we rush from demand to demand. We hurry to finish tasks, help our children turn in good work, and assist anyone who asks. Anyone but ourselves. In the emergency known as life, we often leave our oxygen mask dangling while helping others with theirs. We forget the instruction is to help ourselves first.

Demands for service and attention in every venue of our lives mount until we wake up to find we have become robotic in our thinking and actions. But how can we stop? We are sure we know what needs to happen for those close to us and are positive we are the only ones who can provide what they need, how and when they need it. But it is a huge mistake to not prepare nor treat ourselves with the same attention and care.

If we stop long enough to focus our energy inward, we discover a cave of our own unfulfilled needs, dreams and aspirations, and realize they are dying due to lack of attention. If we are to be of maximum service to others, we can only lead by showing sufficient care and kindness to ourselves before anything else.

Maybe the load we carry needs to be divided. We recognize now that sometimes we are the ones who need help. When this happens, we practice *asking* others for what we need. An honest look at what is important to do, or to let go of, will make this process easier.

What is our basic nature? Some of us are grateful when no one asks us to step up, yet others feel slighted when they have had no invitation to assist. The question becomes, does helping someone else drain you, or does it become your life-sustaining oxygen?

Balance *must* be our first consideration. The control we seek in doing-it-all deprives others a chance to be useful, and so we help sometimes, while allowing others to step up. It's called teamwork. No longer are we a one-man-band.

We pass on gratitude and allow others to fulfill their own long-standing need, the need to be useful.

TODAY'S MEDITATION

Just for today I remember I am no longer running the show. I slow down long enough to ask, can I do this with others, and together we accomplish more than I could have imagined.

"Unfortunately, we do not treat others as we treat ourselves. We should try being genuinely kind to ourselves first and the rest will come naturally, like an 18-kt. Golden Rule." — *Erica Goros*

EXAMINING OUR MOTIVES
MAY 10

Before recovery no one wanted my opinion, preferring instead, to stay as far away as possible. No one could trust me, and people never knew what would happen next when I was around.

Recovery suggests that every thought or action needs scrutiny before we subject it to others, and so we pause when agitated or doubtful.

Examining our motives can feel as foreign as a Centurion coin. Our best thinking is often unavailable, shouted down by the arguments of our self-centered, self-seeking motives. "What's in it for me?" If the answer is self-satisfaction, then we are contemplating action for the wrong reasons.

However, we cannot make a mistake if we do the next right thing, for the right reason. Healthy self-examination as we are preparing to do something causes us to ask ourselves questions: "Is it kind?" "Is it loving?" "How will it help me while doing no harm to others?" Last, "Is it our truth?"

Right reasons are unselfish and pure of heart, an action taken with no thought of gaining something in return. There can be no malice, manipulation, or justification of any kind. These questions become our new barometer for calibrating honesty behind our motives.

Another question, the most important of all is, "What Would my Higher Power *Want* me to Do?" With these and other questions, we cannot make a mistake.

TODAY'S MEDITATION

God, please continue to reveal my true intentions. When I examine my motives, your truth prevails.

"The moment there is suspicion about a person's motives, everything he does becomes tainted." — Mahatma Gandhi

Old Behaviors

May 11

Volunteering in a women's prison, I'm in the humbling position of being able to see and hear myself in inmates who did what I've done, but got caught.

During one visit, an inmate shared her life's story with our group. For many, speaking to this group is the first time they've spoken before their peers and to do so takes courage. During her story, several inmates got up and followed each other out of the room, distracting everyone.

Isn't this the old behavior we exhibited in our addictions? We cut and run believe we were too important; and had too much to do. Bored, we were afraid we would feel something too close to home. Whatever the excuses in or out of prison, these actions are not acceptable.

Old behavior is addictive, regressive behavior. We have a responsibility to ourselves in recovery to go out of our way and do everything different on every level imaginable.

What does that look like? Changing old behaviors begins and ends with our thinking. If we don't know how it's done, then we pause and ask our Higher Power for insight. We examine our intentions by asking, "Is this old behavior? Is what we *think* we need, different? Is it loving and kind, self-seeking, selfish or dishonest; or is it new behavior, often intimidating, but also the right-thing-to-do?"

In our addiction we were sure we knew everything, so we consulted no one. Now, if we are unsure, we talk to others, and we ask questions. Often if the behavior feels comfortable, it is an old behavior and may need to be modified. Consistent practice allows a stronger awareness, and a more resilient and braver person to emerge, as if from dungeons deep.

We break free from fear of doing life different and let faith transforms us as we are certain this faith is emotional growth. We walk away from old, destructive behaviors, and we do this, regardless of where we are.

TODAY'S MEDITATION
Each day I am determined to embrace new, healthy behaviors and let go of the old. Thank you, God, for my continued courage.

"Allow yourself to think only those thoughts that match your principles and can bear the bright light of day...Your integrity determines your destiny."
— Heraclitus

PAIN AND SUFFERING
MAY 12

There is a woman in recovery who seems unable to let go of hurtful situations in her life and so they continue to bring great pain. When she speaks, we hear her self-imposed imprisonment; she is a victim of her own story.

We must remember that no matter what grieves or disturbs us, we have the freedom of choice. Rehashing sad stories reinforces the same addictive thoughts and emotions that brought us to our knees as we cried, "Poor me, pour me another one!"

Recovery is the opportunity to grow and change poor-me thinking into hope and positive energy not only for ourselves, but for those around us to see and to emulate. Sponsors prompt, "Get down from the cross, we need the wood!"

We heard too, that pain is necessary, but suffering is optional. We're told we can change direction and move on by doing something for someone else. We are reminded that our positivity may be the only alternative to poor-me thinking someone may see all day.

We have recovered to be that example for others in our rooms of recovery.

TODAY'S MEDITATION
Please help me God, to exhibit to others life-saving gifts learned through The Steps.

"Some of my feelings have been stored so long they have freezer burn."
— *Beyond Codependency*

PRACTICE MAKES PROGRESS
MAY 13

A tremendous change took hold and has become a new way of life for me. It began by trusting the journey–*my* journey, and accepting a new way of thinking.

With amazement I realized that everything I think, even more importantly, everything I do, begins with practice. The act of positive thinking starts with one thought, and then it repeats. Practice.

Some of us have wasted years shunning activities and tasks because we were stuck in the mistaken belief that perfection was the goal. "If I can't do it perfectly then, why even try?" was the perpetual message we told ourselves. So, we gave up, not realizing that a failed attempt does not predict the eventual outcome, that with practice we could succeed.

In recovery, we know that perfectionistic thinking can keep us sick and emotionally stunted. We embrace progress–not perfection–as a new way of doing. We learn to trust the idea that practice, the mere act of trying, is enough. Why?

Because practice allows us to see that we are doing our part by trying. Without the need or pressure of perfection, we are still moving ever-closer to our goal.

Practice *doesn't* make perfect. Nothing does, but practice *does* make progress, and progress is our goal.

Everything we do begins with practice.

TODAY'S MEDITATION
Dear God. I am grateful I know I am right where you need me to be. I'm glad that perfection is your job and not mine. With practice, I will draw closer to your light each day.

"As long as you live, keep learning how to live." — Seneca

LISTENING TO OUR HIGHER SELF
MAY 14

There are times throughout the day when our thinking becomes open to an inner knowing. We receive clarity, direction. A spiritual connection to our Higher Power works collaboratively to allow innate perceptions to become clear. In this state, there is no doubt as to what we've received. The answer is solid and we trust it. Our heart has received information from our head and now we are sure of our truth. Our knowing makes it so.

In these moments, we are convinced we no longer operate in a vacuum. Daily prayer and meditation allow us to see what we need as we begin our spiritual walk. Faith tells us with assurance that continued practice brings alignment with our Higher Power. In accord with His will, more will be revealed.

These light bulb moments of knowing represent deep and spiritual agreements we make together with our Higher Power. We are Spirit-Centered. As we seek through faith, we become recipients of a knowing heart. Our vantage point is elevated. As we rest in abiding peace, we are positive that who and what we are continues to evolve in a time determined not by us, but through the eternal light of the Universe.

TODAY'S MEDITATION
Dear God, I surrender all that I am to your eternal light of hope.

"Our Higher Self is perfect, Omniscient and Almighty. A fragment of God himself. A pure, transparent, luminous, quintessence."
— Omraam Mikhaël Aïvanhov

REGRETS

There once lived a woman named Regret. She spent every waking moment absorbed in her sad past.

Regret was an example of pride in reverse. She came to regret even her own breath. Her world was dark, hopeless, and suffocatingly small. Her only thoughts were: *Who cares? Why bother?* and, *What's the point?* One day she came to see the painful reality that her best thinking made her sicker and more hopeless with each passing day.

Fortunately, this woman had a change of perspective. She opened her heart and saw the futility of her thinking. Driven to desperation by the realization, she understood that she had to act and take drastic, life-saving action and see her life as if it were a glass half-full. Casting out each negative thought, she called friends to share how much she loved them, asking for forgiveness and help. She committed to writing a gratitude list each day.

Regret had cast a shadow over everything about her life. After the transformation she shared how she had never been this happy and how she never wanted to lose this feeling. Imagine, this entire transformation began and ended with a change in our thinking!

TODAY'S MEDITATION

Dear God, thank you for giving me the courage to change my negative thinking one day at a time.

"The bitterest tears shed over graves are for words left unsaid and deeds left undone" —Harriet Beecher Stowe

NEEDING TO BE HEARD
MAY 16

As I sit in witness to early light heralding a brand-new day, a variety of birds call to each other all around me. One voice is louder than the rest, never ceasing in its chirp, as if needing to be heard. Needing to be the center of attention.

As I wait for the unrelenting chirping to end, I am reminded that this too, was my story. I was *desperate* to be heard, insisting as if my being heard was what was important. Demanding to have the last word with disregard for anyone else, I was blind to the effects of my overbearing demeanor on those around me. And, besides speaking the loudest and insisting I have the last word, came the need to be right.

Recovery shows us how to replace a profound emptiness inside with new beliefs based on truths characterized by a quiet humility instead of the insistence we be heard.

As we mature into ourselves, we comprehend that *we* are the only ones who need to hear or understand our voice.

TODAY'S MEDITATION
Today I recognize my truth is measured by what I do. I no longer need to be heard. I prove the weight of my worth to myself and to my God.

"In life, finding a voice is speaking and living the truth. Each of you is an original. Each of you has a distinctive voice. When you find it, your story will be told. You will be heard." — John Grisham

Right Where We're Supposed to Be
May 17

Today is the single most perfect day of my life. The sun is shining; the air is still as the aftermath of winter offers a gentle hint of spring. I feel a momentary sadness, realizing this is the one and only time I will experience these moments, these thoughts, in the uniqueness of this perfect day.

We are right where our Higher Power wants us to be: in complete peace and acceptance of what is. We concede that even though this may not look as we had hoped, we trust and have surrendered to the moment, appreciating what is, not yearning for what is not.

Quietly comforted, a gentle knowing everything is as it should be cascades over us. The gentle rhythm of life's succession of all things visible and invisible can only be orchestrated through the omnipotence of a Higher Power.

Thanks to that Higher Power, we are safe, protected. In these inspirational moments of clarity, all is reconciled and moving as one, as we follow a force we cannot hear.

We know we are being led and trust a process we cannot see.

TODAY'S MEDITATION
I'm grateful for faith that says I am exactly where I'm supposed to be, just for today. There are no mistakes in God's world.

"Patience is the calm acceptance that things can happen in a different order than the one you have in mind." — David G. Allen

SEX AND RELATIONSHIPS
MAY 18

How many times have we been blind to other aspects of a relationship because of physical attraction? My mother would say, "Don't start something you can't finish," but physical attraction starts things we can't finish all the time.

Our motives and our willingness to trust a potential partner are valid tests to determine whether a relationship will cause short-term ecstasy over a long-term relationship.

We believe sex was designed as the ultimate identifier of pure and enduring love, but relations can become tainted by sexual expressions of anger, jealousy, and selfish displays of power. For some of us, sex becomes an obligation rather than a manifestation of mutual respect and shared pleasure, putting a strain on other areas of the relationship. For some, it is just another addiction.

Recovery encourages balance in every aspect of our life, which requires an open-eyed awareness in an area not experienced before. The Steps provide us with a view of another way of living that elevates self-respect and provides clear boundaries where there were none. We develop personal dignity. What comes with that is an uncompromising trust of ourselves. Maintaining intimate communication with our partner can go a long way to promote a respect that considers the motive, the need and the intent of both parties. Honesty is paramount.

TODAY'S MEDITATION

Today I remember that sexual expression is not what defines me. It is an expression of balance between pleasure and the respect for myself and my partner that I bring to my relationships.

"Real intimacy is a sacred experience. It never exposes its secret trust and belonging to the voyeuristic eye of a neon culture. Real intimacy is of the soul, and the soul is reserved." — John O'Donohue

SPIRITUALITY
MAY 19

"Believing is seeing," a special friend once explained. Imagine the spiritual walk we take day-in and day-out, without sight, yet, trusting that all is well.

As we wake in the morning, the magic of life begins again. Our lungs provide life-sustaining air as our heart continues its work directing blood flow throughout our body. Our senses awaken to our world. We forget one fundamental fact—*our* power orchestrated none of this!

These are gifts, given to us by a Higher Power. Some of us still exist without faith, as others seem comfortable living in the moment only, realizing there may not be another breathe living within us. The instant we cease to exist there is no turning back, no bargaining. We never had power to negotiate these facts and we don't have it now. Not even for the smallest of life that surrounds us.

Who, or what, dictates the timing of our birth and demise? Not having absolutes to control our world is, for some, the issue that brought us into recovery. We assumed a posture of omnipotence fueled by addictions which destroyed us, with or without faith.

We now accept that our best scientific thinking is worthless in understanding or predicting this thing called life. Humbled by how little we know, we welcome this acceptance. With faith, we *Let Go and Let God* and allow a Higher Power we cannot see to just be whatever It is.

TODAY'S MEDITATION
I attune myself to your trust in me My God, a faith that is necessary to begin and complete my day.

"Spirituality is not a function of occupation or calling. ...
Spirituality is determined by personal outlook and priorities.
It is evident in our words and actions." — Dallin H. Oaks

SUBTLE TEMPTATIONS
MAY 20

Each day we are bombarded with external messages. Looked at in the right way, these messages that come at us, often without warning, offer opportunities for discernment and insight.

Recovery teaches us the art of examination and intention. When a message comes in, we stop long enough to become a fascinated observer and detach, taking a step back to see the message for what it is. We become alert to subtle temptations that try to send us places we have no business going, or with people we have no business listening to.

Aware now, we become attuned, honest with ourselves, as we rely upon our knowing what the next right thing is to do.

Prayer paves our way.

Subtle temptations are the messages that appear when we are willing to hear. Why do we need them? We need them to challenge what we think we already know, and to serve as reminders of how far we have already come.

TODAY'S MEDITATION
Spiritual alignment shields me from worldly and subtle temptations that take me off course. Please remind me, God, to walk away from these mires of quicksand.

"Let the heart, then commune with itself and say, "I am poor and weak; Satan is subtle, cunning, powerful, watching constantly for advantages against my soul..."
— John Owen

TAKING THINGS PERSONALLY
MAY 21

How many of us have over-reacted to something someone said thinking it was about us? Dumbfounded, even though we didn't say a word as our body language spoke volumes. Words have the power to hurt us if we see truth in them. We assume that even the most offhand remark must be aimed at us. We are ready to eat the emotional garbage others toss out; we own it.

Dr. Wayne Dyer shared a story about how, while boarding an aircraft, a flight attendant mentioned how difficult this flight would be. Although the delay was clearly not her fault, passengers complained of being three hours late. Dr. Dyer told her regardless of what is said, the words must first penetrate her jacket, her uniform, get under her skin, and reach her heart. He shared that the decision to take on disappointments and negativity of others is ours to make.

The fellowship of recovery reminds us when others speak, what they say, or how *they* react, has nothing to do with us. It expresses their agenda, their thoughts, and their feelings. The more honest we are with ourselves, the less we need to give energy to expectations of and judgments of others. People often go to great lengths to make us feel responsible for their reactions, but we are not. Our truth is all that matters. We are learning to *not* take anything from others personally. However, when there is truth to what is being alleged, then we must rectify our part by clarifying or making amends as needed.

Recovery reminds us that we are a full-time job. We are charged with the mission of discovering and honoring our authentic selves. Today, we own the power of our alignment in faith that enables us to trust ourselves, examine our truth, and watch everything else others think or say drift away.

TODAY'S MEDITATION
What a relief to know that when I remember, I never have to take anything personally – even myself!

"We often add to our pain and suffering by being overly sensitive, over-reacting to minor things and sometimes taking things too personally." — Dalai Lama

THE TRUTH ABOUT HONESTY
MAY 22

I grew up not having the slightest idea what honesty was. I thought it was whatever came out of my mouth. I surmised it had everything to do with telling you what I thought you wanted to hear. I didn't know that the first responsibility of honesty was to be honest with myself.

Recovery tells me that before I respond, I have to put the focus back on me, instead of enlightening others with my opinions. My honesty-with-self lets me surrender to the knowledge that my own intentions and motives for speaking must be considered as I pay attention to those around me. This revelation is central, at the heart of honesty.

The truth lies within us and is about us, and no one else. Our heart and mind work in concert as we seek self-honesty. If we don't have answers to questions, it is always okay to say so. There is no need to minimize or inflate what our truth is. In our prayers and meditation, we practice focusing within and discover that, the more we trust our own honesty, the less need there is to acquiesce to others, or to tell ourselves convenient lies.

We've found our genuineness, our integrity, and rest on this truth because we are no longer alone, nor do we have anything to prove. We walk with a power greater than us and we trust this journey. This is where it begins.

TODAY'S MEDITATION

I remember that while my dreams, opinions, and feelings may change with circumstances, I know who I am inside and out. My truth is non-negotiable.

"We learned about honesty and integrity - that the truth matters... that you don't take shortcuts or play by your own set of rules... and success doesn't count unless you earn it fair and square." — Michelle Obama

THE VOICE OF ANGER
MAY 23

Of all the defects of character we harbor, anger is, without a doubt, the most damaging of them all. The *voice of anger* screams in exaggerated fear, and yells, "How *dare* You!" as it reveals to others, our self-righteous indignation and emotional immaturity.

In recovery, we know that to engage anger is to risk the unthinkable. Anger is dangerous and hurtful, and, too often, intentional. Sometimes the harm it inflicts is physical, and it is always emotional. The object of our anger is to inflict harm, but we are harmed too. High octane adrenalin prepares us for fight instead of flight. Logic evaporates. What appears is a wild-eyed, out-of-control victim, blinded by a self-righteous anger that wounds to the core.

We hear it said anger is best left to normal folks. For those in recovery there is never a sufficient reason to justify anger. And the less sobriety we have, the more dangerous anger can be for us. A powerful scourge that blocks all logic, we strike back as if in a blackout, then turn and pick up our addiction right where we left off.

The solution to anger is a forgiveness that lessens the tension anger produces. After we forgive ourselves, we forgive others and seek the healing that comes with the power of forgiveness, regardless of our emotional pain.

No energy is put into analyzing the intentions behind the disagreement or arguing over who struck first. We remember that we are not the only one upset and disturbed.

Our lives depend on our ability to forgive and let go. Regardless of the magnitude of our anger, or theirs, we realize a change in perception is required. Our goal is to let go of anger so we may reclaim love and tolerance. Our continued sobriety depends on it.

TODAY'S MEDITATION
Just for today I am conscious of my reactions to others and ask, "How important is it compared to my sobriety and serenity?" This is my responsibility.

"Anger is a choice, as well as a habit. It is a learned reaction to frustration, in which you behave in ways that you would rather not... Therefore, when you are angry and out of control, you are temporarily insane." — Wayne Dyer

WHEN IS THE TIMING RIGHT?
MAY 24

I decided I no longer needed my rambling home just for me, and that it was time to sell. What a mess I created! The realtors directed me to remove personal items and to minimize. For two years, I could never find what I needed since I had packed everything away, and my home looked more vacant than lived in.

Thinking I was ready to go, I spent evenings and weekends searching the internet for my perfect home, vacillating between my hometown and other states where I thought I needed to be.

Two years later, I exclaimed, "This is insanity!" I had jumped through realtor-hoops cleaning more during this period than I had in a lifetime! Still, my home never sold.

After lots of talking with my Higher Power what I heard was, this is the wrong time. It is too hard, too stressful; it feels forced.

This exercise reminded me of what I know but had forgotten: life's events happen when the Universe is ready to bring them. Situations unfold on their own accord. All that is required is that we be ready to receive them. The time is right when it is His time, not mine.

This proves we don't know what's good or bad for us. When we surrender to what is, we trust a natural order of universal timing as we're sure more will be revealed. It's in the letting go that our answers become obvious. When in doubt, I do nothing. I pray and wait for the answers that will come.

TODAY'S MEDITATION

I know, God, that you are right on time. Waiting doesn't look or feel the way I think it should. Each time I try to assert my own will, I'm trying to force your hand to move to my command.

"Being infinitely patient means having an absolute knowing that you're in vibrational harmony with the all-creating force that intended you here. You know that everything will happen at just the right time, at just the right place, with just the right people." — Wayne Dyer

STEP EIGHT

MAY 25

*"Made a list of all people we had harmed and became
willing to make amends to them all."*

Step Eight asks that we take our list from Step Four, an accounting of those
we have harmed, as our guide.

By now we've let go of those resentments. Now we must ask, "Are we ready to
forgive ourselves?" After all, we hurt ourselves the most so we may want to put
our own name first on our list of those we have harmed. Our Higher Power will
allow us to see our part when we need to and at the time we become mature
enough to handle it. Our part is to pray for the willingness to be willing.

Making a list of those we have harmed, while citing the facts, prepares us to
commit to everyone on that list. In dealing with some already there, spiritual,
emotional and mental adjustments come, even while the needed healing
between ourselves and others may require a long period of time. Step Eight
is about becoming ready.

We keep in mind that this is about freedom from ourselves, and our isolation
of others. It is self-forgiveness for the harms we caused them. As we make
our list, we are sure some people will be receptive but there will be those who
may remain unwilling to forgive us. Our work in Step Eight is to prepare our
slate of harms done to ourselves and others.

We are thankful for the courage to go the distance for our freedom. What
else can we do? Grateful for our willingness to face the realities of our harms,
we pray for the miracle of forgiveness, regardless of the price we must pay.

TODAY'S MEDITATION
Step Eight is an examination of my lack of honesty and the harms I've done to
others. Today I pray for my readiness to make amends to those I've harmed,
regardless of the outcome, and to forgive myself for my past transgressions.

*"Forgiving does not erase the bitter past. A healed memory is not a deleted
memory. Instead, forgiving what we cannot forget creates a new way to
remember. We change the memory of our past into a hope for our future."*
— Lewis B. Smedes

RECURRING RESENTMENTS
MAY 26

I know, firsthand, how difficult it is to let go of deep-seated resentments. I became agitated, almost manic, when speaking to my sponsor or anyone else who would listen. The more I discussed them, the more powerful my anger became. With power came self-righteous anger, which convinced that I deserved to feel the way I did.

My Al-Anon mentor listened, saying what separates us from others is the program of action we walk in recovery. She mentioned resentments, the first time they crop up, are normal. If the same one comes up again, it's a fluke. However, to bring it up a third time is a pattern that needs attention.

It is imperative we stay vigilant against recurring resentments. As they flourish, fueled by attention, they become invasive weeds overgrowing our psyche as the light of reasoning diminishes. We cannot forget that when *we* are disturbed, there is something wrong within us.

We must be free from anger and resentment. Intolerance, self-centered pride, and an unforgiving heart are all deficiencies which undermine our emotional and spiritual growth. Recurring resentments return us to where we started. Lack of emotional sobriety signals greater underlying issues. Awareness and action are necessary before these recurring resentments morph into something unmanageable and return us to our addictions.

TODAY'S MEDITATION

I am grateful for sponsors and mentors who point out with gentle voices, the danger in my defects. Thank you, God, for allowing them to walk this journey with me.

"Letting go gives us freedom, and freedom is the only condition for happiness. If, in our heart, we still cling to anything - anger, anxiety, or possessions – we cannot be free." -- Thich Nhat Hanh

WORK IN PROGRESS
MAY 27

While active in my addiction, my sense of entitlement rose to staggering heights. My belief I was owed everything had no boundaries. You, and everyone close became the focus of my unrelenting demands, finger-pointing, and accusations. But that demanding ego was evidence of a spiritual poverty. My claim someone owed me everything was nothing more than a cover-up for emotional security that was lacking within me.

In this state of delusion, the expectation was that you would experience the same level of disgust, rage and contempt for me I felt for myself but could never admit.

It took years of help from my village of recovery before I could let go of my denial. To admit I was the one who created the chaos and caused the alienation of those who knew me, took years for me to swallow. It was coming into the light of recovery that helped transform my life.

I am, and will forever be, a work in progress, assessing and reassessing healthy and safe boundaries that nurture and promote personal growth. I am neither more entitled to get my way, nor more deserving of contempt than anyone else. We are *all* works in progress.

TODAY'S MEDITATION
Thank you, God, for the honor of being a work in progress. One day at a time, I grow closer to my ideal and yours.

"Tolerance, like any aspect of peace, is forever a work in progress, never completed, and, if we're as intelligent as we like to think we are, never abandoned." — Ocavia E. Butler

WE ARE BEING LED
MAY 28

I always believed I was just existing. Events and situations happened, good and bad, but always random. My part was to complain and be the victim, but I didn't bother to look for anything greater than myself. Life was just what happened. No one was in charge. But when I quit kicking and screaming and embraced acceptance of what life is, I noticed a gentle shift in my thinking.

That shift starts as a spiritual awakening, an assurance from deep inside that speaks to us of walking, with complete trust, over a bridge of faith. Our faith convinces us to turn away from the twilight of where we've been, while our intentions teach us to see with clarity, there are no coincidences. Our old way of looking at our lives was self-sabotage. And so, we turn away from that twilight and go forward, knowing we are being led over a bridge of faith we cannot see.

The first step we take to cross that bridge compels an instant awareness of all we have ignored for a lifetime, and we feel a safe shield of light surround us. Each step, makes us more certain that there are no mistakes in our Higher Power's world, and the power of a spiritual oneness penetrates our con-sciousness. Convinced without seeing, we are sure we no longer walk alone. We are certain we never were, as there is a knowing that comes with our complete surrender to faith.

We are being led.

Aware now that everything we need is already within us, we reach the other side of that bridge of faith.

A voice whispers, we can never go back to that state of unconsciousness. For those who accept what is, there comes a willingness to follow our intuition. The peaceful, pure joy of all that is reliable unfolds in our Higher Power's perfect timing. We are awake. We are being led, and right where we're supposed to be at this moment.

TODAY'S MEDITATION

I'm grateful for faith that says I am exactly where I'm supposed to be, just for today. There are no mistakes in God's world.

".. In time, as you obey the call first to follow, your destiny will unfold before you. The difficulty will lie in keeping other concerns from diverting your attention." —
Charles R. Swindoll

CARETAKING OF FAMILY MEMBERS
MAY 29

I have a dear friend who grew up without a father in the home. She told how her mother would leave after the children were in bed asleep, not coming back for hours, sometimes not before dawn. My friend took care of her younger siblings and her mother, who could not function after a late night out.

My friend developed an over-exaggerated sense of responsibility for others. She found herself overextended with friends and community efforts, exhausted from keeping up the house, and meeting the needs of her children and husband. She didn't know she could ask for help.

She enjoyed the good feelings her acts generated in others and relished the adoration that rewarded her for her efforts. When asked what she did for fun apart from the things she did for others, she said she didn't know. Had it not been for doing service for others, she felt as if she didn't exist at all.

Al-Anon Family Group is the forum that opened new possibilities for my friend. One stanza of the Serenity Prayer speaks to, "...the courage to change the things we can." She came to understand that no one can make everything right for those around them, and that the most powerful changes a person can make are those that happen within.

She never knew she had permission to put her own needs first, thinking it selfish, even arrogant. As she became a part of the Al-Anon Family Group, new definitions of caretaking and moderation became clear. With this new perspective she realized that her husband felt controlled, and smothered, all in the name of love. She heard that sometimes, her caretaking did more harm than good, and that for too long, she had ignored sufficient giving care to herself.

As she changed the things she could and devoted more time to enjoying a life that had gone unattended for too long, she became happier. She was still a caretaker, but she learned that caretaking began with attention to self.

TODAY'S MEDITATION
When I neglect to put myself, my recovery and my spiritual needs first, they might as well be last.

"One person caring about another represents life's greatest values."
– Jim Rohn, author

ASSERTIVE VS. AGGRESSIVE BEHAVIORS
MAY 30

In conversation we often hear these two words used interchangeably, but there's a difference.

If two wild cats fight in the Serengeti Plains, aggressive will apply; Webster tells us one definition of aggressive is a willingness to fight.

Now imagine two individuals on a platform, each explaining their position on water over-consumption and how to solve it. The word aggressive does not apply. Assertive does.

Assertiveness is a character trait often found in a leader, but can be difficult for some people to embrace. Memories resurface from childhood that say, "Act like a lady." We hear husbands or fathers say, "Quit itching for a fight," when all we want is to be heard. And so, we often remain quietly compliant, rather than risk the appearance of callousness or disrespect for others. We mistake assertiveness for being aggressive.

In the workplace, both men and women hear that less than full compliance is unattractive, unbecoming, unacceptable. Regardless of how cautiously we approach a topic, some make it crystal clear that leaving it alone is in our best interest. We're told to go along to get along, and once again, we are censured to silence.

Recovery provides a safe forum for men and women to become intimate with the meaning of these two words, and to sort out their fundamental differences. We learn this difference in a setting where aggressive behavior is never tolerated.

Instead we learn to be assertive, one component of which is choosing our words wisely. As we gain awareness of our non-negotiable truths, our ability to be thoughtful, yet assertive, grows. As we speak, we let others know how we need to be heard, without resorting to anger. Some boundaries of assertiveness are to "Say What we Mean," "Mean What We Say," and "Don't Say it Mean."

What we learn and practice in our rooms of recovery has a cascading effect. Our assertiveness models strong, but not aggressive behavior for our children, giving them the confidence to achieve their goals with dignity and honesty.

TODAY'S MEDITATION

I am grateful to be born at a time when my self-esteem is validated through assertiveness; for me, my children and for their children to come.

"Truth does not sit in a cave and hide like a lie. It wanders around proudly and roars loudly like a lion." — *Susy Kassem*

CONTROL
MAY 31

My need for control was never greater than when I had the least control of myself: in the throes of addiction. The more stressed and out of control I felt, the more insistent I was in my demands that I control everyone and everything around me.

As a mother and wife in my addiction, I became chief controller, while minimizing everyone else's contribution. Concepts such as *the family*, or *teamwork*, were not a consideration. My inflated ego whispered, "You know no one can do anything as well as you can." I needed perfection and the answers to everything, to stay ahead of everyone's next move. My need to control had no beginning or end.

No matter how logical it seems, control does not work. It alienates others. Control is interfering and demeaning. We never have all the answers, and we're not supposed to.

Control is the illusion that masks our hidden insecurities and fear of not being enough. Exhausting and offensive to others, the effort to control depletes precious energy needed for ourselves. Humility and spiritual alignment create our connection to *Let Go and Let God* so that each person in our lives, starting with us, is free to exercise their rightful autonomy.

TODAY'S MEDITATION
I am grateful that today I can trade control for happiness, where everyone wins.

"Be not angry that you cannot make others as you wish them to be, since you cannot make yourself as you wish to be." — Thomas à Kempis

DEALING WITH LOSS
JUNE 1

Growing up, I watched family members ignore their pain and grief as though dismissing these feelings would be enough to let them go. Years of practice from my doing the same thing made me a frustrated, angry, young adult, unable to cope with everyday upsets and trivial frustrations that are a part of any life. I was miserable, but didn't know why.

The blessed rooms of recovery, and a nurturing sponsor, encouraged me to cry and grieve. I accepted my right to feel all my feelings, not just the laughter. I learned that tears of grief were necessary to cleanse, with tender care, the sore spots of my soul, those painful places made hard through years of obstinate denial.

I imagined tears as little spirits, resurrecting visions of time spent and lost with those I loved. And then my miracle happened. The feelings of loss gave way to a sense of rebirth, a letting go of unfinished business. Years of untapped grief came rushing in as I remembered beloved pets, friends, family, and lost opportunities. Each remembrance exploded in a flood of tears before finding its rightful place in my heart.

As suppressed memories rose from the depths of my past, I acknowledged each one, then set it free, releasing them all from years of emotional entrapment. In opening that door, I, too, became free. I honor all that I am with love and peaceful adoration in a connectedness with those who have gone on before me. In teaching me the lessons of grief, the universe made me whole.

TODAY'S MEDITATION

What freedom there is to give ourselves the gift of honoring the significance of those so loved who have gone before us.

"Life when it ends is still alive, memories are the celebration of what it meant. Grieving is that part, our soul, that can't easily say goodbye" — S.L. Northey

A SPIRITUAL PROGRAM
JUNE 2

When I walk into recovery, I remember the feeling of bewilderment and fear at the mere mention of a *God*. Half expecting to see Him walk into our rooms, I knew there was nowhere to hide, and the only God I knew was a tough punisher, unrelenting, and vengeful.

From my homegroup in recovery came a voice that said, "Choose your own conception of a God." This allowed me to relax, to keep coming back and to seek a God of *my* understanding. There were no exams, no questions, or judgments made. I was free to decide whether there was a spiritual entity presiding over me, or not.

Staying clean and sober in recovery is not dependent on having a belief in a God. We can consider the possibility there is a supreme being of a spiritual kind, and we are not it. Most of us accept this notion with great relief. Some of us concede to accept nothing more. Many are atheists and agnostics and yet, because they become a part-of the solution in recovery, they maintain their sobriety.

On spiritual matters, we feel sure the more we think we know the less we know. In this we don't rely on thinking. We rely on a deeper knowing, a truth that comes from within.

What a relief to find a truth that speaks to each of us.

TODAY'S MEDITATION
Dear God, I am grateful to the traditions of recovery that allow my spiritual convictions to be what they are for me alone, without posing a threat to my recovery.

"By virtue of being human, all people are spiritual, regardless of whether or how they participate in religious observance." — *Margaret A. Burkhardt*

BOUNDARIES
JUNE 3

Life in a dysfunctional home provides little, if any, healthy communication. Anger is the norm, while we try to hide, get away, or retaliate in kind. These actions become our boundaries.

As practice new boundaries in recovery, we redefine and experiment them with others. Changing behavior is not an overnight transformation. Becoming our own best advocate for change, with sponsors and trusted friends as mentors, we learn to trust our intuitive and loving selves. We examine which behaviors are acceptable to us, and probe within for what needs to be revised or let go of. In becoming comfortable with new boundaries for ourselves, we take great pains to treat the boundaries of others with the same thoughtful respect.

Over time, we adhere to new standards for ourselves by constructing and becoming comfortable with new boundaries safe and nurturing to us. We learn to say no without aggression or explanation. Many of us become comfortable with saying yes, grateful to be included. We acknowledge that we belong in recovery where we develop strong and affirming truths. If we are unsure what we need, we ask in prayer, "What boundaries are necessary for my highest good?"

The miracle is that the answer comes, and that for each of us the answer is a little different. But no matter what our boundaries are, they give us the ability to honor ourselves and those around us.

The grace of change comes when we establish safe and loving boundaries and respect the boundaries of others.

TODAY'S MEDITATION
Thank you, God, for the courage to set new boundaries for myself. May I honor those boundaries and be an example for those around me.

"Staying silent is like a slow growing cancer to the soul. There is nothing intelligent about not standing up for yourself...However, everyone will at least know what you stood for — You." — Shannon L. Alder

ACCEPTANCE AND THE NINTH STEP
JUNE 4

For most, this is a step fraught with fear, resistance, and dread. Are we ready to face the wrongs and harms we have done to others and ourselves? We are unsure, but we are certain that to *not* do so is to invite a relapse.

How do we make amends face-to-face and *not* have trepidations? What if our efforts are not welcome or understood? What if making amends opens new wounds? What if our amends aren't accepted? *What if, what if.*

None of these questions matter. They are not our concern. Our job is to go to any lengths. Whether others accept or reject our amends is the business of the recipient. We are agents of change in our *own* lives, responsible for making things right for us. A trusted friend in the fellowship, or sponsor, will help us walk through possible scenarios and examine whether making amends would cause irrevocable harm. We feel sure we cannot make a mistake when we do the next right thing, for the right reason.

The first eight steps prepare us for this moment when we must face the harms we have done to others. Step Nine is the opportunity to seek forgiveness. We don't make excuses. We state the facts of harms we have caused in brief, with kindness, and with a sincere commitment to never have them repeated.

Steps Four and Five have prepared us well. We stand ready to accept the results of our amends today, no matter how they are received by those on our list. Regardless of reactions and feelings, we acknowledge their right to their emotions and recognize they were our targets, suffering untold harm from our actions and injurious remarks.

As with other steps, we work Step Nine with as much completeness as possible with the information we have. When the Universe is ready for us to receive new levels of awareness, amends will be presented at a time determined by our Higher Power. We continue to seek freedom as we make amends and we open the door of willingness.

The Ninth Step Promise that says, *we will experience a new freedom and a new happiness,* will almost always appear to us. By trusting the process of this co-creation with our Higher Power in prayer and taking the appropriate action for each harm, we move closer to wholeness. We do this regardless of how difficult it may be, as we were responsible for making our part of the street clean.

TODAY'S MEDITATION

There is no better way to clean my house than through ninth step work. To have the Ninth Step Promises come true is the change I've worked for so long to receive.

"Sometimes you only get one chance to rewrite the qualities of the character you played in a person's life story. Always take it. Never let the world read the wrong version of you." — Shannon L. Alder

EMOTIONAL INTIMACY
JUNE 5

One of the most difficult things to do is to learn to exhibit compassion for ourselves. Many of us accepted abuse, guilt, and shame, because we absorbed the mistaken belief that there was something wrong with us. But this was not our truth then, and it is not our truth now.

As adults, so many of us have unresolved emotional wounds left from childhood. Until we begin the difficult but necessary journey of uncompromising love of self, emotional intimacy remains a dream. In recovery, as we seek inside ourselves for our answers, we hear intimacy sometimes referred to as *In-to-Me-See*. Oftentimes, trusting others is first experienced through working The Steps with a sponsor or a mental health professional, before we can feel safe enough to attempt intimacy in our day-to-day lives.

Characteristics of emotional intimacy are mutual respect, and a sense of unity and oneness which promotes a bond between two people. This bond becomes a trust that honors the other person with steadfast love and conscious care of the relationship.

Misplaced beliefs can block emotional intimacy and sabotage an otherwise loving relationship. If left unresolved, these old messages replay themselves as our thinking is exaggerated, warped from years of incorrect feedback. From there, it's a short trip to the conviction that the relationship will fail, that we cannot view our partner in the relationship with openness and trust.

Emotional intimacy seeks to provide a safe framework for self-compassion, unconditional love of self, and acceptance for both parties. It requires a dedicated desire to give of ourselves and to provide maximum love and service to another in the spirit of mutual care and compromise. As we give of ourselves in the partnership of emotional intimacy we receive the most treasured gifts of all, self-love and respect.

TODAY'S MEDITATION

Help me to remember, God, I cannot hide from my fears or behaviors because to do so would prevent me from loving and trusting others. Help me to face the truth about myself, just for today.

"Part of spiritual and emotional maturity is recognizing that it's not like you're going to try to fix yourself and become a different person. You remain the same person, but you become awakened." — Jack Kornfield

FAITH IN THE MOMENT
JUNE 6

We have lifetime warranties, free tire replacement, money-back guarantees, maintenance agreements, contracts, legal documents, and more. Promises abound, assuring us we will get what we pay for—forever!

But life is full of broken promises, and not just the ones we are given on paper. What guarantees do we have of living a life in perfect working order?

Life comes with no grandiose forecast that we will live comfortably and eternally, but rather that we will experience life with intention, because we have faith in our moment. Our breath exists in the here and now. There is no life in our yesterdays or even ten minutes from now. We do not exist there. We exist here.

Faith in the moment is a way of keeping our suffering and disappointments to a minimum. We feel relief as we focus our magnifying mind right here, right now. Trust and hope thrive close to us. We are nurtured and protected in the moment of now. This is our lifetime; this is where we live.

TODAY'S MEDITATION
Dear God. Thank you for helping me find faith in the moment. When I'm able to get out of your way, your comfort and faith in this moment sustains me.

"Our faith comes in moments. yet there is a depth in those brief moments which constrains us to ascribe more reality to them than to all other experiences."
— *Ralph Waldo Emerson*

FAMILY FORGIVENESS
JUNE 7

This is an area that tugs at the hearts of many who are addicted, both in and out of recovery. Who knows better than we do the hurt we inflicted on those closest to us as we look at the wreckage of our past? Tortured by the memory of our own transgressions, our need for forgiveness from our families never ever leaves us.

In sobriety, we ask ourselves how long it will take to return our lives to normalcy. As we become convinced we have changed, we wonder why the family doesn't rally around us with pats on the back for doing something that comes naturally to normal folks. We ask, "What will it take for us to find forgiveness?"

The answer is not a straight line. While active in our disease, we harmed everyone. Like a bull in a china shop, we wrecked all hope, trust, and understanding others initially gave us so freely. For many of us our destructive behavior went on for years. Each time we rammed through life, telling lies and blaming others, we isolated ourselves a little more. When we looked up, we found everyone had left.

Some of us protested, "But I did my activities at home, alone!" Our families cried, "Yes, and you didn't need your wife, your husband, or your children; you were never there for us when *we* needed you."

If restitution comes—it won't be on our time.

It took time for our families to lose faith and disregard us. It will take time, now, for them to find the trust and faith they once had and believe in us again. Until then, we stay the course and maintain sobriety no matter what. We accept what is and continue to make living at every opportunity.

TODAY'S MEDITATION

In recovery, we rise to a new level of mutual self-respect and love that cannot be made real without facing and fixing the facts of our harms, especially to those closest to us. We must be responsible.

"Sincere forgiveness isn't colored with expectations that the other person apologizes or change. ... Love them and release them. Life feeds back truth to people in its own way and time." — Sara Paddison

FEAR OF FEAR
JUNE 8

Fear. Worry. Dread. These emotions held me hostage for too long. As a child, I functioned on high anxiety, convinced if I lived the rest of the day, I'd be lucky. I was terrified of living, of interacting with others. I was afraid of everything.

The process through which we uncover, discover, and discard all the lies, denial, and pain that remind us how different we thought we were from others, is slow but liberating. Recovery and the timing of our Higher Power allow us to peel back layers of fear by trading in our fear for a stronger faith. Our fears were never true to begin with! Despite the disasters we imagined, the world never ended. The other shoe never dropped.

Recovery proves the more we change everything about ourselves one day at a time, the less fear overwhelms us. On most days, we remain free from fear, more serene and content than we ever thought possible.

The guiding hand of our Higher Power gives us the courage to move through our fears. Faith gives us courage to face those fears and walk through them with hope and confidence.

What happens when we face our fears? Old boundaries and behaviors that diminished our potential disappear. Positive thoughts and resounding courage expand our capabilities, and we change into the person of integrity and courage we always wanted to be.

TODAY'S MEDITATION
Thank you, God, for tools of honesty, open-mindedness, and willingness. With you, I never have to face anything alone, ever.

"I must not fear. Fear is the mind-killer. Fear is the little-death that brings total obliteration. I will face my fear. I will permit it to pass over me and through me...
Where the fear has gone there will be nothing. Only I will remain."
— *Frank Herbert*

GETTING OUR WAY
JUNE 9

There was a period when I resented the old-timers in recovery share that as the newcomer; I was a liar, a cheat, and a thief, even as I knew they were right. I could sell anyone, anything. I convinced my physician of the necessity of pain medication to overcome ailments I didn't have. I never took no for an answer and got what I thought I needed, when and how I needed it by winning through intimidation.

Recovery changed me. The days of butting heads for the sake of getting my way have passed. It kept you away from me and held me hostage to my addictions. Making amends in Step Nine was necessary for me to clean up the wreckage of my past which meant I could no longer do what I always did.

Can working The Steps of recovery do this for you? Can it give anyone a life recreated beyond their wildest dreams? Absolutely. The principles of honesty, openness, and willingness are the only requirements. We just don't leave before our miracles happen!

TODAY'S MEDITATION
Dear God, I remain grateful for courage to let go of self-centered, self-seeking actions that keep me in the problem. You and recovery are my solutions.

"Words can never adequately convey the incredible impact of our attitudes toward life. The longer I live the more convinced I become that life is 10 percent what happens to us and 90 percent how we respond to it." — Charles R. Swindoll

GROWING RESPONSIBLE CHILDREN
JUNE 10

Our daughter was twelve when my husband asked me, "At what age do we allow her to become responsible for her actions?" It startled me, since I saw myself the victim of my addictions at the time, and knew my ability to take charge was compromised. I didn't know what was right and didn't know what to do so I did nothing.

When we allow our children to own the consequences of their actions, it's agonizing to watch. We want them to grow up without pain in a world filled with flowers, sunlight and smiling faces.

Some of us think that if we make their lives easier, our lives will be easier still. We send our children the message that they can do no wrong and that they deserve everything—*the same message we sent ourselves while in the grip of addictions*!

As adults, we know that without consequences, we make the same mistakes repeatedly. If we take responsibility for our mistakes, we experience emotional stability and growth. In recovery, we struggle to be mature and responsible. Isn't this what we want for our children?

As the parent or adult, we determine boundaries reasonable to everyone, so our children understand they must comply. We determine age-appropriate consequences as early, and as quickly as possible.

When we detach from our children's' negative or risky behavior, several things happen: we take back the cushion they've always used when they fell; we allow them to get up, and to experience the consequences of their actions. The biggest change, however, is we let them fail and give them credit only when it is earned.

We step aside as our adult children decide what they want and need. We allow them to stand up and own their actions, a necessary lesson many of us never learned to implement in our own lives until we found our rooms of recovery.

TODAY'S MEDITATION

With God's help, I'm confident I can be the parent, the confidant and mentor my child always wanted me to be.

"...children themselves haven't yet isolated themselves by selfishness and indifference... Our responsibility to them is not to pretend that if we don't look, evil will go away, but to give them weapons against it." — Madeleine L'Engle

FORGIVENESS

JUNE 11

I remember this woman in recovery I secretly named Angry. She never admitted she was wrong. When others pointed out that she was, she grew sullen, and depressed. The longer she nurtured her resentments, the more toxic she became. Like a cancer, her resentments grew, until they took control of her thoughts. Her thoughts were noxious, and Angry began to die a slow, emotional and spiritual death. She ignored the dangers of relapsing that came with a lack of emotional sobriety; she could not let go of her resentments.

The Tenth Step tells us, "We quit fighting everyone and everything." Working with a sponsor, Angry began to take baby steps in forgiveness. If she forgot to get something someone requested she apologized, and, went back out to get it. If she said something inappropriate, she apologized. Soon, awareness became paramount in her life, and Angry sough opportunities to be helpful to others as if her life depended upon it, because it did.

Gradually, she learned that one way to stay free from the emotional pain of resentments is by giving ourselves the gift of self-forgiveness. The grace of self-forgiveness helps to ensure another day of sobriety. Forgiveness answers the question: Do I want to be *right* or, do I want to be happy? It replaces that question with another: What is His Will for me?

We want, always, to be gentle and forgiving of ourselves, so we can reach out and give forgiveness to others. As we practice forgiveness, an emotional softening becomes us. We replace our anger and our need to be right with kindness.

TODAY'S MEDITATION

Dear God, I am learning that *my* serenity and peace are non-negotiable and can be attained by forgiveness of myself and others. I remember that, just like me, others have problems, too.

"When a deep injury is done to us, we never heal, until we forgive."
— *Nelson Mandela*

HONESTY IN RELATIONSHIPS
JUNE 12

Every meeting we have with another person is an opportunity; a chance to practice honesty. We practice how we listen, share, receive a truth about ourselves, or reveal while active in our addictions. We never considered that our honesty must be appropriate for its intended audience. With co-workers, what we share is much different from the honesty shared with special friends or family. But regardless of who we speak with, what we say must treat those who hear it with kindness, consideration, and honesty.

Honesty with spouses and significant others requires direct and loving communication to sustain relationships. For many of us, though, communication is difficult to practice because it takes time. We return home from work and hit the floor running. We prepare dinner, take children to extracurricular activities, wash clothes, check homework, run baths, fix the car, and fall into bed. Who has time for meaningful interactions? Who took classes in conflict resolution techniques or communication? Busyness becomes the mask that hides our inability to listen or to express ourselves and be heard.

Honesty in our relationships need not take up a lot of time, but it does take courage. What often works best is to be exact in our truth, adhering to the adage, *be gentle, be honest, and be brief.* We recognize that what we say, no matter how gentle and forthcoming, can still feel confrontational when it is not what someone wants to hear. Our emotional balance and serenity rests upon our ability to say it anyway. We are responsible only for the delivery of our truth without malice or negativity, and our own reaction to what is being said.

Experience shows when we pray and ask how we want to be heard to the conversation, regardless of the audience, there are no mistakes, because we're coming from a place of authenticity.

TODAY'S MEDITATION

As I pray today I ask you, God, to keep my words honest, gentle and kind regardless of the issue.

"If you expect honesty, be honest. If you expect forgiveness, forgive. If you expect a whole person, you have to be a whole person." — Kristen Crockett

HAVING TO PROVE OURSELVES
JUNE 13

In my youth, I believed I owed everyone an explanation, and that giving that explanation would win others over. I thought you *wanted* my side of the story and believed that your knowing it would make you like me more.

It backfired. Because I did it for all the wrong reasons, I became confused, even paranoid, as I had no boundaries when it came to deciding what was too much sharing. The reactions of others made me feel manipulated, used, and inadequate. Today I know that it was *my* behavior that was manipulative.

The rooms of Al-Anon give us clarity to see we were always enough without explanation or justification. We learn to detach from our manipulative behaviors and live within mature boundaries. The acronym J.A.D.E. is code for the behaviors we no longer exercise. We do not **J**ustify, **A**rgue, **D**efend, or **E**xplain our actions anymore.

After years of explaining ourselves blue in the face, justifying ourselves to others, we discover that often, ten-words-or-fewer are enough to make ourselves understood and satisfy curiosity. Nothing more is required. Learning to live within the protection of our secure boundaries sends the message we no longer have to prove anything to anyone. We have become sure of our own goodness.

TODAY'S MEDITATION

What a miracle of transformation to not have to prove my worth with a long-winded explanation. I remember just for today, I am enough.

"Strong people have a strong sense of self-worth and self-awareness; they don't need the approval of others." — Roy T. Bennett

STEP NINE

JUNE 14

"Made direct amends to such people wherever possible except when to do so would injure them or others."

There are two steps in recovery that, for many of us, are the most difficult to complete. Step Five, and Step Nine. We have been preparing ourselves all along for Step Nine, beginning with Step One. We are reminded that, "Faith without works is dead." Our real purpose we are assured, is to be of service to our Higher Power and others around us. Sponsors remind us of the commitment we made to go to any lengths.

Our Ninth Step Promises support a newfound goal of freedom that bolsters a willingness to reach a new height. Together with the help of a loving sponsor and trusted friends, practice helps us to become real through the gift of humility in honesty. Each meeting in prayer opens our hearts as we embrace an emerging integrity that happens as we rid ourselves of traits that block us from spiritual and emotional growth. We dust ourselves off and inhale courage and determination to meet another on their terms, while focusing on forgiveness of others.

Walking now with our Higher Power, we are ready to make direct amends no matter how difficult, unless to do so harms them or others. We practiced being brief and honest. Without regard for ourselves, we do this because there is nothing more we can do until restitution is made. This is *our* responsibility. Most of all, this is *our* freedom.

When we have made amends with everyone we think we have harmed we ask ourselves, *have I missed anything or anyone?*

The Promises are re-read in prayer. A spiritual softening in our psyche transpires as we absorb the grace of forgiveness of self. This is the miracle we've been waiting for, a setting down of the burden of the wrongs we have done.

What follows is a restorative, indescribable leap of faith that binds us even tighter to our Higher Power. Together, we do not fail.

TODAY'S MEDITATION

Dear God, thank you for deeming me worthy to experience the fruit of the Promises. I know now they will happen to anyone who acts with your help.

* * *

"Forgiveness is one of the most certain paths to restoration, and it is also one of the most difficult. However, it is an attempt to return to wholeness, once again, by letting go and freeing myself from the tight clutch and heavy burden of caution, anger, resentment, and the desire for revenge and punishment. —
Sharon Weil

* * *

HOW IMPORTANT IS IT?
JUNE 15

By the time I came to recovery, I was over-extended, worn out, and hyper-ventilating just thinking about everything I had to do. I could not sit still; I could not listen. I'd look around and wonder, *can these people not understand the enormity of the responsibilities I have to carry all by myself? How can you laugh and be happy?*

I remember a simple question that helps to measure the problem at hand, "How Important Is It?" At first, this felt like a trick question. Whether picking up papers off the floor, cleaning the floors or taking a friend to the hospital, my days were consumed with important, life-altering things to do, and all of them seemed absolutely critical.

A sponsor suggested I make a list noting every-single-thing I had to do that day, omitting nothing. Then she asked for more columns and the label Monday through Friday. I put an X in a specific column next to the chore that could wait. I was sure something dreadful would happen if everything didn't get done today. But I discovered that when an item with an X lingered a few days, nothing happened.

That exercise became the beginning of a clear-sighted change. I began to see that some chores were not as important as originally thought. I saw how perfectionistic and unrealistic I had been. This act of discernment proved I wasn't as important as I thought I was. Whether I checked a task off or not, life went on. Today my goal is to find an easier way to live, and I do it through The Steps of recovery.

TODAY'S MEDITATION

Thank you, God, for allowing me to see the beginning of a balance that asks, "How Important is it really?

"Your days are numbered. Use them to throw open the windows of your soul to the sun. If you do not, the sun will soon set, and you with it." — Marcus Aurelius

Importance of Meeting Participation
June 16

We're familiar with what happens to those of us in recovery who stop coming back. Most revert to old ways of thinking and doing. Believing they have "enough" recovery, they fall back into the inevitable pit of delusion that brought them to the rooms in the first place.

If we asked people who attend meetings, "Why do you still go to those meetings?" the answers would include, "Because when I'm at a meeting, I find hope," and "Meetings are where I learn to connect with others, just like me." But mostly we hear, "Because I want to."

Coming back, we see what happens to those who choose not to participate in this life-or-death proposition. Likewise, we see miracles of transformation happen to those who keep coming back, even when they don't want to.

As we become part of something bigger than ourselves, a spiritual alteration results in a soul-shift toward a state of hope and acceptance.

Sharing our experiences, our shortcomings, our strengths and our hopes with others who are on the same journey sets us free in a way we may never thought possible. Free from the burden of a self we despised, we are empowered, excited we can become who we always wanted to be. As our thought process rejuvenates, our actions follow.

Recovery is for people who want it more than life itself. Meetings are where it all begins.

TODAY'S MEDITATION

Meetings are a non-negotiable lifeline, a link to help others, to be involved; but always, to connect with you, my God.

"Meetings are the heart of the fellowship. The program is the first 164 pages."
— *Anonymous*

INTOLERANCE
JUNE 17

A friend in recovery had a severe case of intolerance. If she didn't like what someone shared, she would get up and leave. If someone's telephone rang, she made judgmental comments. When someone shared their experience but took longer than she thought acceptable, she crisply redirected the conversation.

Then came the day when intolerance was the topic of discussion, specifically how rude it was for others to exhibit intolerance. By the time the meeting was over, my friend, with her head hung low, apologized to the group. "You've just described me. I see how inappropriate I've been."

It is vital, particularly for the newcomer, that we show respect for others. When we exhibit tolerance, we become representatives of change and an example to the newcomer, testimony to how sobriety is so much more than just staying sober. We acknowledge that, without exception, we are *all* sick people trying to get well. Our literature reminds us, love and tolerance is our code.

As we lead with these core principles of recovery, they never fail to provide the healing touch of tolerance so desperately needed by all who gather in the rooms of recovery.

TODAY'S MEDITATION
Dear God, please remind me this is a program where we grow along spiritual lines. If it were a program of perfection, I feel certain I'd never come back.

"When you discriminate against anyone, you discriminate against everyone. It's a display of terrible intolerance." — Alan Dershowitz

JUSTIFIED RESENTMENTS
JUNE 18

After a painful incident, we often justify the need for a resentment. The emotion itself is not the problem, but rather, what we do with it. Normal people feel resentment, state their anger, and then get over it. They may, after a cooling off period, even make amends if they believe their own behavior warrants doing so.

Those of us in addiction or with mental or emotional instability, tend to weaponize justified resentments, making them as potent as a gun in the hands of a criminal. For those who are not in good control of their emotions, acting out, full-throttle, feels like a right, even a duty. Without self-control, justified resentments tend to be an automatic move to hostility.

In recovery, we do whatever is necessary to diffuse the effects of this emotion before the resentment grows. Justified or not, anger only serves to hurt ourselves or others. Perceived or real, justified anger has the power to cause actual damage. The responsibility for diffusing justified resentments belongs to the person who harbors them.

Waiting 24-48 hours in prayer and meditation, and talking to others before we do anything, can go far to diffuse the threat of retaliation. Asking hard questions of ourselves such as, "What is the truth in this incident, and what is the truth about me?" helps us to see we are not innocent bystanders.

As our anger cools, we let The Steps work us; otherwise, a backward walk through the gates of hell awaits.

TODAY'S MEDITATION
I seek prayer and meditation as the passageway to love and tolerance of others so resentments have no room to fester and grow.

"Anytime you're filled with resentment, you're turning the controls of your emotional life over to others to manipulate . . . Resentments give you an excuse to return to your old ways. This is what got you there in the first place."
— Wayne Dyer

LENDING MONEY IN SOBRIETY
JUNE 19

A wise man said, "When it comes to money, you have no friends." This statement is justified by the behavior of people who borrow money with a silent understanding that they will pay it back, and then never do.

We're told in our rooms we are liars, cheats and thieves, and this three-fold behavior doesn't end just because we find sobriety through recovery. Rarely do we meet someone in early recovery who lends money to another with thoughts of getting it back.

Often, we come to realize we are just one of many who has been asked to give, although there is no expectation to do so. We are always within our right to say no if that is our truth.

Recovery is the vehicle for us to learn to help ourselves. There are some who are tempted to help themselves at the expense of others. A newcomer becomes the perfect prey, as we spot their vulnerability. Women are afraid of insulting someone by saying no. Without a trusted servant or sponsor to guide them, they can fall victim to those with less than honorable intentions; those who borrow and never pay back. Sometimes those we lend money to are never seen again.

Our singleness of purpose in recovery is clear. Our rooms remain a sacred place we rely upon to find and maintain long-term sobriety. Requests for anything other than help with our sobriety are best left outside our rooms. We need not confuse helping others with giving money unless we want to. When in doubt, we have sponsors to advise us.

In our rooms we are not prey, and we do not prey; we pray.

TODAY'S MEDITATION
I'm grateful to be aware of what it means to be a trusted servant, and to be a giver of trusted suggestions to the newcomer.

"While money doesn't buy love, it puts you in a great bargaining position."
— *Christohper Marlowe*

LETTING GO OF CONTROL
JUNE 20

I used to believe I was in charge of everything even as my life spun out of control. By delegating I let you control me, let you be the one to prove I still existed. In exchange for this surrender, the expectation was you would accept and approve of me, listen to me, act in my best interest. It was my personal set-up for failure, and it worked every time—my disappointment was guaranteed. Still, I tried to control everything by controlling others, thinking this would ensure an outcome that met *my* approval. The harder I strove to handle my world by manipulating you, the less real control I had.

Then came a lightbulb moment in recovery. In the Serenity Prayer's last stanza, it says, "…and the wisdom to know the difference." In that instant, I saw I had control, but it could not be exercised by manipulating you. I had to take it back, own it, and be responsible for *me*.

No longer will I look to others to define me. With the guidance of my Higher Power, everything I need is within me. What a blessing it is to realize control begins and ends with me alone. I am free, now, to go the distance by looking deep within and reclaiming the person of worth I have always been but never knew.

Self is the only thing I can control, and I take that control back.

TODAY'S MEDITATION
I'm finally convinced I can only change me, and that is more than enough.

"In dwelling, live close to the ground. In thinking, keep to the simple. In conflict, be fair and generous. In governing, don't try to control. In work, do what you enjoy. In family life, be completely present."— Lao Tzu

MANIPULATION
JUNE 21

It began with our first scream or smile at birth. We observed that to cry, scream or laugh brought attention and relief. Someone came to our rescue. Someone showed us love. Growing up, we learned appropriate and inappropriate methods to get attention.

Sometimes our need for attention or help is born out of a selfish desire to satisfy our sense of entitlement, jealousy, greed, or insecurity.

As children when our needs were not met, we manipulated others until we got attention. In adulthood, this manipulation proved less effective and harmful to ourselves and others. We couldn't be trusted as our deceptions became demonstrably hurtful to those around us. We couldn't tell the truth from the lies we created in the service of manipulation, and when that manipulation failed, we found a sick comfort in our addictions.

As adults in recovery, we temper personal responsibility with compassion. We learn to say what we mean, mean what we say, but say it nice. When we honor who we are by leaning on our authentic selves, the need for self-serving manipulation disappears. With unabashed pleasure at our transformation, we dance with glee in the freedom to love ourselves and others. We have become sincere and thoughtful to those around us. Humbly, we acknowledge that our Higher Power is doing for us, what we could not do alone.

TODAY'S MEDITATION
God, I feel grateful tears as I recognize the closer to your spirit I stay, the freer I become.

"Love comes when manipulation stops; when you think more about the other person than about his or her reactions to you. When you dare to reveal yourself fully. When you dare to be vulnerable." — Joyce Brothers

MY RIGHT TO RECOVERY
JUNE 22

In recovery, we rely upon security, safety, and the spirit of our Higher Power that lives within us; a reliance that strengthens as we grow along spiritual lines. The rooms of recovery are a place revered by those who care to share their experience, strength, and hope with others who share in a common disease and all of its manifestations.

Sometimes security and serenity in our rooms are disrupted. Someone feels threatened. They may not like a group decision or engage in a verbal attack, disrupting the calm and everyone in attendance.

Each of us is different and brings our truth into the light in our own way. Interspersed in the discussions are personal opinions that sometimes lead to arguments. But regardless of the disruptive situation, we must remember *why* we are here. We have earned our seat in recovery not by being a model citizen, but because of mounting consequences, and an inability to stop drinking or drugging.

We are all misfits; emotional, physical and spiritual rejects of society. For some of us, the occupants of our rooms are the only family we have. When disruption comes, we practice love and tolerance even as we, ourselves, sometimes must admit that we are the source of that disruption.

This is not about perfection as we will all continue to learn and to exercise life's lessons, at best, imperfectly. We remember our need to treat each other as gently as delicate china, but especially the newcomer. Together, we strive for a greater good for our most sacred group and its patrons. Together we exercise our right to recovery.

With a Higher Power who walks before us, we humility forgive ourselves and remember our daily walk is never aimed at perfection. We will always be a work in progress.

We hold fast to our right to recover and honor the right to recovery for those with whom we share our rooms.

TODAY'S MEDITATION

I am grateful for reminders that all of us deserve recovery achieved one day at a time.

"Whether I or anyone else accepted the concept of alcoholism as a disease didn't matter; what mattered was that when treated as a disease, those who suffered from it were most likely to recover." — Craig Ferguson

ONE IS TOO MANY
JUNE 23

Regardless of the addiction, we know one of anything that changes the way we feel about ourselves, is one too many, and that one hundred is never enough. One drink, one hit, one sugar-laced cookie, one lie, sets the stage for more, for those of us with addictive personalities.

The obsession to drink begins with our thinking. The delusion that maybe one drink will stop the insanity of obsessive thinking long enough to not feel, is akin to someone who strolls in front of a train to stop their pain.

The journey into personal insanity is launched way before our first drink or drug. Once we've picked up that first drink or drug our disease tells us that if one is good, then ten is better. It's too late.

Our thought process separates us from normal people who can have one of anything and walk away. We are not *like* normal people—nor will we ever be. The only way any of us have been able to keep success is to not pick up even one of the things that has enslaved us.

Our 12-step groups have a solution that addresses our threefold disease of the body, the mind and the spirit. If we want to live more than we want to die, using cannot be an option. One is *always* too many.

TODAY'S MEDITATION
I will remember my mother's adage: "Don't start something you can't finish."

"Recovery is not simple abstinence. It's about healing the brain, remembering how to feel, learning how to make good decisions, becoming the kind of person who can engage in healthy relationships, cultivating the willingness to accept help from others, daring to be honest, and opening up to doing." — Debra Jay

STEP NINE, LIVING AMENDS
JUNE 24

What are living amends? Living amends are the way we change our behavior toward family members and others we have hurt as we practice the principles of recovery in our homes and our community with others. Verbal apologies are no longer an option. They never were enough. We've apologized too many times before.

Over time, we hope the actions of amends we take in our daily living will allow us to regain a respected position in our family. We know that doing the same thing and expecting different results never works, we get the same thing we always got

Living amends is a delicate dance. We have so much to prove, so much to repair, as each family member has been affected by our selfish displays of abuse and neglect. Those close to us expect a day when one slip will, yet again, bring tragic and heartbreaking consequences.

Living amends are proof-positive that we are committed to change. We mean what we say and are resolutely willing to execute whatever actions are necessary to achieve forgiveness.

This is not an overnight deal. However long our addiction played havoc can be matched or exceeded by the time it will take to straighten out our side of the street.

We have no power to take back the harm we've done to others. What we have is a sincere desire to go to any lengths to recover our dignity and reputation and to make amends to those we have hurt. Our greatest amend will always be to stay clean and sober, regardless of being forgiven.

TODAY'S MEDITATION
Today I mourn my indiscretions and continue to show efforts to not repeat them. I will pray for the courage to act accordingly.

"It is the highest form of self-respect to admit our errors and mistakes and make amends for them. To make a mistake is only an error in judgment, but to adhere to it when it is discovered shows infirmity of character." — Dale Turner

PASSING IT ON

A friend, new to the fellowship, took a telephone call from another friend in the rooms. The result was magic. They each heard what they needed to hear.

Anytime someone cares enough to call us, or when we care enough to meet, share, or talk, we pass it on. We pass on what we didn't even know we had to give. We are passing on our experience, strength, and hope with clarity and honesty as we speak the language of the heart: one alcoholic to another.

We are part of a oneness, a spiritual unity that comes to life as we mirror back who we used to be and offer hope as we reveal the person we are becoming. Our self-worth is discovered by reaching out and passing on what was so freely given to us. We don't get to keep what we've been given if we don't pass it on. As we help others find their courage and their will to live, we find our own.

This is the miracle of recovery we carry, day in, and day out, as we practice becoming the person we've always wanted to be. The more open we are to receive lessons from the Universe, the greater our opportunity to see the good in all things, even ourselves. This knowledge comes not from us, but from a higher source, and from each other.

As we share what works for us and as we say a quick prayer, and do the next right thing, we pass it on

TODAY'S MEDITATION
Thank you, God, for allowing me to be a vessel for others. The Universe, in concert with your desires, provides the words from me to others.

"Sometimes when you sacrifice something precious, you're not really losing it. You're just passing it on to someone else." — Mitch Albom

THE PERSON I ALWAYS WANTED TO BE
JUNE 26

I grew up believing my life was over before it began. I trusted no one, least of all, me. I had few friends, and lived a lifetime trying to escape a hopeless negativity. As I got older and my paranoia grew, my world became smaller and smaller.

I sought the rooms of recovery, not to stop my addictions but just to stay alive. I hated who I had become and was desperate to feel, just once, like I belonged somewhere. Recovery gave me this and so much more. As my confidence grew, I gradually became the person I had always wanted to be, but never known where or how to get there.

Recovery taught me that service work is the biggest door to change. We visit the sick both in and out of the rooms and help others any way we can. We work The Steps deliberately, and with focus. As we shed guilt, self-pity, and silly resentments we stored for reasons long forgotten, the miracle of a change in our perception came true for us.

Constant contact, and prayerful rituals enacted each day teach us to walk with sacred grace and thankfulness, one step at a time. We continue until we become the loving, respectable person we always wanted to be. And then we never cease.

TODAY'S MEDITATION

Today, the universe assures me, if I can change my life, then anyone can, provided they want that change more than anything else in the world.

"On your death bed, … You will wish you had ventured out more. That you had spoken up more. Tried some things. Reinvented yourself one more time."
— *Steve Chandler*

THE PURSUIT OF HAPPINESS
JUNE 27

What constitutes happiness is different for each of us. Some expect a never-ending parade of new and different sources of joy, all the bells and whistles that herald each new-found euphoria. Some can't see through a fog of self-disdain to the sunlight on the other side. Yet, still others cry that having everything is still not enough.

However we define it, most of us believed happiness depended on something outside ourselves given to us as if on a silver platter.

Where is the contentment in each wondrous breath we take? Do we not have everything we need right this moment? Happiness and contentment exist in the here and now. We may hope to experience both a week or a month from now but are promised nothing. Only in the immediate moment can we feel bliss, because it is only in this instant that we live.

We always have the option to be happy, and ask ourselves, why *not* now? Sit for a moment with eyes closed. We deserve happiness, regardless of what is going on around us. In our stillness, we open our heart to what is right this moment and breathe in contentment. As we breathe out peace we rest, aware that we are content here where we are, experiencing these wonderful moments called joy.

Engaged in quiet prayer, our knowing insists we are worthy of happiness, and we feel it. Faith and intention produce this peace by keeping us in the moment. We look down at our feet and realize we are grateful, convinced we are alive, right now. This is the essence of happiness.

TODAY'S MEDITATION
I transform my reality. As I define my happiness, I realize I am in control of my own happiness when I keep it simple in the now.

"We discover the vast difference between living and feeling alive when we discover inspiration." The quickest way to true happiness is …by the immediate and actionable pursuit to be inspired." — Elaina Marie

RIGOROUS HONESTY
JUNE 28

I remember my mother's antics when one of my four siblings did something wrong. Lined up in a row, the five of us stood, hands extended. She slapped each hand with a wooden spoon until one of us confessed. I took the blame for one of the other four, grateful that the punishment and the tears would stop.

It is important that we examine our motives behind our honesty. Honesty that points a finger can be hurtful and becomes a deflection away from our own faults. It can be used as our personal agenda, or as a way to blame others.

While nothing counts but honesty, when we lead with our highest good we feel sure the truth we choose to offer is the truth that extends outward with sincerity and love. This happens when our truth is offered with respect. As we practice being truthful and generous in forgiving ourselves without manipulation, we become free to extend the same to others without any other reason than to be truthful.

Recovery shows that balance is the best measure of our truth. We practice delivering honesty with clarity and a gentleness not previously demonstrated. The truth is not in anyone's best interest if it is hurtful or demeaning. We think before we speak and ask ourselves *why* something needs to be said. And when we deliver it, our truth is not distorted, enhanced, or minimized. With gentleness and care, regardless of how the truth is received by others, rigorous honesty becomes our offering that people can count on.

TODAY'S MEDITATION

As I let change begin with me, I become an example of a loving, honest person for my God, and for those around me as I strive not to manipulate my intent with my words.

"There's a lot more to being honest than just not telling lies anymore. There are lies of omission, the things we don't say, secrets we don't share. Those can be as devastating as any outright lie. We don't say we're only as sick as our secrets for nothing. "— Zach W

REGRETS

JUNE 29

Learning to identify feelings remains a challenge. In early sobriety the only feelings I was sure of were anger and regret. Both had to do with the mistaken belief I was a bad, unredeemable person.

Recovery proves it is a short leap from regret to *poor me, pour me another one*. Everyone experiences self-doubt from time to time. But those of us in active addiction suffer acutely, hating ourselves from the inside out. No one knows like we do, how to throw a punch to maximize effect, and the preferred target of that punch is almost always ourselves. It's this sick thinking that returns us to the rabbit hole of self-pity. Stinking-thinking.

As we work The Steps, we become aware of old messages that speed our descent into self-pity. Once identified, we have a personal obligation to stop and change them. We cannot afford the luxury of allowing regret to define who we are. As we look for our successes, we focus our energy on resurrecting and acknowledging the rest of who we are.

Appreciating our strengths and our goodness with the focus on self-forgiveness, we have opened ourselves to the light of a loving acceptance of *all* we are. At our core is an abundance of innocence and purity in intentions that significantly outweigh our regrets. We deserve to be swathed in forgiveness and accept that when we know better, we do better.

Some begin to release regrets by sending a get-well card to ourselves. We list our assets and write gratitudes. With practice, we remember we are so much better than we *think* we are. With trust in our Higher Power, we change the things that we can and we help others. No one can eradicate regret like we can.

TODAY'S MEDITATION
As I work to loosen the grip of my regrets, they haunt me less. Attention to what is good in me provides a freedom I never thought possible, enabling me to help myself and others.

"We all make mistakes, have struggles, and even regret things in our past. But you are not your mistakes, you are not your struggles, and you are here NOW with the power to shape your day and your future." — Steve Maraboli

BALANCE IN HELPING OTHERS
JUNE 30

A friend discussed a challenge in recovery involving her daughter, a teenager in the stage of pulling away. This once inquisitive young adult who never hesitated to ask questions had become estranged from family members. Her mother wanted to get close again, to help her and do for her as she had always done, but her smothering concern alienated her daughter all the more. My friend was distraught, convinced this sudden independence was all her fault, and that it was damaging her daughter.

Another woman told how her partner exhibited this same detachment, becoming reserved, not wanting to talk. Crying as she spoke, she assumed there must be something wrong with her. What did she do to make him like this?

Across the room, a man suggested the two try minding their own business. "Too often, he said, we try to rescue others from their personal challenges when we should encourage them to fix their own discomfort. Let them feel and figure things out for themselves. Unless they ask for help, stay out of it."

At the next meeting, the women were eager to speak. They discussed their newfound courage to not make personal the actions of loved ones. They shared how presumptuous their thinking had been.

As they found their balance in helping others, they gave family members room to solve problems in their own way, even if their method wasn't what the women themselves would have done.

Isn't this what we all want; the autonomy to work things out for ourselves?

By relinquishing our misplaced sense of responsibility, we allow others vital space and opportunity to become independent, mature and logical problem-solvers.

TODAY'S MEDITATION

I'm reminded I don't know what is good for anyone. Today let me balance helping others by allowing them to come up with their own solutions. This frees me up to put the attention back where it belongs, on me.

"Balance, peace, and joy are the fruit of a successful life. It starts with recognizing your talents and finding ways to serve others by using them." — *Thomas Kinkade*

SOLVING PROBLEMS

JULY 1

Under the influence, my egotistical personality prevented me from solving my problems because I never thought them through; in fact, I thought about them little. I tried to drink mine away and focus on having answers to *your* problems. Having solutions to your problems meant I was right and I could ignore the fact I was clueless when it came to my problems. Problems? What problems? *You're* the one with problems.

While in recovery, my sponsor suggested I stop giving my opinion. She told me how mistaken I was to think I had answers to someone else's problems. She said, "That's the job of our Higher Power." She suggested I say something like, "I'm sorry, I can't have an answer for you as I don't know what is best for me."

What never works is giving unsolicited advice to others.

Recently my two garage doors were acting broken. They were old, and both replacement quotes meant spending lots of money. My sponsor suggested I decide after 24-hours of prayer without over-reacting. She assured me more would be revealed. What came the next day was a simple fix might be to change the batteries. New batteries were installed and my garage doors–good as new!

This search for a solution using time and prayer works, especially when we extend that same right to those around us. As we give others the respect and space necessary to solve their issues on their terms, healthier conversations and relationships ensue. It seemed family members got better; but the truth was, we were the ones who changed as we altered our reactions.

No longer is it our job to educate anyone. Instead of controversy we say, "You know, you could be right," and change the subject.

The rewards that come from waiting for a higher intuition from our Higher Power are immense. When we detach, pray, and wait on our Higher Power's time for the right thought or action, we trust the next right thing will happen, because it always does. And we give those around us the same space, along with the recognition we do not have solutions to the problems of others.

TODAY'S MEDITATION

Today I am free from the delusion I have answers to anyone's problems but my own. I turn mine over to God because my life is His anyway, and I ask that He help you with yours.

I can't,
God can,
I think I'll let Him.

* * *

"Some problems seem irrational as they are caused by people's emotional reaction to a set of circumstances or events." — Pearl Zhu

* * *

STEP TEN
JULY 2

*"Continued to take personal inventory and
when we were wrong, promptly admitted it."*

The goal of Step Ten is to free ourselves from the darkness of wrongdoing through a daily inventory that opens our hearts to the sunlight of the Spirit in Step 11. It's called Freedom.

To receive the gift of freedom and the miracle of humility that comes from *Letting Go and Letting God*, we must quit fighting everyone and everything. We let go of resentments, accusations, and fingers that point outward. We already know how to revert to childish, old behaviors, and have come too far to be anything but responsible for all our actions.

Step Ten is our daily check-and-balance opportunity to help keep us free of old thoughts and behaviors and to seek forgiveness of self.

Through daily assessment, we evaluate what we could have done differently, not to grieve over it or to suffer guilt, but to recognize our power in choices. Where amends are in order, we make them immediately, when possible.

We seek to be free from our personal self-seeking bondage as we prepare for Step Eleven where we will be led to continue growing along spiritual lines.

With grace, we will experience the light and spiritual connection we seek.

TODAY'S MEDITATION

Step Ten reminds me, as I clean my side of the street and scrutinize my hurtful behaviors, humility must be ever-present.

*"It is a spiritual axiom that every time we are disturbed, no matter what
the cause, there is something wrong with us. If somebody hurts us and we are sore,
we are in the wrong also..." — 12 Steps and 12 Tradition*

SPIRITUAL GROWTH
JULY 3

Our literature is replete with the need for continuous spiritual growth, growth generated by our reliance on something greater than ourselves. In recovery, we receive ample gifts of the spirit. We couldn't change ourselves enough to stop our addictive behaviors because we had no power. Lack of power is the *real* problem. Our way never worked. The solution is the choice we make. We pray and decide to turn our will and our life over to a Higher Power and we do this, one day at a time. Spiritual shifts are necessary if we are to sustain long-term sobriety.

By the time we learn to quit fighting everyone and everything in Step Ten, we know our life run on self-will brings unhappiness and empty, unfulfilled desires. Without humility, or faith beyond our sight, we know our best thinking brings us stress, anxiety and complications. We stand powerless, unable to obtain sustained happiness and freedom. Many of us continue to die trying to prove ourselves otherwise.

Step Eleven suggests our ability to maintain humility encourages growth along spiritual lines, the gift we sought all along. No longer do we harbor the incessant need to be right or prove anything to anyone. To live and let others live, regardless of opinions or differences between us, is our daily quest. This generosity to others, along with prayer and everlasting faith are all we need to effect spiritual growth.

Just for today, nothing more is necessary. A commitment to our Higher Power and a grateful heart as we seek to be of maximum service, is our path to spiritual growth.

TODAY'S MEDITATION

Thank you, God, for letting me know I cannot be in disharmony and at peace at the same time, and that with harmony comes the blossoming of spiritual growth.

"The easiest way to get in touch with this universal power is through silent Prayer. Shut your eyes, shut your mouth, and open your heart...Prayer should be soundless words coming forth from the centre of your heart filled with love."
— Amit Ray

STARTING MY DAY OVER AGAIN
JULY 4

I knew my day at work would be extremely demanding. Waking up late, I rushed out the door never taking the time to sit and even think about my Higher Power, let alone pray.

When we have days like this, as we all do, we remember to stop and pray right where we are. Remember, we can start our day over again at any time. As we invite our Higher Power into our hearts, we're grateful for our Higher Power to be with us on our journey.

We pause briefly and take a deep breath in to invite the calm of serenity to surround us.

As we connect with our Higher Power, we decide to restart our day, and give thanks for what we can make of this new beginning; a day full of gratitude.

TODAY'S MEDITATION
Thank you, God, for allowing me to stop where I am, say a prayer and begin my day over again.

"We don't develop courage by being happy every day. We develop it by surviving difficult times and challenging adversity." — *Barbara de Angelis*

TEMPTATIONS OF RELAPSE
JULY 5

It was years before I reached my final sobriety date, and after so many false starts, I had to be sure this was the day. And it was.

Since then, I've had yearnings to pick up a drink or a drug again but know I have too much to lose. My obligation to myself and my Higher Power is to stay the course. I do this for me—not for my children or anyone else. If my sobriety is not anchored to what is within, I will fail.

In the moments my husband passed from cancer, I was hit with the realization I had never lived alone sober. I was terrified. I was sucker-punched, wanted to die, convinced I couldn't live without him all in the same instant. As the coroner removed his body from the house, I stepped into his bathroom. The committee in my head exploded with chatter as I looked around the room at the large bottle of liquid Morphine, Oxycodone, Morphine suckers and Fentanyl patches. Whispering, that itty-bitty shitty committee said, "Here you go, this will help. You deserve this. We know how you feel and this will take that suffocating fear of living without your husband away—forever."

In those moments, my God did for me what I could not do for myself. With one foot already in the hereafter, I grabbed the phone and called my sponsor who told me to run outside to my front porch. She came and disposed of everything, and she saved my life.

I'm convinced that relapses are premeditated attempts at suicide that often prove successful. Those of us with a vigilant life-saving gift of sobriety are the lucky ones. Each day we stay clean and sober, regardless of what is happening, we are walking miracles. Those who do not remain sober buy a one-way express-pass to oblivion. There is nothing a drink or drug can make better. I could have been a statistic. Nothing but recovery can compete with the self-medication that drugs and alcohol offer.

Without a regular recommitment to our sobriety, one that comes from strength not from us, but from our Higher Power, relapse crouches and waits for the exact moment to deny us a life filled with miracles of hope and freedom.

I will forever, be indebted to those who came before me, those who continue to pass on what was so freely given to them. Most of all, I am thankful to the will that springs from my Higher Power, that I grasp especially when life gets harsh, to help me stay sober one day at a time, no matter what.

"… this business of resentment is infinitely grave. We found that it is fatal. For when harboring such feelings, we shut ourselves off from the sunlight of the Spirit. The insanity of alcohol returns and we drink again. And with us, to drink is to die." — Alcoholics Anonymous, Page 60

DETACHING WITH LOVE
JULY 6

Learning how to detach with love brings with it fear, uncertainty, and the realization of our loss of control over those around us. Why do we even want to detach with love? Is it necessary? How do we know when detaching is needed? And will doing so mean we love that person less?

When we give more energy to others than to ourselves, when we do for others what they should do for themselves, it may be time to detach with love. Sometimes the act of not engaging is all that is needed. Often, letting go of trying to control an outcome is enough. The power to stop enabling behaviors, breathe, and give ourselves the freedom to detach with love from the behavior of others resides within us. No explanation to the other person is required. We can excuse ourselves with grace or choose carefully which battles to take part in. And we can do it without having to defend ourselves or be right.

We know how to care for others, so detaching with love feels foreign, even uncomfortable. It may seem like retaliation or abandonment but it is not. To detach with love is to respect the space between ourselves and the other person. When we detach with love we allow others to own consequences of their behaviors without judgment or interference. Isn't that what we want for ourselves?

With undiminished love, we offer emotional space for each person to make the best decision for themselves.

TODAY'S MEDITATION

I detach with love without anger or resentment, as I empower healthier behavior and greater responsibility in the person whose choices I have, for so long, tried to control.

"Detachment is letting another person experience their consequences instead of taking responsibility for their problems. It's focusing on yourself rather than rescuing them" — Counselingrecovery.com

TRUST YOURSELF
JULY 7

Why is it that we have an easier time trusting the decisions other people make for us than we do choosing for ourselves? Sometimes we are happy to not have to make tough, difficult decisions, and are content to defer to others, so we go about our lives believing others have our best interest at heart.

Even if they do, having our best interest at heart and knowing what choice is right for us are two different things. Who should know better than we do what is best for us?

When we do not trust ourselves for the answer, we send a message that another's ability to process rational thinking is reliable, but ours is not. It says we cannot trust ourselves to make good decisions.

When we defer to others and allow them to decide what we can live with without our input, everyone is content—as long as the choice they made for us works out. But when we assume they know what is best for us, we set ourselves up for disappointment. Imagine what happens when the decision made for us is one we don't agree with; one that, even though the intentions were good, disappoints us. We become resentful. We blame them. After all, *they* made the mistake, not us. If we are honest, it is ourselves we resent for not stepping up and trusting our own intuition to begin with.

We deserve to be direct, assertive and bold as we take control of our lives and decide what is best for us. Yes, it is unnerving and yes, we can be wrong. *But so can the other person.*

When we're at the helm guiding our course, we're moving forward. We often bounce it off our sponsor, but then we trust ourselves. We take comfort in the assurance that when we consult our Higher Power and pray for the right answer, there are no wrong decisions.

To trust ourselves is to grow up and become responsible. At last, we take ownership for who we are today.

"Know yourself, love yourself, trust yourself, learn to spend time in your own company and listen to your innermost self." — Etta Sawyerr

WHAT IS SUCCESS
JULY 8

Success, for me, was always associated with going to college. The expectation was I would get a degree, land a high paying job, find a significant other or spouse, live in a nice home and, let us not forget, live happily ever after.

None of those things happened. I ran away from home at twelve, barely finished high school but passed with a GPA of 2.2, began drinking alcoholically and drugging at seventeen. For the next thirty years of my addiction career, survival was my success story. The husband, the daughter and the nice house came much later.

Genuine success was born the day I stopped my addictions once and for all, and never looked back.

Today with a sober track record made of thousands of days strung together, success looks different than I ever thought it would: self-respect and a reputation for helping others stands above the rest. Most of all, I earned my seat in recovery through integrity. Success today is my proof of a hard-won authenticity. I have learned the delicate balance between engaging in the world to serve others while keeping the focus on me.

The greatest measure of success is my sobriety. It is the gauge with which I judge myself and it keeps me free from old behaviors.

There is a comfort as big as the Universe that tells me, I am good enough, and when I die I truly will, rest in peace.

TODAY'S MEDITATION

With faith and sobriety, I will continue to be a success, so long as I stay the course while remaining honest, open, and willing to listen to you, God.

"There are women succeeding beyond their wildest dreams because of their sobriety." — *Mary Karr*

WILLINGNESS
JULY 9

Remember when we were too scared, and too unwilling to do *anything* different? Step Three refers to the key of willingness as being indispensable to our journey of recovery. If we close our eyes and imagine life without willingness—where would that leave us? Right where we are anchored in place, without a chance for spiritual or emotional growth.

Willingness plays a huge part in our recovery. For many of us, willingness is the platform on which all growth begins. Our willingness is an unspoken contract we make with ourselves to accomplish dreams and goals by trusting a process we cannot see.

Each morning begins with a willingness to get out of bed, to do the next right thing, to trust our Higher Power. Some days we must pray to be willing.

As we become involved with others; we become willing to be a *part of* something bigger than ourselves, instead of the outsiders we were when we sat on the sidelines of life, criticizing those who were taking part, but unwilling to risk anything. Willingness is the miracle that propels us closer to the person we want to be.

TODAY'S MEDITATION
When I have willingness, it brings courage that says no matter how I feel, today I'll try. I do it whether I want to or not, whether I like it or not. When I have the guts to carry it out, I grow beyond my wildest dreams.

"The willingness to grow is the essence of all spiritual development." — *Bill W.*

ASKING FOR HELP

One of the most difficult things for a newcomer to do in sobriety is to ask for help. By the time a newcomer walks into recovery, they are frightened, desperate, and they do not know what to expect. Beaten down, often still under the influence, they prefer to hide in place.

Sometimes we scare or overwhelm the newcomer when we offer our help, surrounding them with love, suggestions, phone numbers, and conversation.

The newcomer may be court-ordered, not happy to be there to begin with, and may just want to be alone. There are times, too, when the newcomer might like to ask for help, but is too terrified to risk getting close to anyone. Embarrassed and uncomfortable, they ask for nothing.

What the newcomer doesn't know is that, just like them, we came to these rooms desperate and in need of help, and often unable to ask for it. They don't know how grateful we are to have someone ask us to do anything at all! Many of us haven't been invited to do anything in years because we couldn't be trusted to do anything. Recovery is our opportunity to give back to others. To be requested to help is a confirmation of our usefulness.

If you are new to recovery, we hope you will reach out when you're ready, and take the hand we offer. You will not be judged, instead, you will be supported and encouraged. Soon you feel like us, secure and comfortable, knowing you belong in our rooms, doing what we do. If we are to be useful, productive and sober members of society, we must help by giving to others what was so freely given to us.

TODAY'S MEDITATION
God, please help the newcomer to see the love and hope we have for them. When they ask for help, their miracles have already begun.

"Don't be afraid to ask for help when you need it. I do that every day. Asking for help... shows you have the courage to admit when you don't know something, and then allows you to learn something new." — Barack Obama

BEING GENTLE WITH OURSELVES
JULY 11

It feels natural for us to take care of others. We know intuitively what they want or need and we're there to provide it. With those we love and care for, we are especially gentle and kind.

But what about us? When was the last time we treated ourselves with a kindness equal to what we give to those we love and care for? Some equate being gentle with ourselves with being deserving. Those new in recovery rarely feel deserving. Often, they may turn away from being gentle with themselves with negative messages that say, "That's silly!" "I don't have the time for that."

Somehow, we always have time for others. Many of us just never give ourselves permission to attend to our own self-care. We who do so much for others, deserve a personal self-check.

Learning to be gentle with ourselves is a commitment, a personal declaration that says we are *worthy* of self-care. Nurturing must begin with us if we are to have the inner resources to give care to those we love.

Maybe the best we can do is a thirty-minute soak in the tub, or a ten-minute break with our feet up. For some, a personal hug at a tense moment in the day is a reminder of the need to be kind to ourselves.

Setting personal limits, exploring new boundaries for ourselves, and learning what we can do and what we can let go of, reminds we are no longer, all-or-nothing people. Maybe a simple "I'm sorry I can't do that, but I could do xyz," is in order when others ask for our help. We get to be in charge of what gentleness to ourselves looks and feels like.

Accepting loving-kindness from ourselves is the beginning of self-compassion. Sobriety is the permission we've always needed to see how much we deserve to make self-care a priority.

TODAY'S MEDITATION
With your help, God, I remain convinced of how deserving I am. Today I will not minimize the importance of taking care of me.

"What do you do when life blindfolds you and spins you around? We think it's our fault, that we're to blame, when really we should be focused on being gentle with ourselves." — Melody Beattie

CHANGE OR DIE
JULY 12

A man walked into recovery complaining, that while she was not in active addiction, his life remained unmanageable. He was angry at the fellowship for not giving him what he expected as he over-ate, spent money, and gambled. As he unleashed his anger, he declared, "I was happier when I was drinking!"

Unfortunately, for some of us in recovery, the only change we see is the letting go of the addiction. This man never stuck around long enough for his miracle of self-transformation to work. Instead of focusing on our similarities he designed his own recovery, picking and choosing what he thought he needed as if recovery were a smorgasbord. He took pieces of The Steps, and completely omitted the life-changing Fourth, Fifth and Ninth Steps.

Recovery, irrespective of intellect, best thinking, or will-power, teaches tough truths about us. Short-cuts are how we lived before recovery, when we insisted on having our way, doing only what was convenient and easy, and in the process remained an emotional destitute.

Faced with our addiction we have two choices: resign ourselves to changing everything one day at a time—or die. We may fool ourselves by substituting one addiction for another, but the excruciating, isolating pain that comes from self-loathing signals the truth, that nothing has really changed.

In order for recovery to work, we must concede through complete and total surrender, that our best efforts will *never* be enough to conquer our disease. Many die every day trying self-selected halfway measures.

The unity, courage, and success we find in recovery works, but only if we work for it.

TODAY'S MEDITATION

Today I know so long as I trust a process I cannot see, and follow a few instructions, my life continues to change for the better.

"If you're not changing, evolving with the times, there's a pretty good chance that you're stagnant, dying, already dead, or just a rock in someone's shoe."
— *Ray Palla*

ACCEPTANCE OF SELF
JULY 13

"Today is the first day of the rest of your life!" my Uncle John liked to exclaim. I used to laugh at him when he'd say this to me, totally missing its significance. Each new day really *is* the first day but you have to embrace it, and to do that you need to embrace yourself by accepting all that you are right this moment.

I used to think acceptance was what happened for everyone except me. I often wondered what it meant to accept myself and then be content with what I saw.

Recovery proves the person in the mirror before us is worthy of our acceptance if for no other reason than because we live. And because we live, we have a purpose.

We accept that we are, at times, self-centered, impatient, and jealous; emotions that throw us off balance when we give them power. From there it is a short step to self-loathing.

Accepting ourselves begins with the admission that we are not perfect. Acceptance of ourselves, as-is, gives us the peace to become more patient, loving, and thoughtful.

Conversations with our Higher Power confirm we are right where we're supposed to be, taking baby steps and making progress a day at a time. If this is the first day of the rest of our lives, we have ample opportunity to go on accepting ourselves today, tomorrow, and the next day.

For those who seek it, acceptance of self grows a little each day.

TODAY'S MEDITATION
Thank you, God, for accepting me as I am. You give me permission to accept all of me.

"I think happiness comes from self-acceptance. We all try different things, and we find some comfortable sense of who we are. We look at our parents and learn and grow and move on. We change." — Jamie Lee Curtis

ANGER'S POISON
JULY 14

I grew up an angry child. The older I became, the more resentful I was with everyone. I trusted no one. Absorbing the hate of those around me, I became a hateful, self-destructive victim. Without tools to cope with frustration and anger, I descended into hopelessness. Addictions suppressed my anger, as it festered and grew stronger. I didn't want to feel; I wanted to escape everyone including me.

Anger was _A Nasty Getting Even Response_, and I had it down to perfection. After years of hatred, eating anger's poison and hoping others would die, anger told me, "I'll show you, I'll kill me!" Recovery came not one minute too soon.

For as long as we blame everyone else do we stay a prisoner to our misery, convinced that anger is the only way we can get attention or sympathy. We stay the victim with self-imposed _rights_ to remain that way. Working with professionals and loving sponsors helps us to accept responsibility for the harms we've done to others, as we begin to let go of selfish, self-centered anger that hurt no one as much as it hurt us. As others walked away, we were the ones who hung on to the power and excitement of anger's poison.

When we ask, "How important is anger?" we remind ourselves that our hard-fought serenity and peace are non-negotiable, without exception. Anger must go. We promptly admit when we are in the wrong and make amends to correct the situation. After all, this is _our_ program, no one else's.

With practice, we learn to pause when agitated or doubtful and remember that _This Too, Shall Pass._ These actions, together with constant contact with our Higher Power help to ensure the distance necessary to dissipate our anger, and the poisonous damage it causes us and others.

TODAY'S MEDITATION
The degree to which I place my serenity and sobriety first determines how often my character defect of anger takes a back seat. Thank you, God, for showing me how to _Let Go and Let God._

"You will not be punished for your anger, you will be punished by your anger."
— Buddha

COMMUNICATION
JULY 15

Many of us believe we have to explain ourselves to be understood, but those explanations can be volatile and defensive. Some of us have a history of pointing a finger at others to avoid having to see painful truths about ourselves.

Recovery teaches us to speak with kindness, to be brief, and to be gone. It means we take an honest look at what we are about to say and why we are saying it. We speak our truth as we know it, with directness.

Sometimes that means not speaking at all–excusing ourselves rather than taking part. When we do speak, we have the responsibility to do so with respect and with concern for how we want to be heard.

Talking around an issue doesn't work. Being subversive, passive-aggressive, or imposing sneekish, manipulative agendas doesn't work either. What does work? Saying what we mean with directness, honesty, love and kindness, and saying it clearly. Helpful communication is not aggressive; it is assertive. It stands up for itself, but it never bullies.

When communication becomes difficult we've learned in recovery, "… to pause when agitated or doubtful…." as mentioned on page 87 of the Big Book of *Alcoholics Anonymous*. Why is this important? The pause helps us to communicate with respect and clarity, instead of rushing in without thought, trying to control the conversation.

When we do not understand, we ask questions until we do. This may feel uncomfortable at first, but the results of being heard and the respect we show when we listen to each other's words is comfortable and reassuring. Helpful communication is the beginning of mutual appreciation and understanding.

TODAY'S MEDITATION

Dear God, when I want to be accusatory, please put your arm over my shoulder and your hand over my mouth.

"You have everything you need for complete peace and total happiness right now."
— *Wayne Dyer*

BEING TRUE TO SELF
JULY 16

To Thine Own Self be True. Active in our addiction, we never understood what this Shakespeare quote meant. Some thought it referred to a personal selfishness, but we could not have been more mistaken. Being true to self can only be measured through knowing all of ourselves, appreciating both strengths and weaknesses. In recovery we come to terms with who we are as we nurture the gift of self-love.

We never stop working The Steps. As we move through the shadow of ignorance, we become students of new life principles designed to sustain and strengthen our core character; that self we must be true to.

Armed with new knowledge and a Higher Power who walks before us, we observe our own unfolding and come to rely upon our intuition and judgment. We accept with honesty new revelations about ourselves and trust these and our decisions based in faith. Reliance upon our spirituality brings confidence that we are no longer alone.

Walking in our truth has no regard for how other people perceive us. Some will disagree with our position; that is *their* choice. They may need to leave a relationship with us, they may feel threatened, or take our decisions personally. We are worthy of differentiating between what is open to compromise and what is non-negotiable.

What truths have we become willing to stand up for? In sobriety, we learn to stand firm for those things that are non-negotiable. We are not responsible to others who may not agree. We recognize that these are their issues, their opinions, not ours.

We deserve to write our own version of Shakespeare's, *to thine own self be true* as we nourish our deepest strengths and come to terms with our weaknesses.

TODAY'S MEDITATION
Clean and sober, we are learning to face everything with grace and integrity, regardless of what life brings to us. We are learning to be true to ourselves.

"I prefer to be true to myself, even at the hazard of incurring the ridicule of others, rather than to be false, and to incur my own abhorrence." — Frederick Douglass

BREAKING THE ILLUSION OF CONTROL
JULY 17

Control is an illusion, and for many, our personal addiction. Our belief that somehow, we have information, power, or influence to control an outcome is akin to playing God. Others call this egotism, an over-exaggeration of one's abilities. We call it our disease.

Whether we think we control the stock market, children, or another's response to plans for tomorrow, the results are disheartening. Somehow, we felt sure we held the answers for our children, our beloved, and extended families. Since we don't know what is best for us, how can we possibly know what is best, or right for anyone else? Some of us have heard it said, "If you want to make God laugh, tell Him your plans."

Surrender acceptance are the antidotes to control. One measure we take to break an illusion of control is that we stop trying to control others. It's never worked before, so why should it work now?

One gift of recovery is the ability to surrender control and begin to live in the moment. We turn our desires over to a Higher Power. Control begins and ends when we accept that of ourselves, we are powerless. How our life unfolds must be our only focus as we do what is in front of us to do. We waste precious energy on the pretense of knowing what is right for others as it brings us no closer to the harmony and peace we seek, regardless of preparation.

When we live in acceptance of what is, we have no expectations or need to control anything. We trust the result of our moments is the next right thing for the highest good, or it would not be happening at all.

TODAY'S MEDITATION
Each time I forget and insist I have the answers for you, I'm reminded I do not. Were this true, the outcome would also be mine. Then, surely, I would be God!

"Many of us rely on our own illusion of control. But when God makes it known to you that you're not the one steering the ship, be thankful. He has removed the illusion, and forced you to rely only on Him." — Yasmin Mogahed

FEEL THE FEELINGS OF OUR PAST
JULY 18

Often, we find our way into the rooms of recovery sick and frozen on an emotional, spiritual, and physical level. As if mesmerized, we were held captive by fears we tried to hide from, as though to feel would give them the power to come alive in our heads. Drugs, alcohol, or other addictions were our escape from a life of painful memories, but there was no escape.

If we are to find sustained peace, we must allow ourselves to feel uncomfortable. We must push fear aside and experience the discomfort of past feelings to let them go. Stuffing them deeper keeps us sick and addicted. Sponsors tell us no one has ever died from the effects of feeling their emotions.

We begin to trust this process of feeling as tears of uncovering and discovering come from a deep place called courage. With repetition, we are stronger emotionally and gain a confidence that tells us, feelings aren't facts, and our past is not now. A dawning awareness makes clear we are not the same person we were then.

We observe the spiritual shift of our newfound resilience as we let work The Steps. With eyes closed, we breathe in tenacity and feel *all* our feelings. A determined awareness and acceptance let us discard them repeatedly. Soon, the power they once had, and the resentment and hurt they once produced, dissipates.

This Too, Shall Pass, becomes a reassuring truth, as fears once etched in our souls change to gentle waves of acceptance. Sometimes we recite this in the Fifth Step with a sponsor, a trusted servant, or with our Higher Power. We can use this ritual anytime. Some write their fears on paper and watch them dissolve, burning the paper as we let them go.

Our memories no longer control us. With excitement, we reach for the gifts of self-forgiveness and confidence. Although not forgotten, we see our past through clear eyes now, and feel a gentleness of self for just how far we've come. This spiritual path we walk, led by our Higher Power's compassionate grace, becomes lighter, more confident and we are grateful.

At last, we can live in relative peace. No longer are we afraid to feel our feelings because we've faced and shattered their power over us. In dealing with terrors of the past, we cannot walk around them, only through.

TODAY'S MEDITATION
Thank you, my God, for this incomparable gift of peace and freedom to feel and face all my feelings without exaggeration.

"...Try to raise up the sunken feelings of this enormous past; your personality will grow stronger, your solitude will expand and become a place where you can live in the twilight, where the noise of other people passes by, far in the distance..."
— *Rainer Maria Rilke*

CONSCIOUS CONTACT
JULY 19

To be *conscious* is to be in a state of awareness. *Contact* is the act of getting in touch.

In his book, *"Getting in the Gap,"* Dr. Wayne Dyer explains that as we meditate, we return to a silence where everything is created. "This awareness," he says, "puts us in that space where we return to our Higher Power."

Knowledge of the power from which all of us come is the result of having made this conscious contact with our Higher Power.

In recovery, the ability to contact our Higher Power is a spiritual experience where thoughts and rituals pass through us. Meditation and prayer to a God of our understanding begins, for many, a daily connection of hope that transcends our human egos.

Conscious contact is the awareness that elevates our otherwise incomplete and often misguided thinking, assuring, through acceptance, that we are right where we're supposed to be. We are on time. It reminds us of our humanness, fraught with imperfections and failures, yet connected through a spiritual portal back to our Higher Power.

Conscious contact reminds us of our rightful place, our rightful voice, and our never-ending need to ask for clarity, spiritual guidance, and the uplifting peace that comes to us in the silence of awareness.

TODAY'S MEDITATION

Today I embrace the silence in between the notes of life's symphony. Conscious contact raises my vision and humility and lets me see above my ego, as I give thanks for the gifts of this embrace.

"The most effective intention is a desire for a conscious contact with your soul, a deeper connection to your Self. This is the most powerful purpose to intend every time you meditate, pray, or do any spiritual practice." — Derek Rydall

CONTROLLING BEHAVIORS
JULY 20

I worked hard doing for my family what they should have been doing for themselves. I became the Queen of Questions. Terrified of surprises and the unknown, I thought that having answers to everything was what made me a good wife and mother.

I made it my business to know every movement, intention and proposed plan. The problem was, it wasn't appreciated. My husband and daughter became experts in hiding information from me and shut down emotionally when we were together. I became hurt and resentful at their need to keep me at arm's-length. Obsessive and jealous, fear said I should exert *more* control. Fear was the forceful tool of my control and it worked; but the price was a forced separation in my home, from those I loved. It never made a situation better. We were trapped with nowhere to go, and no way to grow.

Recovery proves we are no one's keeper but our own. As we let go of control and return the focus of our lives back to ourselves, we learn to let people be who they are. They deserve to experience their failures and successes without critique or criticism.

Practicing to *Let Go and Let God*, helps us to set down the rock of self-righteous control for a gentler, more humble position. Understanding that control is an old, displaced belief, we turn our family over to the care of our Higher Power.

TODAY'S MEDITATION
All I want today, God, is to be useful and kind to someone else. I see now, I never had any control to begin with, but you do. What a miracle.

"Codependents are reactionaries. They overreact. They under-react. But rarely do they act. They react to the problems, pains, lives, and behaviors of others. ."
— *Melody Beattie*

PRACTICING STEP TEN
JULY 21

Part of my daily ritual is to invoke the grace of Step Ten. I am reminded to quit fighting everyone and everything as I have become accountable to my Higher Power. This Step tells me that moment-to-moment, I no longer run the show. Before I take any action, I must ask, "How Important Is It?" When I forget, I know my grandiose, ego-centric thinking is hard at work seeking that weak spot to change my thinking to drinking thinking; the thing that brought me into the rooms of recovery.

A sincere Tenth Step begs for a continuous watch for selfish, dishonest, resentful, or fearful behaviors. As the first of three maintenance steps, we know that to rest on our laurels is an invitation for disaster. We are given a daily reprieve based upon the maintenance of our spiritual condition, not credit for the work we have done in the past. This means every day we stay clean and sober, we do so because we've come to our Higher Power and asked, "How can we can be of service to others?" We examine motives and actions and ask, "What amends can we make today?"

Our imperfections require us to be alert when offenses occur so we can make amends right where we are. Sometimes, we make amends even if the wrong is nothing more than a misperception on our part. When in doubt we make amends to stay free of remorse and guilt.

Step Ten is our daily reminder that love and tolerance is our code. This humility reminds us of the importance of honesty. We keep our attention on what needs to be restructured within us and stay in our moment. As we acknowledge that our Higher Power has the final word in all of our affairs, we have peace we are right with our world and the people in it.

TODAY'S MEDITATION
Self-examination allows me to remain true to myself just for today as I keep my side of the street clean

"It's one of the greatest gifts you can give yourself, to forgive. Forgive everybody."
— *Maya Angelou*

EARNED SELF-RESPECT
JULY 22

I remember reading a self-help book thinking, *how does someone gain self-respect?* My sponsor reminded me that if I look within, every answer I need is there waiting for me.

Looking within, this is what I found.

We know how easy it is for us to cater to others and give them the respect we hope will come back to us. To earn respect from others, we must first know it is already within us to give away.

Self-forgiveness replaces the negative energy that consumes our psyches. With practice, our pain is transformed by the softening caress of self-respect. Maintaining a gentleness with ourselves when coming to terms with past failures enables us to discover we are worthy of forgiving ourselves, and we move on.

When we extend the same forgiveness to ourselves that we extend to others, we become right-sized with our fellow men, no better and no worse than anyone else.

Our thinking changes one thought at a time. Speaking in a positive, uplifting and loving tone, we rule out negativity. This new gentleness with ourselves gives us permission to accept loving care from those around us. Our new-found self-respect says we deserve it.

With this attitude change, we notice that people in our new and sober world smile more, are approachable, and open their arms for a hug. Sponsors laugh and say, "Others haven't changed, *you've* changed!" The power of a love of self with self-acceptance, invites others to enter our personal space and meet us where we live.

With our new earned self-respect, our insides match our outsides. What others see, is our authentic selves.

"Stand up for who you are. Respect your Self and ignite the divine sparks in you. Access your powers. Choose your rights and work together with others to bring blessings into the lives." — Amit Ray

FINDING EMOTIONAL MATURITY
JULY 23

Early in recovery, sponsors pointed out my lack of emotional immaturity. While not a newsflash, hearing it said out loud felt like a punch to the gut. Grudgingly, I accepted their verdict. I knew I had zero coping skills and always blamed my shortcomings on everyone but me. I admitted my inability to accept criticism, along with my overindulgence in self-pity, and resistance to change. I owned the fact I could not face tough situations without acting out.

A plan of action was put into place with my sponsor. Instead of crying and pouting I was instructed to call my sponsor, take direction, and stay in the solution. The Steps were essential for me. They changed my perceptions and nurtured an acceptance of what is. I no longer felt entitled to a life that matched expectations.

With practice in faith and gratitude, my relationship between my Higher Power and myself became forgiving, even gentle. I opened the door to emotional maturity.

One of the greatest transformations experienced in recovery is the dawning of integrity. We bring what we say and do into alignment with what we need and watch as vibrant action replaces good intentions. Discipline over convenience, and love-of-self over self-neglect become our highest good.

Emotional maturity means a sacrifice of short-term gratification. It means facing a conflict head-on without evading or minimizing, while working with our Higher Power for the desired outcome. What we see in the mirror is a calm and satisfying integrity.

TODAY'S MEDITATION

Profound gratitude is the roadmap we carry in our quest for emotional maturity. It guides us to be the very best person we can be.

"One of the characteristics of emotional maturity is when you can take personal responsibility for your own sin." — Joel Nyarangi Akoya

LETTING GO OF EXPECTATIONS
JULY 24

In the role I played as wife and mother, a pattern emerged as I let go of my denial. My exaggerated expectations were the cause of most of my frustrations.

I expected others to do what I wanted, when I wanted it. I always thought it was the other guy's job: "Can't you see this needs to be done?" or, "Why do I have to ask you to ___?"

For me, love and affection were conditional, based on expectations being met. If you got it right, then everyone was happy, but only for a little while. Days were consumed with my doling out orders and outlining expectations of what needed to follow, as everyone around me grew more resentful and argumentative.

This relationship problem sounds familiar to many in recovery. It is self-inflicted. It is ours alone. We expect perfection in others but ignore that same measure in our own lives because it was too much work for us.

One exercise in letting go of expectations is to make a list of expectations in one column. The second column header asks *How Important Is It?* Each expectation is assigned a number. Number one is least important and number ten is most important. A third column header asks, "Is this *my* business my responsibility?" Answers are either yes, or no. After each line and response is checked, we end the exercise with a prayer: "Dear Higher Power, please take this from me."

It doesn't take long to see that the quicker we focused on what our business was as opposed to our expectations of others, the happier and more content we remain.

TODAY'S MEDITATION
Dear God. I know the less expectations I have of me, the less I have of others. I know now those expectations were a setup for failure.

"In order to be free, we must learn how to let go. Release the hurt. Release the fear. Refuse to entertain your old pain. The energy it takes to hang onto the past is holding you back from a new life. What is it you would let go of today?"
— Mary Manin Morrissey

FEAR OF ENDING RELATIONSHIPS
JULY 25

Sometimes we continue in a relationship we should have ended a long time ago. Many of us never had the courage, afraid that hurting someone else's feelings would be worse than staying in an unhappy relationship. If we were in active addiction, a fear of the unknown was often enough to keep us stuck.

Ending relationships, whether business or personal, sometimes speaks to our personal lack of tolerance or lack of self-respect. Separation is necessary when we realize there is some difference of opinion that can't be reconciled, or the damage from a personal affront that shook our psyche can no longer be ignored.

No matter how justified, ending a relationship can be painful. Still, we must open ourselves to the signal given to us by our intuition that says ending this unhappy relationship is in our best interest. We hear our inner voice say, "It's time," and we must listen. The voice of our intuition speaks in concert with our Higher Power. Sometimes the universe has other plans, other options, or other people it needs us to engage with. But always, without exception, more is revealed.

The end of a relationship is just one final moment. It is the jolt of awareness that has been with us for a long time, but now we are ready. This moment of moving forward can be met with great angst, anger, or painful expressions of regret; or it can be met with acceptance.

We understand this separation is occurring in the manner and the time it is supposed to happen, or it wouldn't be happening at all. We use our intuition for our highest good, invoking freedom and the courage to face the unknown we're about to embrace.

We are stronger and more resilient than we know. Maturity helps us to face our journey and avoid losing ourselves in the quagmire of regrets and second guesses. Our Higher Power, with arms outstretched, stands ready to soothe our journey We are not alone. Competent, loving and kind, we can do this, and we will.

"The end of a relationship is not always a failure. Sometimes all the love in the world is not enough to save something. In these cases, it is not a matter of fault from either person. Some things cannot be, it's as simple as that."
— Ashly Lorenzana

FINANCIAL INSECURITY
JULY 26

There was a time in my marriage when I could never put two dollars together. I remember my husband reminding me about gasoline I used to take our three-year-old for socialization at a McDonald's playground. Financial insecurity played a significant role in our lives.

There is a pivotal scene in *Gone with the Wind* that changed me. Scarlett O'Hara, against the backdrop of a dramatic sky, pushed to her feet in a desolate potato patch. Hand clenched, she declared, "As God is my witness, I will never be hungry again!" As I clenched my fist reaching for the heavens, I promised myself, "...I will never be *broke* again!"

Not having enough money can be devastating; it makes us feel powerless. But we are not completely powerless. When it comes to money, no matter how much or how little we have, we *do* make choices. We have to be careful that we aren't frivolous with money and get ourselves into greater debt. We must not forget the financial distance we went in our addictions to get what we thought we couldn't live without.

Those who work a 12-step program make financial restitution part of cleaning up the wreckage of their past. It often looks and feels worse than it is.

But sometimes, it is worse than it looks, making us hopeless, ready to give up. Then we remember we agreed to go to any lengths for our hard-fought sobriety, and financial debts are part of the paying-back we do as we claim our hard-earned freedom.

There is nothing that cannot be redeemed when we clean up, sober up, and suit up for life once more. Financial insecurity is difficult to face and is solved with the same determined dedication we gave our alcoholism.

Sometimes we need professional guidance to make our financial situation whole. Adjusting to a strict budget may be necessary, building new habits, accepting deferred gratification. We can do this. We trust we will be given what we need just for today.

"We tend to focus on assets and forget about debts. Financial security requires facing up to the big picture: assets minus debts." — Suze Orman

SELF-FORGIVENESS
JULY 27

To forgive ourselves is the most intimate, loving gift of compassion. It enables us to accept both parts of us, the part we treasure and the part we dislike. As we forgive ourselves, we experience a spiritual healing of our heart, a letting go of anger and the resentments we held for too long. In his book, "Releasing You from the Past," Steve Richards says "When you initially forgive, it is like letting go of a hot iron. There is initial pain and the scars will show, but you can start living again."

As we give ourselves permission to walk this journey of self-discovery and self-love, we find forgiveness doesn't undo damage done, nor does it minimize our pain, because self-forgiveness is not a feeling. Self-forgiveness is the choice we make to pardon ourselves for real or perceived wrongdoings. This decision, born from pain, sets us free from our obsessive thoughts of retribution, self-pity or the omnipotence of martyrdom.

Years of stinking-thinking blocked self-forgiveness, as we insisted we didn't deserve to be forgiven. These old, mistaken beliefs infiltrated the core of who we were and in response, we felt shame. This destructive thinking has the power to leave us emotionally vacant, replete with paranoia, and not good enough when it comes to the love-of-ourselves and those around us.

The degree to which we judge others, is the degree to which we will be judged. Self-forgiveness is a cry for freedom from the captivity of our own disapproval.

With help from our Higher Power, self-forgiveness penetrates the dark walls of the soul and provides a gentle healing of a rejuvenating light of hope. We become complete as the repressed pain of self-persecution is dispersed by recognition of our basic goodness.

TODAY'S MEDITATION

Dear God, your example gives me courage to change my thinking. As I release others in forgiveness, I also release myself, and in letting both go, I become free.

"Without forgiveness and love, you will live with resentment, bitterness, malice and strife which result in more pain. You can never love without forgiving. Forgiveness deepens your ability to love and frees you from pain." — Kemi Sogunle

HONESTY IN THE WORKPLACE
JULY 28

"Wait a minute," we say. Many of us cannot imagine dishonesty in the workplace. We are hard-working examples of collaboration and teamwork. We show up on time for work and meetings. We are reliable, trustworthy, and thorough.

A closer look, however, often reveals a pattern of displaced honesty. Prior to recovery, we would never have admitted to being guilty of deceptive acts. In a pose called dedication, one small but intentional act propagates into a new norm. Some of us bring work home along with paper, pencils, pens and blank CDs. Then there is the work we never quite got around to as we made a big show of putting it in a brief case, then keeping the materials we so conveniently "borrowed."

Some of us pad actual time worked, come in late in the name of overtime, as others call in sick. We rationalize acts of theft or omission because we were doing what we always did, which was committing to a less-than-stellar performance with false claims. We did what we could to look overworked and dedicated. These behaviors are another manifestation of our sick addictive behaviors.

In recovery dishonesty, no matter how small, represents a risky step toward self-sabotage. Fortunately, the grace of the Twelve-Steps and our hard-won sobriety activates our moral barometer. Sobriety says we can lose everything over a few filched pencils, hours not worked, a sick day spent with our addiction, and many do. It's called self-justification. From here it's a short hop to bigger and bolder deceptions.

Short-changing anyone, for any reason, hurts us. Honesty in the workplace means we must not allow old self-righteous thinking and ego to run, unrestrained, as the excitement of getting away with something becomes a self-perpetuating thrill that expects more of the same. We have come too far, we know too much to jeopardize our hard-fought integrity and sobriety.

TODAY'S MEDITATION

I'm grateful, God, for a consciousness that includes you to discern intentions, motives, and actions. I cannot justify a poor decision any longer, nor turn in a less-than performance in all spheres of my life.

"If you're in a workplace you don't like right now, be encouraged because God will use it for your good. Think about it this way: He wants you to be a light in the darkness - and He's putting His confidence in you!" — Joyce Meyer

I AM ENOUGH
JULY 29

It is a beautiful Saturday morning. I slept in a bit, got up and went to the store. Putting the food and dishes away, I hear a whisper, *Look at you. It's almost noon and what have you accomplished? Nothing!*

Who is that I hear in my head? Is that *my* voice? No, the voice belongs to my mother, chiding me to do more, be more, or to somehow be different than I am.

Fortunately, in recovery, I've learned there are few things that require a reaction. Negative messages top that list. Growth along spiritual lines tells me to ignore those messages unless they have a ring of truth. If they are untrue, the choice is mine to react, or to do nothing at all.

We are all enough today, regardless of how much we choose to do, or not do. With agreement from our Higher Power, we no longer have to act out of shame, guilt or any other mistaken belief. Instead, we embrace comfort in our confidence and lean on our Higher Power when in doubt. We are, right this moment, doing exactly what we're supposed to be doing. This means on any given day if all we do is remain clean and sober and stay close to our Higher Power then—we are enough.

Remember, nothing ever looks like we think it should look; and no one measures up to impossible expectations.

We are not less–than. There is no standard we must meet to be worthy. Our Higher Power accepts us right where and exactly as we are!

TODAY'S MEDITATION
God, your love tells me I am enough. I know, because you allow my journey to unfold exactly the way it is, or it would be different.

"The fear of not getting the reward becomes the fear of rejection. The fear of not being good enough... is what makes us try to change, what makes us create an image." — Miguel Angel Ruiz

GOD'S WILL FOR ME
JULY 30

Some of us have never heard discussions about what God's Will is for us and so we wander alone and blind.

Others among us, walking our path in recovery, come to believe a power greater than ourselves can restore us to sanity. As we accept new beliefs and move away from black or white thinking, hope opens a door to a new knowing, a conviction grounded in the spiritual realm. Recovery looks to willingness to suspend our thinking and asks that we trust as we keep doing the next right thing, somehow the *next* right thing will follow. And it does.

This process of hope is the expression of God's Will for us. We believe our Higher Power wants us to be gentle and kind to ourselves and to others. Recovery literature assures us our Higher Power wants us to be happy, joyous, and free. How can we test this? Our actions prior to recovery proved that our way of thinking and doing, didn't work. We were hopeless, without a connection to anything other than our misery. No matter what we did, we couldn't stop nor could we change our addictive behaviors. Misery and defeat were the only things we had faith in.

As we rest, instead, on our relationship with our Higher Power, miracles become our reality. Recovery offers an easier, softer way of life, if we do the work.

Our literature tells us we can no longer sit and do nothing waiting for life to come to us. We must take control of what needs to be done. We help others, trust God and keep our side of the street clean. As the next right thing reveals itself, we come to rely upon this as God's Will for us. We do the work and let go of the results of our efforts as outcomes belong to our Higher Power.

TODAY'S MEDITATION
We're reminded that while we may not always get what we want, we always get what we need.

"Decisions become easier when your will to please God outweighs your will to please the world." — Bella Montreal

THE GIFT OF GIVING IT AWAY

What is it we give away when we are giving of ourselves? Every time we speak to someone regardless of whether we're gentle or harsh with our words, we're conveying something about ourselves.

I used to think giving it away meant material things. What else could someone new in recovery have that others would need or want? Could there be anything at all? We came into recovery because we were broke, many of us on a financial, spiritual level without hope. We were absent emotionally and our physical self, in dire need of help. Surely, we had nothing at all to give others; we thought.

Miracles happen when we give of ourselves to others in the rooms. We give away our experience. Even when we have no strength or hope left, when we walk into the rooms, we have our experience that brought us to our knees. It is *this* experience that qualifies us as being competent to help others. We allow others to see ourselves through our mutual experiences.

We cannot *give away* what we don't have. This proves that whenever we share about ourselves, we become real in a way that we were not, before we spoke. We look to others for experience, strength and hope so that someday soon, we may have what they have. We take from others what we need, and like everyone else, leave the rest.

When we speak from our heart, we are being authentic. How does that work? We are authentic when we don't edit, judge or manipulate a conversation for what we think others want to hear. Some spot this authenticity, but almost always, many others *feel* it. How many times have we spoke and then said, "I don't even remember what I said!" When this happens, we are sharing from our hearts as together, our highest-self and Higher Power work through us. You don't think those words came from you alone, do you?

Sometimes what we seek is the ability to listen, to be non-judgmental or to find patience. When this happens, we show others what they want to aspire to. Sometimes what others see in us, is our ability to give of ourselves by being there. By becoming a part-of.

Most of all, when we give a piece of ourselves away through any myriad of examples and opportunities, the act of giving is the essence of a faith we cannot see. We are learning to become *other centered* instead of self-centered.

242 • HARRIET HUNTER

Giving it away doesn't have to cost money, be flamboyant, grandiose or loud. It can be a silent and random act of kindness that no one takes credit for. It can be as simple as a telephone call, a pat on the back or an offer to accept a harm committed by someone else. We give away our *humanness* to be an equal-among-equals. As we keep coming back, we find we are becoming whole.

TODAY'S MEDITATION

Help me remember, God, that when I sit in my rooms of recovery, I may be the only big book someone will see or hear.

"The meaning of life is to find your gift. The purpose of life is to give it away."
— *Pablo Picasso*

LEARNING TO SAY NO

How many times did we want to say no, intended to say no, but instead heard a voice—our voice–issue a resounding, "Yes?" Where did that come from?

Many of us find it easier to go along in order to make others happy and avoid conflict. Often, we minimize and dismiss our truth saying, "It's okay," or, "It's not *that* big a deal." We do this day-in and day-out. It becomes automatic until one day, it feels demeaning.

Every time we go along when we want to say no, we relinquish a piece of our essential selves. What others see is people-pleasing. People-pleasing says someone else's happiness is more important than ours. Without being aware, we swallow our truth in the name of kindness while our subconscious keeps score. Little-by-little we become resentful; we feel taken advantage of, even victimized. Since we can't see our way out, we blame others for our unhappiness, as we disappear into ourselves.

When we say no, we change the balance between pleasing others and a healthy sense of self-worth. One way we do this is to accept that what is important to us should never be negotiated away unless we agree. This new thinking takes practice and an examination of our priorities. Some of us have been saying "yes" for so long we have forgotten what those priorities are!

We deserve to say no when no is our first thought or intuition that leads us in that direction. As we say no without rancor, we are empowered, strong enough to accept assertiveness and the ability to say no as our personal right.

We may need to practice saying no in front of the mirror. How does our voice sound as we say no? What does our non-verbal appearance transmit? Anger? Gentleness? How do we want others to see and to hear us? Do we say no with kindness, but also with conviction? As confidence in our ability to say no grows, we discover a softer, more gracious voice that carries the force of truth while conveying that truth with kindness. Practice makes speaking our truth as comfortable as breathing, without feelings of shame or guilt. When life-changing decisions present themselves, we are ready now, to say no with grace and courage, without regard for interpretation. We are emotionally grounded, what we say is our truth, and we own it. We have grown.

TODAY'S MEDITATION
Dear God, when I'm able to be true to me, you allow my decisions to come to pass without recrimination or rejection because others feel my certainty.

"Happiness is when what you think, what you say,
and what you do are in harmony." — *Mahatma Gandhi*

LIVING IN ABUNDANCE
AUGUST 2

A friend shared her gratitude to be living in abundance. Although facing the severe financial consequences of her past addictive behaviors, she told of how right here, right now, she had everything she needed. Her heart was content.

It takes a determined vision, consistent faith, and action at work to rise above the valleys of despair that hold us to our "have-nots." Many of us in recovery come from the depths of a personal hell and live with the aftermath of disasters we created ourselves. This is where we demonstrate readiness to face everything and walk a warrior's path with dignity and gratitude.

The wise choices we make in recovery assure an abundance of growth and uplifting faith. With a few words that affirm we are now living in abundance, we change our perspective and find strength. Our attitudes change, and our thoughts give abundance to the space it needs to engulf us.

Abundance manifests in the vision we've created within, expanding like magic each time we share gratitude with others and give abundance away.

TODAY'S MEDITATION

Dear God, I am open and grateful to powerful life-changing messages from those around me. They allow me to see that I too, am living in abundance just for today.

"Your most precious, valued possessions and your greatest powers are invisible and intangible. No one can take them. You, and you alone, can give them. You will receive abundance for your giving." — W. Clement Stone

THE MAGIC OF MESSAGES
AUGUST 3

Trust God, Clean House, Help Others. Sounds simple enough, and it is, but only if we keep that message in mind each day.

Making prayer the priority of our day lives in the phrase, *Trust God*. It is in prayer to a power greater than ourselves that we find our strength. As we internalize guidance from a Higher Power, we are reminded we're living where our feet are; safe in the moment.

As we move through our 24-hours efficiently and with purpose, we practice the ritual expressed in the phrase, *Clean House*. We make lists in order of importance and do what is in front of us to do. When in doubt we return to prayer, seeking guidance and discernment as we continue to clean up the wreckage of our past. Amends may be in order, and if so, we make them. We stay clear of other people's business.

Help Others is the life-sustaining link that unites us in our usefulness to others. We ensure our sobriety for another day by helping others and giving away what was so freely given to us. This spirit of unity is the anchor that keeps us in the solution, our recovery.

By trusting God, cleaning house, and helping others we live another day free from the bondage of self, and sober.

TODAY'S MEDITATION
Dear God, thank you for the community that is recovery. Just for today I can keep life simple as I *Trust God, Clean House, and Help Others.*

My favorite six words in recovery are: trust God, clean house, and help others
— Matthew Perry

MISUNDERSTOOD EXPECTATIONS
AUGUST 4

People who have expectations are often disappointed. Unmet expectations cause frustration and misunderstandings. Expectations are a set-up for dis-illusionment. They are ego-centric and harm relationships. The expectations most likely to hurt us the most are the ones we never voice.

Then there are those expectations we demand *others* fulfill, "When are you," "Why haven't you," or "You should know what I want by now!" These are a few of many expectations met with mouths open and eyebrows knit together in exasperation because they were the last to know.

Recovery teaches us that expectations are resentments waiting to happen. Manipulative, and hurtful, we *expect* others to know what we need, when, and how we need it. When our expectations don't materialize, we feel cheated, let down, betrayed. Over time, we develop resentments and as they accumulate, they are a short hop to full-blown anger.

The answer to unmet expectations is communication. When we *ask* while being clear and exact about what we need, we reduce fear. This approach encourages understanding and allows for having needs met without a verbal tug-of-war. No one can read someone else's mind, regardless of the closeness of the relationship or how long the relationship has been going on.

The closeness of a relationship brings no guarantee that unspoken wishes are understood without clear communication. Mutual respect requires we *ask* for what we need and leave the response up to the other person. When we do this, we can embrace ourselves lovingly for having shown courage to ask for what we need clearly, and for the respect we've shown in honoring the answer given. We do this instead of spewing grievances based on unspoken requests and expectations that went unmet.

TODAY'S MEDITATION

Just for today, God, I will practice saying a prayer for honesty and ask for what I need without manipulation or expectation. I will leave the results in your hands and respect the outcome.

"Expectation is the root of all heartache." — *William Shakespeare*

PERSONAL GROWTH
AUGUST 5

It is said that when the student is ready the teacher appears. But how many times over the course of our lives did we turn that teacher away or fail to see opportunity before us?

We don't hear what we need to hear, until we hear it, until we become aware. With awareness we move thoughts from head to heart, having what some call, a spiritual experience. We sigh in recognition as the information reaches our soul and becomes a part of us. Together, the heart and mind are tuned to a higher form of knowing. *Now* we get it!

No longer are we afraid of the unknown. Set free by what has been revealed, we become fascinated observers of our own unfolding. One revelation appears, then another, and another, and we are transformed. With this growth comes the assurance that so much more will be revealed. We open our hearts and welcome these inspiring shifts in our awakening.

We know now that we've always been deserving of goodness and light. It has always been there, we only had to turn toward it. The difference today is we expect it; we honor and embrace all that we are. We are enlightened and willing students, worthy of receiving what we need, when we need it. Our teacher has appeared.

TODAY'S MEDITATION
With a child's excitement, God, I embrace all that I am. I honor energy gifted by you and look to your perfect timing in the journey of my evolution.

"Often, it's not about becoming a new person, but becoming the person you were meant to be, and already are, but don't know how to be." — Heath L. Buckmaster

RELATIONSHIPS WITH OTHERS AT WORK

AUGUST 6

The work environment is not designed to promote emotional intimacy. Personal and professional boundaries often prevent casual talk. Customers and a fast pace require constant attention and adaptation to an ever-changing climate of rules and procedures.

What if the job requires close collaboration with others as part of a team? Is the company one that encourages familiarity or one that demands associates remain detached, strictly business? What does it mean to be a part of something far more rigid than family or friendship, part of an enterprise that is designed to generate profit, not relationships? In recovery, we have to examine the self we present in the work environment and be willing to adapt accordingly. As part of our journey we must reevaluate our expectations and motives in the relationships we build at work, both individually, and as a team member.

Does our self-care match what we want others to see in the workplace? If we ask questions and dress for success, chances are our demeanor, voice, and the words we choose will follow. How do we want to be heard in this competitive, business environment? If we are not sure, we practice in front of the mirror. We ask ourselves how we want to be seen by others, as we develop a style that matches our sobriety and suits our place in the work force.

Relationships in the workplace can be a delicate dance. With an awareness of boundaries and expectations specific to our work place, and respect for ourselves and our coworkers, we fulfill important roles. Roles that allow all of us to succeed with professionalism and dignity while serving the higher good of our own sobriety.

TODAY'S MEDITATION
Today I remember why I am here. I will practice staying focused on the quality and reliability of my output and the necessity of a teamwork mindset with others.

"When we work together, we achieve more. Character is not a concept that is simply spoken about, but actually manifests itself through our actions."
— *Jose A. Aviles*

Step Eleven
August 7

*"Sought through prayer and meditation to improve our
conscious contact with God as we understood Him, praying only
for knowledge of His will for us and the power to carry that out."*

For those who persist in prayer, The Steps afford wisdom that could never be
achieved without conscious contact with something greater than ourselves.
By the time we reach this step, most of us enjoy a personal relationship with
our Higher Power. We've reestablished a desire to know and to do His Will.
Prayer is how we speak to our Higher Power, while in meditation we listen
for the answer we seek.

As we work through self-examination with our Higher Power, we become
aware of new perspectives, suggestions, and a grace that replaces the darkness and despair we came from when we walked into recovery. Step Eleven is
the departure from drinking and thinking behaviors. Here we exchange fear
for faith and bring faith to life through action. We use prayer and meditation
often throughout our day to bring emotional balance in all things.

Pages 86, 87 and 88 of the Big Book of *Alcoholics Anonymous* give us a blue-
print of actions to take beginning at night and again upon awakening. We
learn how to live with focus and intention within our 24-hours. This is the
backbone of a conscious contact.

Conscious contact with our Higher Power strengthens our reliance on intuitive messages of faith that bridge the gap to knowing the next right course
to take. Failure to exercise our faith with the same ease we use our muscles
invites a fall from grace, plunging us back into the abyss of our delusions,
closer to the insanity of our addictions.

We work this step, strengthening our spiritual connection, one day at a time.
Practice moves us toward the illumination of a Higher Power, one who has

never left us; remembering we were the ones who turned our backs on that light. We have come to trust and rely upon the light of the spirit.

TODAY'S MEDITATION

Dear God, I drop to my knees in a humble prayer of thanks. As you prepare me to receive, I know more will be revealed.

"...Prayer does not demand that we interrupt our work, but that we continue working as if it were a prayer. It is not necessary to always be in meditation, nor to consciously experience the sensation that we are talking to God, no matter how nice that would be. What matters is being with Him, living in Him, in His will." — Mother Theresa

A MASK OF DISGUISE
AUGUST 8

Growing up, I felt safe wearing imaginary masks that hid me from my world. I couldn't bear for you to see how little I thought of me, and how much self-loathing I suppressed.

At work, I'd wear the interchangeable mask to present the face I thought each coworker needed to see. I hid my inferiority while engaging socially with others, although I much preferred to be left alone. Then there was the mask of perfection that hid my mistakes. These disguises kept others from knowing the real me.

And then I began working The Steps.

Those of us who have worked The Steps, are free from disguise; our masks are gone. We no longer hide behind anything or anyone. We are comfortable now with who we are. Embracing weaknesses and coming to terms with imperfections, we become less critical and judgmental of everyone else because we have found compassion within. We allow ourselves to be imperfect and extend that permission to others.

As our hearts open to forgive others, pieces of our life's puzzle fall into place. We see now, our insides match our outsides, and we continue to trust the process that is recovery.

TODAY'S MEDITATION
Dear God, so long as I continue to stay the course, my eyes will be opened and I will be set free, showing my true self to the world, not a mask of disguise.

"God changes his appearance every second. Blessed is the man who can recognize him in all his disguises." — Nikos Kazantzakis

In sacred rooms of recovery throughout the world, framed reminders of what works for the millions who have come before us grace the walls of 12-step rooms. Wherever we meet, our shared language of the heart is there, on display, boldly posted to help keep us on track.

The slogan *Easy Does It* reminds us we no longer need to take on the world.

We learn to *Take it Easy*, to be content with just a little recovery and a little humility each day we're clean and sober.

First Things First and *This too, shall pass* both provide reassurance that taken one at a time we will achieve our goals, and that, in time, everything changes.

The phrase *Easy Does It but Do It*, assures us that our journey is not about perfection, and that "doing it" is always a 24-hour commitment, nothing more.

These are just a few of the universal slogans of our program, loving reminders that in The Rooms of recovery, we are all on the same journey.

Wherever we are, our slogans are there to remind us we are home, safe in sobriety and on the right course.

TODAY'S MEDITATION

When I stumble in my journey, the A.A. slogans hang bright and bold, displayed on the walls of our rooms of recovery, there to help me, as they have helped others all around the world to stay the course.

"Be as enthusiastic about A.A. as you were about your drinking." — *Anonymous*

LEARNING TO LIVE IN THE MOMENT
AUGUST 10

I am learning to feel comfortable living in the moment. But this was not always the case. I would allow obsessive thinking to run wild, living in a world of what-if's. Incessant thinking about the future made me sick. Consumed over my tomorrows, I was over-controlling, over-bearing, and, as if in quicksand, too stuck to move. I terrified myself.

Instead of struggling in the web of what-if's, we can put ourselves in an imaginary hula-hoop. Everything inside the hula-hoop represents the power and manageability we have over what we think and do today. Everything outside the boundary of our hula-hoop belongs to our Higher Power.

To remind ourselves to stay in our 24-hours, some of us put a rubber band on our wrist. Each time obsessive thoughts reach outside the bounds of today, a quick snap brings us back to where our feet are, right here, in this moment.

Others make lists of what we need to do each day, all the while asking our Higher Power to help us keep our thinking focused and compact.

This is where we live and breathe.

With practice, we stay within the circle of now, and our lives become efficient and easily manageable. We are competent, pleased with ourselves for changing what we can, accepting that we are responsible, just for the rest of these 24-hours.

TODAY'S MEDITATION
Everything I am I owe to recovery, this village of like-minded people helping each other live sober, just for today.

"Each day means a new twenty-four hours. Each day means everything's possible again. You live in the moment, you die in the moment, you take it all one day at a time...You try to walk in the light. "— Anonymous

ASKING FOR WHAT WE NEED
AUGUST 11

As a child, my mother would say, "Little Girls should be seen but not heard." Living in our dysfunctional household was difficult for all of us. As the oldest of five, I was the loudest. I never learned to be gracious, deciding at a young age that, one way or the other, I would be heard!

In my marriage, while engaged in active alcoholism, I handed my power to my husband. He was chief manipulator, answering every question, it seemed, with, "no." This, coupled with money and control issues, became a perfect excuse for my shutting down, avoiding conversations, and feeling insignificant. I was living my mother's edict. I was seen, but not heard.

Some of us prefer to wait for the universe to provide for us. Many of us expect that others should know what we need.

To not ask, is to not receive. Not asking for what we need is to acquiesce to a mistaken belief that we are not good or deserving enough to receive what we want or need—that we should be seen but not heard!

When we take charge of our destiny, we deserve and expect to have answers to questions, and to ask with tact and kindness for what we need. When we trust our own voices and honor our authentic selves, asking for what we need becomes as easy and as important for us as it is for others.

These intentions position us with clarity and exactness as we act as if we deserve to be heard, because we do. Regardless of the answer, we accept the results will be the Will of our Higher Power. Our responsibility is to do the footwork, and that means being *heard* as well as *seen*.

TODAY'S MEDITATION

Dear God, please help me to say what I mean, mean what I say, and to say it with love and kindness.

"The truth is that we won't receive the support we need until we ask for it... And when we don't speak up about our needs, we're asking our loved ones to read our minds—and then we resent them when they fail our test...". — Jessica Ortner

FEAR OF THE UNKNOWN
AUGUST 12

I remember my divorced parents stealing two or three of us five kids in the middle of night. I was left behind, hiding in waiting, as if death would find me. I was petrified, away from the others having to play a game that wasn't funny. I grew up terrified of the unknown, my antenna always on high alert, sensing my surroundings for imminent threats from people, places, and things. Sleep was almost impossible; I was convinced someone was out to get me.

Alcohol worked well to calm the fear and panic that rose often and threatened to strangle me. It provided a false sense of security. Years of professional intervention along with recovery helped to quell my fears.

Today, I know feelings are not facts and that what I imagine does not influence reality.

Today I am no longer afraid.

I embrace the darkness and trust that while I cannot see, I know I am not alone. I am so grateful The Steps have changed my thoughts and actions.

TODAY'S MEDITATION

Today I am relieved to not know what is to come. God is in control, I am powerless, and I like it that way.

"To live for your dreams, you have to be fearless in life." — *Lailah Gifty Akita*

AWARENESS IN THE MOMENT
AUGUST 13

It may happen to you. That day when you wake, feeling restless, confused without knowing why. As you begin to refocus, you realize your feet are on the floor and you are thinking about your day. You're still breathing and, on some level grateful for that breath, but you seem to be having an odd experience, Not out-of-body, but not quite anchored to your world either. It feels as if you're floating somewhere in between, detached from everything, including the day ahead.

On mornings like this, experience shows me to focus on one fact—that we are held in the awareness of here and now. Closing our eyes, we see and feel what we are doing in that moment. We're aware our own weight as we sit on the edge of the bed. Upward we stretch while inhaling, allowing ourselves to reenter our own lives.

And then we push to our feet.

Although not euphoric or thrilled to start our day, we know that getting up and moving despite how we feel, will change the day for the better. As this day begins, we act as if we believe all is well as we put one foot in front of the other. Acting as-if, we move and breathe in comfort.

Today we are free to change our perspectives about everything. We are in control of our emotions, reactions, thoughts, and actions, living safely in this moment.

It feels reassuring to know we are better than we *think* we are, at least in these moments.

TODAY'S MEDITATION
I'm grateful that when I am able to see the goodness within myself in this one, unique, moment.

"Look at a tree, a flower, a plant. Let your awareness rest upon it. How still they are, how deeply rooted in Being. Allow nature to teach you stillness."
— *Eckhart Tolle*

Preparing Ourselves for Change

I vaguely remember as a child how I handled changes in my life which, for me, began with kindergarten. Overwhelmed with fear, I exhibited behaviors of abandonment. I hid in corners, screamed, cried, and wet my pants. This same behavior with variations continued into my 20's.

Recovery asks that we prepare ourselves for a change of huge proportions, the change from addiction to sobriety which we can only do one day at a time. We hear this statement and want to run, forgetting we have prepared for this day our entire lives through all kinds of changes. We met challenges of change in our work place, in family relationships, changing cars, priorities, and so much more.

Recovery is the biggest change of all. It feels like we're being asked to give up the self we know. What will be left of us? Will we resemble the hole in the donut? We kick and scream just thinking about the enormity of it all and balk our way out, back into the arms of our only real love: drugs and alcohol. We forget that, as we took our first swing with a driver on a par-nine fairway; it was the practice that dictated just how far we'd hit. Change is difficult, and yet, time and time again we did it anyway, didn't we? We took whatever steps we had to, to swing like a pro and never looked back.

Recovery from a seemingly hopeless state of mind and body is no different, although we are more scared than we have ever been in our lives. Our addicted self is the only self we feel comfortable with. We listen and absorb just enough each day to move us toward a necessary change, not more. We are not changed overnight, nor do we become healed in a day. We prepare our course and do the things needed to begin this lifelong transformation of self. We don't dive off a high-dive without learning how to first hold our breath and then swim. We don't quit our addictions without finding how to get through just one day sober. One sober day prepares us for the next, and the next, and change comes.

TODAY'S MEDITATION

Thank you, God, for strengthening me so that I can change my footing and perceptions and become stronger in unity with you and my world just for today.

"All changes, even the most longed for, have their melancholy, for what we leave behind us is a part of ourselves; we must die to one life before we can enter into another." — Anatole France

BE WHO YOU ARE
AUGUST 15

I was always in a frenzy of people-pleasing, and while I thought I wasn't a door-mat, my actions proved otherwise. Fear and insecurity ruled my emotions. Each thought was directed outward, contrived with you in mind. I became a mental strategist, searching for the right facade to hide behind to keep you from disap-proving of me. *If you're happy, then I'm happy too*, was the adage I lived by.

To be who we are is the greatest gift we can give ourselves. It means we've stripped away everything that kept us from being real. While we consider the opinions and needs of others, their happiness belongs only to them. It is their responsibility.

We no longer betray the truth of who we are to please anyone other than ourselves.

Genuine authenticity requires we never abandon our truth, regardless of cir-cumstances. We avoid deception and deference to others. To defer to others is an affront to our personal integrity we've worked so hard to achieve.

We deserve this precious gift of self-acceptance and welcome with arms stretched wide, the trust and confidence that comes from allowing ourselves to be authentic. Life unfolds when and how it is supposed to because we have let go of approval-seeking and manipulative behaviors.

We have tailor-made our authentic selves and with assurance, we can be who we are.

TODAY'S MEDITATION
Today I radiate with a love of self, knowing I deserve to be who I am.

"Be who you are and say what you feel, because those who mind don't matter and those who matter don't mind." — Bernard Baruch

Breathing through the Panic
August 16

We all know the feeling that is panic. Faced with a threat, we stand, frozen in place. Sometimes the mere thought of a stressful situation is enough to raise our blood pressure and produce symptoms of a heart attack.

In that moment of panic, we stop, and just breathe. We close our eyes for a moment, and feel the control we gain as we focus on where we are, right here.

Panic is a feeling, not something tangible. It is an extreme manifestation of the fight-or-flight instinct. We imagine we are cornered. Feeling trapped or threatened by a lack of control in a situation, our hearts race, our palms sweat. As if there is no way out, we panic in anticipation of what will come, but there is always a way out. Even as nothing materializes. Freezing in place isn't helpful. Panic is a psychological *reaction* to fear that keeps us stuck.

This too, Shall Pass.

Some things we do to reclaim our balance is to breathe deeply from our diaphragm and exhale, counting to five. Do this more than once. We confront this panic and take back control with new commands as we change our perspective. What used to be debilitating terror becomes our portal to freedom when we embrace fear as a personal friend, an intuitive nudge that tells us we have work to do to get to the other side.

What else can we do? We remind ourselves fear is a feeling, not fact. It is *false* evidence that appears real. Redirection, prayer, and calm feedback helps us to develop new pathways to change us from a victim, to a survivor. We repeat our mantra that says, "I deserve to feel the fear, examine the facts, and let it pass," or another of your choosing. We see ourselves safe in our hula hoop of time, and look down at our feet to confirm that right here, right now, all is well.

TODAY'S MEDITATION
Just for today I trust myself to take charge and not panic.

"Being under stress is like being stranded in a body of water. If you panic, it will cause you to flail around so that the water rushes into your lungs and creates further distress. Yet, by calmly collecting yourself and using controlled breathing you remain afloat with ease." — Alaric Hutchinson

BREAKING THROUGH DENIAL
AUGUST 17

It's taken thousands of days adding up to many years for the denial of my alcoholism to subside enough for me to admit that any life that revolves around drinking and drugging is not normal. Obsessing over how to get my next drink, calculating how long before I could have another; checking how much was left, and whether I had enough money to get more were just a few of the delusions that consumed my obsessive-compulsive thoughts.

Breaking through denial took walking into the rooms of *Alcoholics Anonymous* and asking for help. It took humility and an honest readiness I never knew I had. All I consciously brought with me was my desperation. But as others shared their experiences, strength, and hope, I saw so many similarities; I wasn't the only one who had arrived desperate.

I am not alone in the relief I feel when I walk into those rooms. For the first time in our lives for many of us, what we feel is hope. There is hope that if we keep coming back, life will somehow change. Hope that if this roomful of people, laughing and smiling, has found the answers they need to stay sober one day at a time, then, maybe, we can too. We're convinced that if we stay the course and do what others did, we will get what they got.

One of the great truths learned in recovery is, together we stay sober, alone we die. This is the natural course of the disease if we do not break through our denial and seek that place where we come together to heal.

TODAY'S MEDITATION

Thank you, God, for giving me the rooms of recovery and the courage to recognize I must keep coming back, no matter what.

"Gratitude unlocks the fullness of life. It turns what we have into enough, and more. It turns denial into acceptance, chaos to order, confusion to clarity..."
— *Melody Beattie*

COMPARING

AUGUST 18

Who remembers from high school all the silly competitions we engaged in with friends? We measured a puffed-up imagine of our self-worth based on how we looked compared to others, what they said—especially about us, our relative accomplishments, or lack thereof. If this still has the ring of validity, maybe it's because we're still caught up in comparing.

Comparing ourselves to others is a manifestation of our insecurity. We resonate on some level with the whispered judgment of others that we are not enough. If we set aside those judgments, what is the measure we've created for ourselves? When is what we have, or who we are, enough to satisfy ourselves?

When we compare ourselves to others or take their judgments to heart, we are using a false material-measure of who we are that is rarely satisfied. This externally-based appraisal is constantly in flux and represents no truth at all. Comparing is a self-inflicted standard we developed as children to feed our over-nourished ego and our under-nourished self-esteem. We know better now, then to engage in this self-defeating ego-stroking past time.

When we are sure of our truth and of who we are on the inside, and who we are in the eyes of our Higher Power, being enough becomes our new reality. As our need to compare wanes, we get comfortable with who we are.

We are fulfilled, validated by a connection to our spiritual-selves which tells us that as our Higher Power's children we are equal.

TODAY'S MEDITATION

I only need to compare myself to you, God, my reminder of so much more spiritual growth yet to come. Keeping the focus on what you think, and not others, helps me achieve this goal.

"Try to keep your mind open to possibilities and your mouth closed on matters you don't know about. Limit your always and your nevers." – Amy Poehler

CONTROLLING EMOTIONS
AUGUST 19

What does it mean to control emotions? Can it even be done? How do we stop the rush of feelings that demand our attention? What do we do with overwhelming emotions like fear, grief, and anger?

Slamming the door shut on our emotions is not the answer. We must learn, instead, how to regulate them. Regulating emotions takes practice and insight. Even as our hearts beat faster, anticipating what will come, we find we have the ability to control our reactions and find our calm center before we respond.

We are always accountable for our behavior, but where the emotion is extreme or inappropriate for a given situation, we have a responsibility to adjust our response. Recovery teaches us to count to ten. During that slow, deliberate count, we detach ourselves from what we feel, and gain perspective by taking a step back and pausing. We stop in that instant and focus on our breath.

Prayer also enables us to short-circuit old, knee-jerk reactions and respond with controlled politeness. By focusing on something else, we regain our emotional footing. We remember, when there is no truth in what others say; we need not own it by responding.

As we move gracefully away from a volatile situation, we celebrate this much needed outcome. We work the Tenth and Eleventh Steps right where we are, realign ourselves in prayer, and let it go. Progress and forgiveness are the goal. The ability to control our emotions is a continual practice in all our affairs.

TODAY'S MEDITATION
With your help, God, I am ready, regardless of circumstance, to feel my feelings and then watch them pass. As I practice in quiet reserve, I trust my emotions will pass, as they always do, whether I act on them, or not.

"Comfort in expressing your emotions will allow you to share the best of yourself with others, but not being able to control your emotions will reveal your worst."
— Bryant H. McGill

Don't Worry, Be Happy
August 20

A friend named Ms. Contented had a neighbor named Ms. Miserable. At a neighborhood party, Ms. Contented heard disparaging things said about Ms. Miserable; calls to the police, nasty encounters with neighbors, and threats made were just a few of her escapades. It seemed at every turn Ms. Miserable was just plain miserable. She just didn't know any other way of engaging.

Ms. Contented realized people were not born mean and nasty. Being new to the neighborhood, she wondered if she should make introductions, maybe even become a friend of Ms. Miserable. She decided to try. Ms. Contented, in recovery herself for several months, knew she had to do something nice for Ms. Miserable, and do it without expectations. Ms. Contented prayed about what to do and then visited Ms. Miserable.

The air was crisp and dry as Ms. Contented held her courage and a beautiful home-grown orchid, both with loving care. Ms. Contented's orchids all had names, the one picked out for Ms. Miserable was named Happy. That was her prayer of the night before, that Ms. Miserable would find happiness somewhere, in something. One foot perched as a brace on the step above, and the other down on the step below, Ms. Contented was ready to run if she had to. Hand shaking, she knocked on the door, hoping she wouldn't be assaulted, or the door slammed in her face.

The front door cracked open. She could see Ms. Miserable's frown, heard the anger in her voice ask, "Who are you and *what* do you want?"

Ms. Contented forced a fearful smile, extending her arms to Ms. Miserable with an orchid in her hand, and made introductions. Ms. Miserable said thanks, took the orchid, and with the hint of a smile, closed the door.

Not only was Ms. Contented practicing love and acceptance of others, she did so without judgment, or the expectation of a reward. She afforded Ms. Miserable the chance to be happy. Ms. Contented is an example of a brave woman in recovery, offering love and kindness. She may be the one person to change the course of Ms. Miserable's day with an attitude adjustment.

We have lots of decisions to make in recovery. One important decision is, do we want to be happy, or do we want to be miserable? What a gift it is to have choices, and the power to carry them out!

TODAY'S MEDITATION

I don't want to worry, I want to be happy. Just for today I will look for opportunities to help someone else find their own happiness.

"...Don't worry about things you can't change. You can't change the traffic in the morning. You can't fix everybody at work. You can't make all your family members serve God. But you shouldn't let that keep you from being happy..."
— *Joel Osteen*

Denial of Feelings
August 21

If someone were to ask you if you are in denial, what would you say? How would you know? Can you even recognize denial?

Denial has a chorus of voices, each offering a criticism of its own. One voice says, "My life would be so much better if only you would…." Another says, "I don't know." For me, denial was profound, the voices loud and clear. "Don't Trust!" "Don't Feel!" "Don't Tell!" For what felt like a lifetime, I denied responsibility in my relationship as a mother and a wife. In my addictions, I was a perpetual liar and became known as someone who couldn't be trusted or depended upon.

Recovery, and the influence of The Steps, encourage us to face and to be responsible for the hurts we've inflicted both to ourselves and others through our denials. We listen to our one honest voice and awaken a truth that is stronger now than any act of denial. In recovery, we are too aware to not listen and respond.

Written gratitude's allow feelings to be what they are without judgment, raising the possibility that denial is a manifestation of extreme fear. This awareness opens the door to acceptance followed by action. We know that if we spot it, we got it, so we already have what we need to change. Once we exchange denial of our feelings for acceptance, we become a powerful, awakened instrument of change, our own goodness expanding.

TODAY'S MEDITATION

I have little denial in my life today. I am free to share with others the real me, as I have been set free.

"You can't wake a person who is pretending to be asleep." — *Laurie Limberg*

EMOTIONAL SECURITY
AUGUST 22

Walking into recovery, it was no surprise to be told my addiction career had set me back emotionally thirty years. I reacted to life much like a seventeen-year-old, which is what I was when my addictions began to take hold.

Emotional insecurity roared, proof positive of my relentless inability on any level to cope with negative life situations in healthy and acceptable ways. I was a mental-incompetent, and blamed myself, for every upset real or imagined. I had few examples of what normal was and possessed no resilience against fear. I stayed frustrated, depressed, angry, and scared. I stayed seventeen.

An emotionally secure person maintains a sustainable level of self-esteem and confidence with appropriate emotional maturity for the age. They handle situations with consideration for self-care while apologizing with ease. They catch negativity as soon as their inner-critic tries to sabotage their efforts. Emotional security begs the question of *"Do I want to be happy, or do I want to be right?"*

The satisfaction that comes with the ability to sustain emotional security continues to be a life-long discovery process, as I leave seventeen behind and become the mature adult I was always meant to be.

TODAY'S MEDITATION
The degree to which I walk along spiritual lines, determines the harmony I feel with my soul and the universe.

"Emotional security is how we feel about our self, how good we feel in relationships with other people who are important to us (e.g. family), and how confident we are that things will turn out well for us." — Dr Anil Kumar Sinha

EXPERIENCE AS THE TEACHER
AUGUST 23

Even in adulthood, I imagined I had nothing to offer anyone. My sad life story was stamped into my psyche. I believed it was who I was; a consummate victim. Believing I was worthless, I convinced myself that I deserved to be shunned, and, as a result, I was.

This is an example of the insidiousness of our disease and the damage our delusional thinking can do. The false belief that we will *always* fail and a deep self-loathing have the power to keep us immobilized, stuck in this illusion of hopelessness.

As we become sick and tired of being sick and tired, recovery, for those who are the lucky ones, opens the door to hope. Hope extends to our emotional and spiritual growth. By Step Nine, a profound shift in our thinking leaves less room for negativity as new pathways and uplifting thoughts give us courage. Strong principles redefine the person we have become. We hold proof-positive, a knowing that we never *were* that person we told ourselves we were.

As self-centered fear diminishes and our truth and self-esteem now self-evident, we embrace new certainties. We stop focusing on our failures and realize that becoming useful to others is paramount if we want to live happy, joyous and free. We have moved away from selfish, self-centered thinking, if just for today.

No longer immobilized, we walk forward, motivated by our usefulness to others. As we let go of the lies and stinking-thinking that held us hostage for so many years, a real purpose, which is to be useful to others, takes its place. Experience continues to be my best teacher.

TODAY'S MEDITATION
Today God, I am so grateful to know that you have me right where you want me: putting others in my life so I may be of service; sharing my experience, strength and hope.

"The best teacher is experience and not through someone's distorted point of view" — Jack Kerouac

FEAR OF ACCEPTANCE
AUGUST 24

I often struggle with accepting the friendship others offer. I hear a voice saying, "Hey! You have no friends, they're just pretending to like you!"

We tend to make life more difficult than it needs to be. Sometimes we feel alone and confuse it with being lonely; we tell ourselves we haven't felt loveable for some time, so why should anyone love us now? Even as an adult, sick-thinking can transform us into that scared child again, the one who is sure she has no friends, and that even if she did, she'd never be accepted.

What body language do we let others see when we are in that lonely place? Are we standing alone, arms crossed, or sitting away from others, waiting for them to come to us? What do our facial expressions say? Do we share a welcoming smile, or are our eyebrows knit together, our mouths down-turned, as we walk into a room? Chances are, as we scare ourselves with the thought others are shunning us, we scare others away at the same time!

We don't have to see ourselves as less-than, or not good enough any longer. We don't have to prepare ourselves for rejection every time we meet others. Instead, we should expect and be prepared to offer the best of who we are. This acceptance of ourselves must come first.

We are not defective, we may simply have been looking in the wrong places for approval. As we practice embracing ourselves as we are, we open the door to accepting others, silently inviting them to do the same for us. Our fear of acceptance will, over time, become a non-issue.

TODAY'S MEDITATION
I know today, that as I accept myself, am I accepted by others.

"Love is what we were born with. Fear is what we learned here. The spiritual journey is the relinquishment, or unlearning, of fear and the acceptance of love back into our hearts." — Ritu Ghatourey

HONESTY, OPEN-MINDEDNESS AND WILLINGNESS (H.O.W.)
AUGUST 25

In the realm of recovery, these three words deliver the essence of meaning not otherwise heard before. Used and practiced together; they are indispensable.

Experience shows what happens when we don't exercise complete *honesty* in our lives. Without sugar-coating, minimizing or accommodating others, we strive to say what we mean, mean what we say, and not say it mean. With help from our Higher Power, we pause before we speak and ask: is what we're about to say honest, is it necessary, and did someone ask for my opinion?

Without *open-mindedness*, we would be powerless to accept a Higher Power and principles crucial to recovery. As we dilute our black and white patterns of inflexible opinions, open-mindedness ignites our higher-self and we begin to embrace the grey. *Never-say-Never* becomes our new awakening.

Willingness is our route to a personal integrity we refine each new day. When we pray to have selfish, self-centered or dishonest thoughts removed, willingness aligns with our Higher Power. The energy manifested within our core of goodness moves us forward throughout our day. Our life changes because of our willingness to make it happen.

We are strengthened in courage as H.O.W. positions us to maximize the sunlight of the Spirit. As we trust our own unfolding and prepare to receive, to believe, and to accept what-is right where we are, we see we are right on time.

TODAY'S MEDITATION
God, please bless me today with honesty, open-mindedness and willingness. Tomorrow I will begin again, as I trust it is Your Will for me.

"Honesty, open-mindedness and willingness are the three primary principles in laying down a solid foundation for recovery. Honest with oneself. Being open to Power Greater than ourselves and willing to take certain steps."
— Author unknown

FINDING YOUR COMPASSIONATE SELF
AUGUST 26

Many of us shy away from the topic of examining our compassionate selves because we fear what we will find. The idea of giving compassion to that true self, scares us even more. We feel, deep down, that we are unworthy of anyone's compassion, even our own.

Over time we developed a troubled relationship with ourselves and others and then we withdrew, preferring numbness and indifference to pain. Some of us found comfort in depression, while others nurtured various forms of abuse, perfectionism, self-criticism, and stress. This familiarity only bred more negativity; still, we lived with what we knew.

To find our compassionate self, we must believe there is an abundance of goodness already within us waiting to be resurrected. As we become convinced through recovery that none of us is born bad, we begin to grow up and learn acceptable and affirming coping skills. We exchange old patterns of negative thinking and exchange behaviors for goodness and remember we were born pure, a centerpiece of loving innocence.

Each of us can come to accept that we are strong, loving, and courageous on some level. In so doing we come back to life. We grieve, laugh, respect and honor those people and things we love.

What if we became as an innocent child accepting everything that is true about ourselves; thoughts, feelings, and actions, good and bad, coming to understand that they represent all that we are? Now picture your innocent inner-child accepting your every thought without criticism or judgment. This is self-compassion. For without compassion for ourselves, how can we find compassion for anyone else? It is this essential gift of our love of self, that reminds us that we are worthy of embracing our strengths and acceptance for our compassionate self.

TODAY'S MEDITATION

I continue to explore and extend compassion to others as an example for them to see their own reflection of who they want to be.

"You can search throughout the entire universe for someone who is more deserving of your love and affection than you are yourself, and that person is not to be found anywhere. You, yourself, ... deserve your love and affection."
— *Buddha*

GETTING RID OF PERFECTION

My life was consumed with never measuring up. I saw myself as never good enough. As a child, each time I tried to clean my room or assist in any other way, I was marched back to the task at hand and told it wasn't good enough, and to do it again. Maybe it was mom's way of getting me to be more thorough, but what I heard was, it wasn't *good enough*. What I heard was, I needed to be perfect.

The older I became, the more rigid were my thoughts and actions. Convinced no one could work as hard as me, I became a critical, overbearing perfectionist. Everyone around me bore the brunt of my compulsion that they too must be perfect. It wasn't long before I was labeled an opinionated and boring know-it-all.

Al-Anon asks us to unveil the child within and return to the time when we first began to suffer from our labels; in my case, not good enough. As we evaluate what we think we knew about past situations and our mistaken beliefs, we embrace the pursuit of *progress*, not perfection. Today, we no longer have to take anything personally because we know that the labels others put on us, the standards they insist we live up to, say more about them than they do about us.

In recovery, we turn perfectionism over to a Higher Power where the weight of having to be not just good, but perfect, becomes as light as the air we breathe.

As we focus on letting go of old perfectionist behaviors and our all-or-nothing thinking, the easier our lives become. We become free to embrace ourselves and others with a new gentleness that honors our imperfect selves. We acknowledge in peace, that we are now and always will be a work in progress. What a relief!

TODAY'S MEDITATION
Thank you, God, for doing for me what I could never do alone. You lifted the burden of trying to be perfect. I acknowledge now that perfect is for You alone.

"Perfectionism is not a quest for the best. It is a pursuit of the worst in ourselves, the part that tells us that nothing we do will ever be good enough that we should try again. "— Julia Cameron

LEARNING TO ACCEPT
GRIEF AND LOSS
AUGUST 28

The death of a loved one, and the relentless pain that accompanies that loss, is often paralyzing. The experience often leaves us numb, in a state of shock.

Gradually, this state of numbness is replaced with an understanding that the loss is real and it is permanent. While we reconcile ourselves to our loss, everything else becomes a burden, the simple day-to-day rituals are more than we can handle. We are exhausted, very often depressed. Our loss disables us, and it takes time to accept what has happened and move on.

As we allow ourselves to feel grief, we also face our own vulnerability. We are mortal too, and so are all those we love, but we must not push grief aside and go on as if nothing has happened.

Tears soften and soothe the never-ending ache and pain in our hearts. As we cleanse, nurture and care for ourselves, a spark of gratefulness is kindled. Our tears represent the magnitude of love for our lost one, transforming feelings of devastation into a balanced mixture of gratitude and sorrow: gratitude for the love and precious time we shared, sorrow as we recognize missed opportunities, and the fact we will never share our days with our loved one again.

As we experience grief we are gentle and loving to ourselves. We feel, process, and heal in our own time, no one else's. We deserve to be attentive to our unfolding, and give ourselves permission to mourn our loss fully, recovering at a time and pace known only to our Higher Power.

TODAY'S MEDITATION

Dear God, I am grateful that sorrow and tears are equal in importance to joy. Tears reflect the depth of love for the deceased, as sorrow is the admission of selfishness, for never wanting to be without them when I know they have returned safely to You.

"People are like stained glass windows. They sparkle and shine when the sun is out, but when the darkness sets in, their true beauty is revealed only if there is a light from within." — Elizabeth Kubler-Ross

SELF-DECEPTION
AUGUST 29

There is a passage in our literature that speaks to self-deception. "The delusion that we are not *like* the alcoholic has to be smashed."

Self-deception is one of the hallmarks of active addiction. Adept at minimizing our lies and denial, we delude ourselves, convinced that since the consequences of what we did were borne by others, the blame was not ours, the problem was someone else's. We are *not* alcoholic, *not* addicted.

We conveniently overlook the fact that money was stolen, lies were told, appointments broken and jewelry hocked, all by us in an effort to feed our addictions. Day-after-day, we bought whatever lie was necessary to avoid a truth we worked so hard to evade, the fact we were addicted.

In his book *Vital Lies, Simple Truths,* Daniel Goleman notes, "The mind can protect itself against anxiety by diminishing awareness. This mechanism produces a blind spot: a zone of blocked attention and self-deception."

Until we become willing to face the darkest truths and demons central to our addictions, we are doomed to live in a world of self-deception. This facade keeps us stuck, emotionally, physically and spiritually, a delusion that insists the alcoholic is that other guy. Not me.

TODAY'S MEDITATION

Dear God, please help me to think before I speak and ask myself, "Is this true?" I will practice rigorous honesty in all of my affairs.

"People who believe that they are strong-willed and the masters of their destiny can only continue to believe this by becoming specialists in self-deception."
— James Baldwin

IT'S YOUR SIGN
AUGUST 30

At a party, several of us in recovery played a silly game called It's Your Sign. "If you do (this), then you *may* have an addiction." We went around the room, laughing at how many abnormal, sick, or damaging things we've done that led us to recovery.

One participant said, "If on a dinner date someone leaves a third of their wine untouched and we drink it, we may have a drinking problem." Some nodded in recognition and the litany of "signs" traveled around the room: We could have a drug problem if we look in others' medicine cabinets to see what they have and what we can use.

You could be an alcoholic if you believe near-beer or wine coolers are safe.

If you wonder whether or not you are addicted, well—that's your sign.

If bottles are hidden around the house, in the car, at work, behind the toilet, or under your pillow so no one will find them, that's your sign.

If you find you can't walk away from a drink or drug after the first one, or if your personal creed is "more of anything is better," you may have an addictive personality.

Those of us with an addiction can add to this list endlessly. We know, too, that to a non-addict/alcoholic, these examples sound pretty far-fetched and never thought about.

Maybe going to an open A. A. or N.A. meeting is all that is required for some to determine their sign. The new friend you make at the meeting who shares their sign may, in the process, tell you yours!

TODAY'S MEDITATION
If I want to be honest, I will evaluate my thinking and behaviors to look for patterns that signal addiction. I know if I spot it, I've got it.

"When you can stop you don't want to, and when you want to stop, you can't..."
— Luke Davies

THE KEY OF WILLINGNESS

"We only have to be willing, to be willing," a friend assured me early in my sobriety. Willingness implies an open mind, a withholding of judgment. It affects how we perceive our world and those around us.

We can apply willingness to anything and everything. Imagine for a moment, the lack of willingness to move out of the way as someone cuts us off in traffic. Or envision when someone needs help, and without willingness we watch instead.

But willingness can also be an excuse. Some people use willingness as a way to avoid responsibility and allow others to make decisions for them. Some use willingness as the measure of their own goodness, feeling they must be willing to help others regardless of the consequences.

In recovery we're told we need to do something different for our sobriety. Even when we don't understand and would prefer to close our mind to an idea, we pray for the willingness to become open in our thinking. We're not being forced to change. We're being asked to suspend what we *think* we know and listen. Willingness opens us to new possibilities without condemnation or debate. It suggests, anything is possible and stays away from the extremes of black and white.

Give it a try. See how it feels. Try wearing it like a soft sweater on a cool day, Willingness is the perspective that accepts others could be right. It encourages wisdom and growth outside the rigid box of, *this is the way I always do it,* and, *they're just trying to push me around.* To be willing is to listen without judgment or paranoia and try on whatever idea has been offered, or not!

TODAY'S MEDITATION
Today I will wear the soft sweater of willingness. I will make adjustments taking it off, putting it back on as I practice listening without judgment.

"We must be willing to get rid of the life we've planned so as to have the life that is waiting for us." — Joseph Campbell

THE GIFT OF PAUSE

SEPTEMBER 1

I used to laugh when I heard people use expressions such as, *look at that knee-jerk reaction*, or, *insert foot in mouth*. As I sobered up, I realized I was that person people were talking about. I never knew when to quit, how much was enough, or when to back down. I pushed. I did things my way.

Winning through intimidation was second nature for me, exciting and emotionally satisfying. Negative attention was better than none at all. I was oblivious to the hurt and embarrassment I regularly caused friends and family. Most of all, I never saw the self-degradation or the damage it did to my wounded soul until I entered recovery.

Here, as we touch that knowing place of shame and self-loathing, humor leavens the hurts we inflicted with our cold anger and righteousness. Our unthinking reactions unleashed because we didn't care if we hurt ourselves and others.

In recovery, we engage a simple principle called pause. With each breath, we are told to stop long enough to detach from our emotions in silent meditation. Encouraged to count to ten or twenty, if needed, we take in a deep breath of faith as some of us say, *This too, Shall Pass*.

Recovery shows as we pause long enough to think, we are protected from the emotional adrenaline that surges when reacting in the moment. In the pause, we achieve emotional maturity.

We allow our Higher Power to redirect our thinking through this wonderful principle of pause. We pause—and then we do.

TODAY'S MEDITATION
No words or actions can compete with the magnificent grace of pause.

"Practice the pause. Pause before judging. Pause before assuming. Pause before accusing. Pause whenever you're about to react harshly and you'll avoid doing and saying things you'll later regret." — Lori Deschene

STAYING THE COURSE IN SOBRIETY
SEPTEMBER 2

I remember those first few months in recovery. I rode a pink cloud of sobriety where days were steeped in gratitude and that feeling that I had arrived, were ever-present. My family wondered when my meetings would end. "Just how long do you have to go to these meetings?" they asked. Although I no longer wreaked havoc, took control or made selfish demands of their waking hours, they never noticed food was on time, clothes washed, and the house clean, previously long neglected. I was changing, yet the family stayed confused, waiting for repeat performances of my drunkenness.

First instincts said, "Just go pick up a bottle. Maybe they are right." The way to sobriety was a slippery slope and the difficult changes necessary to maintain my sobriety only seemed to alienate me from my family. The fellowship and a sponsor encouraged me to stay the course and remember that I was the one needing to understand my disease, no one else.

We keep our program and many conversations of recovery to ourselves and walk our new walk with resolve while allowing family members to own whatever they feel. We remind ourselves each morning in prayer how powerless we are over everyone, except ourselves.

Today the most important thing we can do is to detach from fearful expectations and behaviors of others, and practice being the best person we can be through living amends. We change our *behaviors*, and something bigger than us is in charge of how this change affects others.

On good days, we are convinced our lives will unfold the way they are supposed to, without our interference. As we practice living life sober, we see these good days come more often. Continued forgiveness of ourselves makes it easier for our Higher Power to guide our lives in a way we alone never could.

We go to meetings even when others think we are cured. We know what we really have is a 24-hour stay of execution based upon the maintenance of our spiritual condition. Today? Anything could happen, and so we stay the course.

TODAY'S MEDITATION
Dear God, thank you for encouraging me to attend to my behaviors and disease, instead of insisting my family and everyone change to suit me.

" *I'm hopeful knowing that I broke the cycle for my children. They will never suffer having an absent nor an addict parent.*" — *recovery.org*

SOMETHING WITHIN ME
SEPTEMBER 3

During a walk, I realized there was something causing me general distress. I blamed the weather for my irritability and quickly became a victim, trapped in my home without money to spend, feeling unrecognized, unloved and alone while the rain fell outside my window.

I deserved to treat myself to something! I drove out and got my usual fix, vanilla ice cream, and hot fudge. A moment of contentment washed over me as I ate my first bowl. As I filled my second bowl, that same disconnect surfaced yet again.

I realized that this craving was an inside job. There is something within me that needed attention. As I sat the spoon down, I noticed I had the same expectations as I do when I am in my addictions, thinking this bowl of ice cream will put a lid on the shortcomings I refused to recognize. Emotional nourishment, satisfaction, and happiness are things I try to give others, but I can't give away what I don't have.

The problem is *always* within us; a growing dissatisfaction deep inside. Some of us become judgmental or grandiose, seeking to blame anyone or anything, as long as we don't have to look inside for our answers. We forget that when we stop expecting others, or indulgences such as multiples of anything to make us whole, we might get a glimpse of what is missing in ourselves. Like any other addiction, indulgences and distractions become the smokescreen overshadowing the real issue: our perception and expectations.

When we remember it is our Higher Power who removes old beliefs, inappropriate thinking, and behaviors, we begin a slow journey of replacing these with what is emotionally appropriate and sustaining. Together with prayer and meditation, pathways for change and healing become formed, but changes and healing come in the timing of our Higher Power. Working The Steps and working with others, restores those places inside that leak toxins of loneliness and self-pity. As we commit to work with our Higher Power to do the next right thing, we become convinced more will be revealed. It continues to work when we work it.

Dear God, my imperfections are the signposts needed to point me to you. You are the only answer to my sanity, and ultimate contentment.

"I've always wanted people to know who they are from the inside. Then they can create the life they desire and deserve.". — Iyanla Vanzant

LIFE ON LIFE'S TERMS
SEPTEMBER 4

I always thought my life would never change. I figured my parents would live together forever; that I would stay disappointed with myself, and that people could never be trusted. I grew up alone, isolated, and afraid.

The more life spins out of control as we try to manage the unknown, the more insane our lives become. Professional help and recovery teach us to take baby steps in accepting life on life's terms. We learn to keep our attention on ourselves and let our Higher Power control everything and everyone else. We allow life to unfold around us, with our Higher Power in our side pocket. We don't condemn ourselves to extremes of *always* or *never*. Each day is unique.

We learn we deserve the same care and thoughtfulness we so freely give to others. As we learn to love and nurture ourselves, we are shored up with patience, as our lives now are re-created in peace and understanding.

We position ourselves to be where we are supposed to be, accepting the fact that we are a full-time job, prepared to face and handle whatever comes before us. We free ourselves to let go of what we don't need, including the need to control, along with the belief that our lives would never change.

What freedom there is to be a warrior, facing, handling and taking care of *our* life as it unfolds just for today. With the help of our Higher Power we deal with whatever comes for this is the essence of life on life's terms.

TODAY'S MEDITATION
Today with welcome serenity, I accept what is. I embrace life as it unfolds right this moment. I don't have to like it; I just have to accept it.

"If we believe that tomorrow will be better, we can bear a hardship today."
— *Thich Nhat Hanh*

TURNING IT AROUND
SEPTEMBER 5

I remember never seeing the flip-side of anything. I never wanted to. By making a situation the other person's problem, my reward was to stay self-centered, prideful, and full of justified resentment. In my self-pity, other people's feelings never mattered. My version of events was the only one that mattered.

One of the gifts of sobriety is learning to see another person's side of a situation, even if it differs from my perception of the same event. Recovery gives me the ability to see that very little is as it seems through the eyes of one observer. It's been difficult, but learning this lesson has helped me see differences between my sisters' memories, growing up in her dysfunctional family and my own. Turning it around has given me compassion enough to see that we each have differing perspectives, and that is okay.

A wise sponsor reminded me that everyone has their own take on events based on their vantage point, and personal circumstances. Although our stories differ, each of us has the right to tell our story as we remember it. After all, our story is *our* story.

Today with some emotional maturity, I am open to listening, to detaching with loving kindness, and to accept experiences and feelings of others on their journeys, even if they differ from mine.

Just like me, my sisters deserve their own story as it was for each of them. My job is to honor their journey and perspective in the same way I would like to have mine understood and honored by them. In turning it around, I practice principles before personality in all of my affairs.

TODAY'S MEDITATION

I'm grateful and accept that although we came from the same family, interpretations, emotions, and memories, are different from my own, *but no less relevant or true.*

"Our task must be to free ourselves... by widening our circle of compassion to embrace all living creatures and the whole of nature and its beauty."
— *Albert Einstein*

PRAYER AND MEDITATION
SEPTEMBER 6

Part of my personal dysfunction was the inability to see a God of my understanding. I crawled into recovery, broken, without a God, yet blaming Him for not coming to my rescue. I had long since given up meditation or praying to anything, period.

As my eyes opened in recovery, I understood the spiritual process in front of me. It was clear what was missing in my life was a power greater than myself. Previously, I positioned myself at the right hand of something that wasn't there. The only strength I recognized was my own—and I knew I had no strength at all.

At some point; it becomes obvious we have been playing God. As we become right-sized, we see we are a child of a Higher Power who reigns omnipotent. It never was me, although I abandoned my faith.

Step Two shows us *believing is seeing* in the spiritual realm.

Step Three encourages us to turn our life and will over to the care of our Higher Power.

Step Eleven asks that we seek, through prayer and meditation, to increase our conscious contact with our Higher Power. This step implies some faith was there all along or we couldn't *see* it now.

Our daily ritual becomes, *Trust God, Clean House, and Help Others.* Prayer and meditation are the portal to a conscious contact with our Higher Power, emotional stability, and the balance we need to live in peace. Faith is the anchor to our here and now. Our Higher Power is the rock that provides stability on our spiritual journey even when life's turbulent waters rise. Conscious contact through prayer and meditation remind us we are not alone. If our Higher Power brings us to it, He will get us through it.

As we open our heart and become willing to listen, our Higher Power points to the next right thing for us to do.

> ## TODAY'S MEDITATION
> Prayer is the anointing act of lifting up our voices. Meditation is the silence that brings answers to our questions home.

"We live, in fact, in a world starved for solitude, silence, and privacy and therefore starved for meditation and true friendship." — C.S. Lewis

WHAT IS ENOUGH
SEPTEMBER 7

How many times have we asked ourselves the same old questions: did I do a good enough job? what's missing? or, how much more should I do? Sometimes, no matter how much we do, the doing gets followed by a question that implies, our efforts were not enough. Maybe, we think, they are never enough. We become obsessed with the act of doing, caught in our trance of busyness, with no end in sight.

Insecurity is often the reason we fail to see that we have already done enough. Expectations of ourselves are skewed through years of misaligned messages. Rather than rely on our own intuition when deciding what constituted enough, we let others determine what enough was for us.

If we are honest, we already *know* our saturation point when it comes to how much is enough for us. Our subconscious takes a step back: observes and reports, "This will do." This is our heart's way of communicating to the head that we can stop now. We've done enough. When the mind replays its usual messages that we must do more, we tell ourselves, not only that we have done enough but that we *are* enough. So, we stop right here.

Regardless of what it is we're doing, we are certain we are enough when *we* accept that we are. Our value is carved in our being, not doing. Recovery shows how to give up people-pleasing antics by owning our power of decision-making. The more we look within for answers, the greater our truth and clarity becomes. It's called trust.

Today we get to define what is enough for us. No one has the knowledge or insight to know what we must know for ourselves. We rest in our intuition.

TODAY'S MEDITATION
I'm conscious today, of how thoughts influence my actions. As I detach from old messages, I create new ones to accommodate who I am now and my actions follow, satisfied that I am enough.

"Love yourself enough to set boundaries. Your time and energy are precious. You get to choose how you use it. You teach people how to treat you by deciding what you will and won't accept." — Anna Taylor

FORWARD MOTION

SEPTEMBER 8

"Why am I not there yet?" "How long will it take before I get it?" "What am I doing wrong?" Like a child, we stomp, "But I want it NOW!" These and other statements cry out for answers on our journey in recovery. We think we deserve answers but they are none of our business. When no answer comes it is often because it's not our turn to understand. Patience, tolerance, and letting go, these are the principles tested as we approach our light of knowledge. As we wait in line for an answer that doesn't come, we accept we already have everything we need.

The process of recovery, although ever-changing, is as profound as our Higher Power whose sovereignty is as encompassing as the ocean's tides. By doing the next right thing, we're already right where we're supposed to be; safe, as we connect in thought to the spirit who presides over all.

We are moving forward, in the timing of our Higher Power, not ours. This forward motion doesn't *look* like we think it should look but we continue to trust the process.

There are no mistakes, only a perfect unveiling of our actualization. We are no longer free-floating. We are connected to something greater than ourselves, and because we are, knowing this is enough. We trust that if we remain clean and sober, we've become a miracle of forward motion.

Today we are bathed in the assurance of being led and accept, with trusted confidence, that more will always be revealed as we move forward, and it is. The continued rise and fall of our consciousness with our Higher Power assures this is so.

TODAY'S MEDITATION

God, as we continue to work together in faith, I accept I am no less a miracle when I lack the answers I think I need. I am a work in progress of forward motion. I walk on faith.

"Man maintains his balance, poise, and sense of security only as he is moving forward." — *Maxwell Maltz*

FEAR OF REJECTION
SEPTEMBER 9

In early addiction, I was consumed by rejection as I rejected everyone around me. My home was without plants, pets, or family. I had too few friends and came home each day to utter isolation. To others, my way of life appeared normal, so few would suspect the underlying problem which was a horrific fear of rejection. Although I anticipated hurtful words, my body language and facial expression projected indifference.

Many of us experience this same fear both in and out of recovery. Some people isolate and use protective rituals while connecting with others with hesitancy and only do so from time-to-time. Others replay messages of confidence, hoping to soften our expectations of rejection, but we are still sure rejection will come.

The fear of rejection often stifles any hope for emotional growth, but what can we do to change how we feel?

The Steps are tools of action that work to change our perspective and reject fears which, for many, appear real. Because we *believe* in these fears, they become self-fulfilling. Real or imagined, rejection deserves to be examined with compassion.

Instead of expecting rejection and letting it incapacitate us, we use the power of inner-knowing and make decisions based on a broader perspective. Rejection doesn't have to define us. Rarely, if ever, is it an indication that we are flawed, as everyone experiences rejection for something routinely.

Used constructively, rejection can signal the need for a deeper, kinder attention to ourselves, an acknowledgement of our fear of rejection. We change our thinking by seeing rejection as our personal exercise in detachment, by letting it go. We trust our Higher Power, clean our house of inner-false beliefs and confusion, and we help others.

One day at a time we let go of rejection and know rejection is fleeting, that *This too, Shall Pass.*

TODAY'S MEDITATION
Dear God, please help me to live each day without fearing rejection. Give me the power to change the things I can and leave the rest with you.

"Most fears of rejection rest on the desire for approval from other people. Don't base your self-esteem on their opinions. "— Harvey Mackay

BEING OURSELVES IN RELATIONSHIPS
SEPTEMBER 10

I thought marriage would answer all my problems. My knight in shining armor would come bursting through the door and carry me off into that blissful existence that, as little girls, we often thought marriage would be, that, "happily ever after."

Recovery and The Steps allow our eyes to open enough to see how far we are from "happily ever after," and that, oftentimes, an overhaul in our relationships is sorely needed. This admission, along with the willingness to change, gives us the courage to set aside pride and accept that, one day at a time, we will work on that overhaul, either alone or together.

While change isn't about perfection, the love we feel for those we cherish propels us closer to the person we want to be. As we become comfortable in our own skin we feel ourselves transform in sincerity, trust, and honesty. Recovery provides skills to make these new truths evident to those around us.

Each time we dive deeper into the sea of willingness, we rise with a new awareness of where we are responsible for negative traits we see in ourselves. Willingness has the ability to convert those traits, by trading them for compassion and trust. These traits were already within us, and as they strengthen, fear is left behind.

Acceptance and honesty are the meaningful changes in how we treat others, and how they treat us. We feel safe to be who we are. As we practice giving each other what we need without expectations, we become free to embrace our authentic selves.

That is the place where all authentic relationships begin.

TODAY'S MEDITATION
Each time I delve deeper into the waters of change, I surface more aware. I see both myself and you, with greater clarity.

*"Being deeply loved by someone gives you strength,
while loving someone deeply gives you courage."* — *Lao Tzu*

CREATING NEW BOUNDARIES
SEPTEMBER 11

I struggled with boundaries while in active addiction. I never knew how to say no, nor did I care to. All my boundaries were set by you and I didn't like them much. I was afraid you would withhold something I wanted, or worse yet, get in between me and my addiction.

If I recognized boundaries that caused me to see I was at fault, then I could no longer accuse you of anything. And what if my boundary offended you? I was scared to give myself a voice. I felt I was dishonoring you, that you had different expectations, would judge me, and not like me if our chosen boundaries conflicted. If I was looking for them at all, I was looking for boundaries set by you for me. I was too scared to set any of my own and terrified of confrontation.

It is okay to create boundaries acceptable only to ourselves, even if they are different from those embraced by others. We must choose boundaries for *ourselves* made with us in mind. Practice voicing our new boundaries helps give ourselves conviction so they don't feel foreign, or uncomfortable. Our apprehension is normal and should not deter us from honoring the boundaries we have set.

How someone else hears what we have said is their business. So long as we say what we mean and don't say it mean, no apologies are necessary. We are learning to execute exactness in our responses, for our greatest good. Speaking our truth, defining and redefining what we need to clarify, becomes stronger each time we stretch our voice with purpose.

The process of teaching others what we need to feel comfortable is ongoing; we continue until we are sure that we have been heard. We hope others will understand, but if they do not; we know it is not about us. A decision to remove ourselves from that relationship may be next in order. We are determined to develop and nurture a healthier, more self-reliant, self, one who sets, protects, and then honors their own boundaries.

TODAY'S MEDITATION

God, thank you for standing with me as I practice what is kind and true for me. I accept my interpretation of where my boundaries lie, and leave others' expressions, with you.

"Compassionate people ask for what they need. They say no when they need to, and when they say yes, they mean it. They're compassionate because their boundaries keep them out of resentment."— Brené Brown

COPING WITH CHANGE
SEPTEMBER 12

I watch a little girl stomp her feet, swing her arms and, through tears, cry, "I don't want to move, Mama. I don't want to move!" As this scene plays out, I am reminded of all the changes in my life, and how I fought against them. Fear of loss, abandonment, and starting over, threw me into an emotional meltdown. Like that little girl, I defiantly stomped my feet, but change came anyway.

Fear of change has the power to restrict breathing, as suffocating thoughts of what-if assail us. For many, the word *change* brings up bad memories. Some of us got divorced, lost children, lost jobs; others lost homes and everything material. Some lost their faith and themselves, along the way.

We know change is inevitable, but suffering is always optional. Knowing this doesn't make change any easier. What helps diminish the stress of change is to look at how far we've come by facing some of our greatest challenges. As we change our perception, we see how much better we are at handling changing situations and adapting than we have ever given ourselves credit for.

Most of us must deal with change, regardless of how we feel. In recovery, change is our only option if we want to live a contented and peaceful life in freedom. By now we have dealt with great changes and have come so far that to go backward would be self-defeating. We know too much about ourselves to not face this next hurdle of change and do it anyway. Staying put emotionally, spiritually in recovery must be non-negotiable, for our addictions never sleep.

And so, we change our vantage point. We have no choice but to grasp a faith we cannot see and throw ourselves into the light of hope.

As we lift our faces to the promise of spiritual alignment, we feel a presence. A warrior once more, we change ourselves to meet our conditions. Stronger now, we have become resilient enough to face whatever comes next and we do. We are a miracle off change!

TODAY'S MEDITATION

I am in charge of decisions that affect me directly, every day. When I employ the power of my God, I have no fear of change because he is walking before me, leading my path.

"Scientists have demonstrated that dramatic, positive changes can occur in our lives as a direct result of facing an extreme challenge - whether it's coping with a serious illness, daring to quit smoking, or dealing with depression. Researchers call this 'post-traumatic growth." — Jane McGonigal

EMBRACING OUR DIFFERENCES

I grew up believing there was just one way to do life right. And so, began my stringent, predictable, and controlled way of doing chores, child-rearing, and relationships. Differing opinions were strictly frowned upon. Didn't these people know there was a *right* way to do things? Why couldn't we just go with my program and do things my way? I was certain there was only one way to do things; it was called My Way, which meant I was always right.

The big world proved me wrong as I saw that everyone had an opinion and a unique way of thinking and carrying out their daily lives. Still, I spent many years fighting with everyone over those differences. It took a long time to realize that, no matter what the goal, there are many ways to get there. I looked long and hard to discover not one path was labeled, "The right way."

Recovery teaches that everyone deserves their opinion. The way we get from point A to point B *is* the right way, as long as it produces the desired results without causing harm. Our ability to step away from judgmental and fearful thinking and embrace our human differences is healthy.

Emotional maturity has roots in facing differences of opinion with grace, accepting others with forgiveness for who they are, and letting go of our my-way-or-the-highway need to be right.

TODAY'S MEDITATION

I'm grateful, God, for the ability to embrace differences, at last convinced that acceptance is the answer to all my problems today.

"...As we learn to embrace our diversity, we become stronger, more tolerant. The differences are beautiful. The differences matter. It's what makes life an adventure." — Ryan Potter

Step Twelve

"Having had a spiritual awakening as the result of these steps, we tried to carry this message to alcoholics, and to practice these principles in all our affairs."

This step identifies us as a responsible member of society, one who helps others. I used to think service work was relevant only to people in recovery, something I could leave behind once recovery was achieved. We are called upon to be of service whenever and wherever anyone needs help. Thousands of opportunities to serve others exist in and out of our communities, our homes, our hospitals, or while visiting friends and families.

Helping others is what we do to help ourselves stay in the solution and sober. Calling a friend on the telephone is service work. Setting up speaker tables, chairing meetings, or assisting with what we can in and out of our Rooms is service work, and is no less important. When we assist others, we focus on their needs instead of our problems. Instead of isolating, we become part of the community linked by a universal oneness.

Giving money, finding housing, and doing something others should be doing for themselves should first be discussed with a sponsor or trusted friend. It is always okay to say, "Let me speak with my sponsor about that," when we are unsure what to do.

Step Twelve tells us, as we rely on the direction of our Higher Power's most perfect patience and principles, that being of service to others liberates us from selfish desires. Helping others is the cure for feelings of worthlessness and self-pity that continues to haunt us in recovery. The ache of emptiness and uselessness is replaced by fulfillment as we work in the service of others.

TODAY'S MEDITATION

My daily reminder of your everlasting promise of forgiveness, God, propels me into service as I do for others. Trust God, Clean House, and Help Others are the answers to my salvation.

"The purpose of life is not to be happy. It is to be useful, to be honorable, to be compassionate, to have it make some difference that you have lived and lived well." — Ralph Waldo Emerson

FAITH IN THE FACE OF SURRENDER
SEPTEMBER 15

I will never forget the brightness of the beautiful day my husband passed away. He had been struggling to live with cancer. Hospice was here at our home. My denial of what I already knew, made hoping that my love for him, the doctors, their remedies and special medicines, would be enough to keep him in this world.

As I drove to our beautiful lake and collapsed to the floor of the dock in tears, it was here denial left me. What engulfed me was a depth of grief never before experienced. Unable to see through my tears, I threw my arms up to the heavens, as I knew that all bets were off. I surrendered to my own powerlessness.

Pleading would do no good. I surrendered to this realization at a level not felt before. For the first time, I faced my inadequacies with absolute awareness. No matter how hard I had tried, how perfect a wife I had become those last few months, I knew in that moment, my God would not grant him one more second of life. It was over.

Within the hour of my returning home, he left. In that last hour I sang our favorite song, told him how much I loved him, how strong he had been, and I let him go. It's odd how that works. I allowed him to leave me, and he did, as if waiting for my approval. It was his time. My sobriety, my faith in the face of this profound surrender, sustained me then and continues to do so, in the miracles that are my today.

TODAY'S MEDITATION

Thank you, God, for carrying me that frightful day. In times like these I am forever reminded that there is nothing in this world a drink could possibly make better; only You can sustain me.

"Once you have surrendered yourself, you make yourself receptive. In receiving from God, you are perfected and completed." — Fulton J. Sheen

EMOTIONAL SOBRIETY
SEPTEMBER 16

Five years into recovery, I had a difficult month of disappointments. It was clear after sharing in the rooms that I was experiencing a dry drunk. I wasn't drinking, but I veered off the emotionally-sober path feeling lost, and acting restless, irritable, and discontented with everyone and everything. It never occurred to me I was spiritually detached. Without awareness, I had moved into the driver's seat of life again. With an elbow sticking out, I had edged my God out the door.

A renewed dose of humility is all it takes to help get back on track. As we seek advice through prayer before doing anything, we find our solution when we ask who is in charge.

Emotional sobriety has everything to do with humility. By getting out of our way, we feel the security that comes as we change our perspective and pray. We return to our 24-hours and keep our thoughts close enough to grasp. Here, we are safe, assured, hopeful.

Our instructions for living just for today, as found on page 86-88 of the Big Book of *Alcoholics Anonymous* gives us direction. We ask our Higher Power to show us the foothold needed to regain emotional balance while examining our motives throughout the day. Continued prayer shows we are beginning to, once again, grow along spiritual lines. This progress is not perfect by any means, but continual practice and awareness returns us to a position of contentment and peace.

TODAY'S MEDITATION
I'm grateful to recognize the rut of emotional backsliding today. As I remember the answer to fear is faith, I lean on the promise of my God's love for me.

"If we examine every disturbance we have, great or small, we will find at the root of it some unhealthy dependence and its consequent demand. Let us, with God's help, continually surrender these hobbling demands. Then we can be set free to live and love: we may then be able to gain emotional sobriety." — Bill Wilson

BEING GENTLE WITH OUR WORDS
SEPTEMBER 17

As a child, my mother would implore me to think before I spoke because once spoken, words can become a permanent affront, not just to another, but also to our higher-self.

Recovery teaches us to take what we need to hear and leave the rest. Most often, what people say has nothing to do with us. Knowing this reminds us just how little we need to take anything personally.

Since we are not responsible for what others say, only for how we receive what they say, the important lesson is to control what we can, and that is the words that come out of our mouths. A.A. teach us how to speak from a place of kindness rather than self-righteous arrogance.

Remembering this journey is practice, not perfection, we continue to think before we speak and work to let our knee-jerk retaliations go. As we pause, we allow ourselves time to observe our motives for speaking, making sure our opinion was asked for. Being gentle with our words becomes easier over time. Our attention to this practice allows us to not take anything personally. We ask ourselves, "How do I want to be heard?"

We have an obligation to ourselves and others to speak from a place of compassion and integrity. In delivering only direct and kind feedback, we become trustworthy. What is important is the delivery of our language of the heart, and that we do it gently and with sincerity.

TODAY'S MEDITATION
I must be responsible for my words today, that they reflect to others what my God would have me say. Anything else is old behavior.

"Wherever there is a human being, there is an opportunity for a kindness."
— *Lucius Annaeus Seneca*

WALKING THROUGH GRIEF
SEPTEMBER 18

On a spiritual retreat, I was exposed to lessons in mourning. I was instructed to allow myself to feel whatever was there without prodding, manipulating, or apprehension. Eyes closed, I suspended thoughts and with an open heart, gave myself permission to embrace whatever came forth, letting the feelings be what they were, not judging them as good or bad. What came were deep feelings of loss and separation, and an appreciation of the lessons grief taught me previously.

Losing a child is a reminder to stay in the present, watching emotions go as tears flow. I allow pain to just be what it is. My tears represent the years we'll spend together one day, while in the present, I find gratitude for the gift of time we had together.

In our pain and grief, we must strive to live the rest of our life for the highest good which is where energy to recreate ourselves lives. We begin to experience joy right where we are. Grief, like laughter, is the elixir that fuels our compassionate selves. Tears honor loved ones, but laughter balances the soul and allows others to see how to face their demons and find peace.

Peace washes away fear and, in its place, shines a mountain of everlasting faith.

In our grief, we are sure a return to addictive activity must never be an option. It does not heal us. It hides the source of our pain and restarts our disease which, under these and other circumstances, controls us with a vengeance.

Acceptance of our loss frees light, illuminating our spirit as we connect with the grace needed to walk through and release our grief.

TODAY'S MEDITATION
Although I cannot see you who are now lost through death, your spirit assures me you are never far away. In prayer, I promise you will never be forgotten, but I will go on. This is all I need to know.

"I realized that grief is metabolic: it crawls through you like a disease and takes your energy away. Then it gathers and hits like a sudden migraine, like being hit by a car, like having a large, flat rock hurled at your chest." — Laurie Colwin

HOPE FOR A NEW WAY OF LIVING
SEPTEMBER 19

Growing up, I told myself I must be a loser because my parents said I was. I heard I would never amount to anything because that is what I remembered when I went to sleep at night. I made the connection right then that my parents' unhappiness was all my fault. I was filled with guilt and shame.

Alcohol and other drugs were my solution and, as if in a dream, I watched myself act out in ways I wouldn't have thought possible. The more I drank the closer to destruction I came in my unconscious quest to self-destruct. I was determined to prove my parents right.

When I reached out in my darkest hour, recovery was there for me. A soothing haven of hope encouraged me to trust a new way of life with others. Armed with friends who applauded my successes and, with the help of a Higher Power, my life and my story changed.

Today I no longer resemble that pitiful victim who walked into the rooms of recovery long ago. I no longer hear the voices that told me I was nothing. My life is a miracle, an example of strength, love, and truth as I trust my faith for a new way of living.

TODAY'S MEDITATION

I am so grateful to be convinced that since The Steps work for me; they can also work for you, if you are willing to work for them.

"Rarely have we seen a person fail who has thoroughly followed our path..."
— *Alcoholics Anonymous*

HURT PEOPLE, HURT PEOPLE
SEPTEMBER 20

I don't know anyone eager to admit wrongdoing, especially when those wrongs inflicted pain on a so-called loved one. Oftentimes it is our pride that is most affected—it shocks and humbles us that we have turned love into a weapon.

The Steps soothe the flame of raging defiance and hostility, overcoming our natural resistance to trust anything at all. We work The Steps because we suffer from sinking guilt and suffocating shame. Hurt people, hurt people. We work them because, by now, we're ready to see, and own, the harm we caused others. We work them because the knowledge of our indiscretions has been too much for us to bear. Trusted friends remind us that since we know better now, we have an obligation to ourselves to *be* better. In this our choice is clear.

Freedom from the bondage of self is what we're after. Having worked The Steps, our insides match our outsides. We move forward with the same intensity with which we used to secure our next drink or drug, but we move forward with a gentle awareness of the needs and feelings of those around us.

We are responsible, and remember the lengths we agreed to go to experience life-saving miracles of recovery. Engaged with our Higher Power, we seek a personal co-creation. With courage to do the work, we absorb life's serene blessings. As our hurt leaves us, the need to hurt others does too. Another miracle of recovery happens as we wake up without revenge on our mind.

TODAY'S MEDITATION
Thank you, God, for the honor and grace it takes to continue to make amends. I've come too far now, to turn back.

"The deepest wounds aren't the ones we get from other people hurting us. They are the wounds we give ourselves when we hurt other people."
— Isobelle Carmody

INTEGRITY
SEPTEMBER 21

Of all the attributes I wish to exemplify, integrity is the most important. With years of abhorrent behavior and a reputation for dishonesty, integrity represents everything I've always dreamt of, but never believed I could achieve. I had no grounding, no guts, no truth, only a codependent need to please others.

Integrity is a state of being whole, of being a person of good moral character, one who doesn't waiver. We earn self-respect and integrity by examining our motives at every turn. With our Higher Power, we explore our actions and intentions under a moral microscope and ask: does what we expect to do or say pass the test of being honest? Will it serve the greater good? Is it built of strong enough moral material to stand against all assaults?

If the answer to these questions is yes, then the planned course of action meets the definition of integrity with dignity and grace that is steeped in humility, because we've done the footwork.

Our Higher Power knows when we do the right thing for the wrong, selfish reason, the act is still wrong. Only when we see through the eyes of integrity, and examine our motives using our Higher Power as a measure of truth, are we sure we are right.

TODAY'S MEDITATION

I am grateful to have found an integrity that is not situational, nor swayed by compromise. With the guidance of my Higher Power, my integrity allows me to build a recreated life on solid rock, not sand.

"To give real service you must add something which cannot be bought or measured with money, and that is sincerity and integrity." — *Douglas Adams*

IF I AM NOT THE PROBLEM...
SEPTEMBER 22

A beloved long-time member of our fellowship died several years ago, but because he shared his cherished gift of sobriety with thousands, his testimony lives on today. Indelible and heartfelt his mantra remains with us, "If I am not the problem there is no solution."

Upon hearing this the first time, I remember I asked to have it repeated so I could grasp the meaning. I was told regardless of the situation, when I am disturbed, the problem is me! I could no longer blame anyone or anything for my own discomfort. Regardless of the facts, or other people involved, the only hope for change began and ended, with me.

To have reminders such as this that keep pointing to the answer is a great comfort. The reminder, *if I am not the problem,* combined with a sincere desire to see my reaction in a situation realistically, helps to keep things honest and simple. I can't blame the rain, my boss, my spouse, or anything or anyone else for *my* discomfort, for my problems. It belongs to me and I am the only one who can fix it.

I am grateful to be the solution today. As such, I get to choose and control how I perceive the problem. Since the problem is within me, I get to apply whatever step is necessary: make amends, let go, and practice Steps Ten, Eleven and Twelve. *Trust God, Clean House, and Help Others.*

TODAY'S MEDITATION
Dear God, please help me remember to keep the focus of change on me. The only hope I have to improve my life is by recognizing I am *both* the problem and the solution.

"You are the community now. Be a lamp for yourselves. Be your own refuge. Seek for no other. All things must pass. Strive on diligently. Don't give up."
— Gautama Buddha

LEARNING TO NOT SUFFER
SEPTEMBER 23

A woman named Sorrow was a born sufferer. She was pathetic with her constant cries of misery and negativity. She often found it hard to put one foot in front of the other. In recovery meetings, it felt like all we talked about was her suffering!

During one meeting, Sorrow revealed her misfortune of the day. After, a woman approached her and suggested that every time she heard herself whine, Sorrow should take her notebook and write the question, "What Choices Do I Have?" At first, Sorrow looked stunned, saying, "That's nonsense! What choice do I have?" Still, she accepted the suggestion, discussing it with her sponsor. The moment she complained, her friends held up a little sign that said, "What Choice Do I Have?"

Her sponsor told her to get down from the cross, "We need the wood." It wasn't long before Sorrow got the message and changed her approach to life's problems. She found a solution she could share with others. Over time she learned that suffering was optional and, so was the way she changed perspective. It wasn't long before friends put their signs away. Sorrow echoed the encouraging suggestions and support given by others, smiling and laughing as she shared. What she gave them was her experience and gratitude in learning to not suffer.

What she had learned was that happiness is an inside job. It is our choice to change or shrivel up and die.

TODAY'S MEDITATION

I'm grateful for people like Sorrow, who taught me how powerful we are when we make choices to change attitudes and move forward helping others to do the same.

"Well, child, you may do whatever you like with your suffering," ... "It belongs to you...I grasp it by the small hairs, I cast it to the ground, and I grind it under the heel of my boot. I suggest you learn to do the same." — Elizabeth Gilbert

THE NEED FOR SPEED
SEPTEMBER 24

Most days we get up and hit the floor running. In our minds, we're already obsessing about task number three. How do we become efficient at juggling, switching dates, commitments, kids, camps, cars, work, babysitters? And where's the money for all the things on our must-do list?

Many of us come into recovery exhausted and guilt-ridden, overwhelmed by the belief we are in charge and bear responsibility for everything imaginable. In recovery we are told to *Take it Easy*, or *Easy Does it*. We hear it is okay to take a deep breath, to eat, to sleep. Sponsors say, "You're just not that important," and newcomers ask "What does *any* of this have to do with our addictions?"

Absolutely everything.

We learn in our rooms of recovery how to change our obsessive behaviors one day at a time. We are reminded to slow down. Take a break. Take a nap. Then slow down again. Just because our mind is racing, doesn't mean *we* have to. And when we slow down, our mind follows.

Nothing is important other than adjusting to this new world of sober and slow. If we don't trim our sails, slow down, and learn to pick our battles, then we get what we always got: more out-of-control insanity, and a must-do list that drives us there.

TODAY'S MEDITATION
Just for today I will remember to pause, take a deep breath and ask, "How important is it?" Then I will do the same thing again, each time a must-do insists I pick up the pace.

"The road to recovery will not always be easy, but I will take it one day at a time, focusing on the moments I've dreamed about for so long. "— Amanda Lindhout

PROCRASTINATION
SEPTEMBER 25

I used to live by the motto, "I'll do it tomorrow." Needless to say, day-after-day, that "tomorrow" never comes. My inaction says that nothing is important enough to do in the moment, and that everything can wait. I remained listless, unfocused, without a sense of purpose in my life.

Procrastination devours all hope of forward motion and strips us of healthy self-esteem that comes with accomplishing things, and so we stay stuck. Balance, and the proof that we can improve our lives insists that we get up and practice active-doing.

It's as simple as that. To cure procrastination, we must do something. We don't have to like it. We don't even have to *want* to do it. Our Higher Power gives us the grace to move and we must. Not all at once. A little at a time is fine. Sometimes the fear of falling short of perfection is enough to keep us immobilized.

Easy Does it, But Do It. We must do enough to change our mistaken beliefs that have commanded our thoughts with, "we can let things go indefinitely."

Like it or not, we do it anyway. When we do, we get to feel emotional satisfaction and experience a sense of empowerment and accomplishment. Some of us make lists of what must be done today and in the next column we ask, "How important is it?"

We deserve to make choices on where and how we need to act. We also deserve to *Take it Easy,* remaining in balance even as we move forward.

TODAY'S MEDITATION
I am grateful that, although my inclination is to procrastinate and let things slide, with strength from my Higher Power I can dust myself off, pick myself up and take appropriate action. This is recovery at work.

"Amateurs sit and wait for inspiration, the rest of us just get up and go to work."
— *Stephen King*

SHAME

SEPTEMBER 26

Way down deep in the soul of so many of us, lie hidden the wounds of shame. Shame screams to convince us we are something we are not. It remains a loud voice in our heads, making sure we still believe the lie, "You really *are* good for nothing!"

The voice insists we are defective, delivering its punch to our core time and time again. Belief in the truthfulness of that inner critical voice is so entrenched that, for some of us, it serves as a wall that separates us from others, tells us we don't belong, that we don't deserve to be a part-of anything. Shame is the excuse to hate ourselves for who we think we are: losers, damaged beyond repair.

The good news is no matter how deep, how rehearsed, or how strong the messages of shame are, we have, within us, the ability to defy shame. Sometimes it takes help from trusted professionals. It takes great courage and the guidance of our Higher Power to shatter lies that bind us to a life of resignation, self-sabotage, and failure.

Our Higher Power gives us an abundance of intuition and survival skills, among them the ability to examine what-is critically empowering within us. When was the last time we challenged ourselves to look at shame for what it is? If we're honest, we must admit that, thanks to recovery, we are no longer the same person we once were, one absorbed in self-pity and negativity, one drowning in shame.

There is hope as soon as we recognize that change is within reach. Re-creating our life without shame requires us to embrace positivity and use it against the negative messages we have lived with for so long. With practice, shame is replaced by truth and honor. This change in perception deepens our faith.

That faith walks with us, assuring us that we deserve emotional freedom. We now have a heart convinced shame was nothing but a story we heard and believed. Today we are strong enough to let shame go, once and for all.

TODAY'S MEDITATION

Dear God, I am filled with a newfound love of self. I understand that with your help I am the creator of my story. As the originator, author. and main character, I get to choose my truth. Free from ties that once bound me to shame, I walk in your light.

"Today I am strong and with God I can be free. Today I will not be a victim."
— *Sammie F.*

TRUSTING THE PROCESS, ONE DAY AT A TIME
SEPTEMBER 27

During a prayer and meditation session, I thanked my Higher Power for allowing me to trust my life right this moment.

Even though we do not know what an hour from now will bring, we embrace blind trust in a power we cannot see or understand. Our soul is anchored, steadfast in a knowing that says regardless of the outcome, our Higher Power will get us through, whatever we face.

We become so confident in this thinking we accept that no matter what a situation brings, two universal truths will always prevail, if our Higher Power brings us to it, He will get us through it; and, if a situation was supposed to be different, it would be.

We no longer need to obsess, manipulate, and control, driving ourselves and others around us insane, as we try to influence what *we* think an outcome should be. This letting go is not easy. Some of us are convinced we know better than anyone else, including our Higher Power, and persist in this delusion. Those who learn this lesson come to trust this moment, to understand, we are where we're supposed to be. Our job is to trust the process of our unfolding as we are the ones being affected.

As we trust the process of living and breathing in this moment, awareness gives enough light to allow us to continue on this path in peace. Regardless of distractions, we are being led. Trusting the process is the easier, softer way.

We, *Let go and Let God.*

TODAY'S MEDITATION
God, you are my first example of real trust. Today, I trust my life in your hands.

"The more you go with the flow of life and surrender the outcome to God, and the less you seek constant clarity, the more you will find that fabulous things start to show up in your life." — Mandy Hale

VICTIM VS. MARTYR
SEPTEMBER 28

Some of us wake up realizing that in this play that is life, we have been cast in roles we never asked for. The roles we play are those of the victim, or the martyr.

The martyr is often the source of their own suffering, which grows out of a need to champion an idea, a person; to stand up for something. They never drop their torch of martyrdom, hoping someday recognition and adoration will fall upon them. The loyalty of others is demanded, sometimes accompanied by forceful threats.

Plagued by low self-esteem and narcissism, nothing is ever enough for the martyr when they can tie their demands to a worthy cause. They expect constant acceptance and a pledge of allegiance to no one but them. The martyr exerts complete control regardless of what is being asked of them and takes no responsibility for the behavior others exhibit in the service of the cause, or for their own. They don't have to because they govern from a place of self-proclaimed perfection and authority. In their eyes, they are never wrong. They hide their narcissism behind noble goals.

The victim arises from a place of indifferent ignorance. All they know for sure is that they are being picked on, and nothing is their fault. Scared and timid, they've painted themselves in this role for so long they believe nothing else. Often from dysfunctional families, the victim has embraced the idea that others will always push them around while blaming them for anything that goes wrong. Where martyrs command absolute conformity and obedience, victims are entirely passive, defeated before making any effort. Victims adhere to the adage of the three D's: *Don't talk, Don't Feel, Don't Tell.*

Whether we are martyr or victim, recovery is our last hope. We never knew we had the courage to change until we walked into our rooms. We never knew that by opening the door to willingness we would see similarities between our stories and those of others in recovery and that our lives, too, could miraculously change.

We *can* change and forever leave behind the martyr and the victim. It happens in recovery; it can happen for you too. We only have to keep coming back until our miracle happens, and it will, but only if you want it more than anything else.

"The difference between a professional victim and an empowered person is NOT what has happened to them, but the way in which they REACT to what has happened to them." — *Miya Yamanouchi*

WAITING FOR OUR TOMORROWS
SEPTEMBER 29

Looking back over time, I wonder how many times I deferred doing anything at all for another day. My mantra, "I'll do that when *this* happens," became justification for a myriad of personal failures. One by one, the list of failures just kept growing and growing.

I'm beginning now to shift my thinking to the importance of doing. During my years as the great procrastinator, I had no insight, knowledge, or inclination to change my perspective. I was satisfied just existing.

Today I see value in *not* waiting for life to happen, not when I can seize the moment now. Living means making a difference right where I am: here and now, doing what is in front of me to do. This gives me purpose as my intentions are validated and I watch them come to pass. I do something.

The positive energy created in forward motion engenders positive thinking. Our self-esteem rises each time we embrace the power of now as we take care of today, what we used to put off for tomorrow. We swell with earned accomplishment having participated in life today!

There is no power, no energy in our tomorrows, only the dead-end realization that procrastination leads to more of the same.

So, why not today?

TODAY'S MEDITATION
God, I don't want to lie on a gurney to see life as nothing more than days lost, dreaming about a tomorrow that never came. My tomorrow is today, right now. Now is all there is.

"A good plan today is better than a perfect plan tomorrow.
Don't wait for an inspired ending to come to mind. Work your way
to the ending and see what comes up. "— Andy Weir

DETACHING WITH LOVE
FROM OUR ADULT CHILDREN
SEPTEMBER 30

One of the most painful events life presents for some of us is to detach from our struggling adult children with love. The thought of not engaging on any level is enough to thrust the knife of betrayal into our hearts. It feels abnormal. It feels like we're dying inside, it feels, it feels, it feels.

Similar to those of us who have walked into recovery for the first time carrying a favorite addiction, we must detach from the problem and behaviors that come with it. We detach because we have no choice. We do it because we concede our life must, often for the first time come first, or we will continue to watch our own lives spin out of control. Most of all, we detach with love because we understand that until we do, we enable delusional thinking that comes from the ego. It says something that we do holds the needed magic to change someone else, and that's the greatest misconception of all. Changing ourselves is hard enough!

Until we accept we are the only problem we can fix we will struggle to manage a life that is not our own. A step back into our breath gives us the space necessary to see that to *not* detach is as dangerous and troublesome for us as our child's behavior.

Detaching means we understand that we've reconciled few answers for ourselves, let alone our children. We accept that our children belong to a Higher Power who helps those who help themselves. Regardless of how hard or long our journey is of sacrifice and care, detaching with love is the kindest, most mature act of unselfish, enduring love we can give.

Will detaching guarantee that our children will take responsibility and stop abhorrent behaviors? It's not our business.

Will it mean our children will stop loving us? No. It means their personal journey is no longer about us and hasn't been for a long time. Detaching from our children is about *their* self-reliance and allowing them to find freedom from their demons and to crawl up out of the cave of darkness into the light of hope. We relinquish authority and allow our adult children to find their way according to their dreams and desires, regardless of how we feel.

Detaching with love from our children isn't easy. But allowing them autonomy without strings is often the missing link to the self-confidence and self-respect they seek as they look to find their own truth and to change their behaviors. We've done our job for eighteen years or more. As we love them from a distance, we make their job of becoming accountable easier. Through detaching with love, a new-found respect for each other begins.

TODAY'S MEDITATION

Just like parents whose children go off to war, I practice detaching with love. I remember the quality of my life depends upon how well I can do so and stay out of God's way.

"When you realize it's not personal, there is no longer
a compulsion to react as if it were." — Eckhart Tolle

GETTING RID OF ANGER
OCTOBER 1

Have you ever been so upset you felt anger pulse through your body? Anger is a poison that ravages us when we lose control.

Before reaching full-blown anger, we experience bothersome resentments. We claim to have let them go, but as the irritations mount up, resentment is triggered again and again. Our brain acts like a computer, filing the resentments for future attention. We minimize, discount, or pretend we don't care, but we keep track subconsciously. We think each incident is forgotten but as we are bombarded with new irritations throughout the day, our brain runs out of filing space. The next small irritation becomes the trigger to explosive anger.

In recovery, we know we have to diffuse this hurtful emotion as it has the power to destroy our hard-fought serenity and sobriety. Anger must not be ignored.

What can we do to eradicate this lethal emotion? We first must ask, "What was our part in it?" Intentional focus on ourselves helps to soothe a raging ego. Prayer, meditation, or discussion with a trusted friend help bring about a calm and thoughtful resolution. We seek to rid ourselves of self-righteousness and stubborn pride as we ask for the forgiveness of others after forgiving ourselves.

As we let go of anger, what appears in its place is often the beginning of a spiritual awakening. We thank our Higher Power for showing us the way to peace.

TODAY'S MEDITATION

Today I will open myself to the solution instead of rage. As I breathe in peace and breathe out anger, I commit my anger to God and surrender my self-knowledge to humility.

"Holding anger is a poison...It eats you from inside...We think that by hating someone we hurt them...But hatred is a curved blade...and the harm we do to others...we also do to ourselves." — Mitch Albom

ACCEPTING WHAT-IS
OCTOBER 2

When we carry dissatisfaction because we want to change someone or something to suit our way of thinking, we have two choices. We can become aggravated and controlling as we work our one-person crusade, manipulating and coercing others to see our point of view. Or, we can choose acceptance of what is.

Acceptance is the easier, softer way. As we practice acceptance, we experience organic changes within us. Our blood pressure decreases. We assume a posture of humility as we ask our Higher Power for acceptance. Our general sense of well-being increases as more emphasis is directed to living in the moment, than in trying to change our world and the people in it. Stress leaves us, and breathing becomes easier.

We quit fighting everyone and everything and practice the mantra of *Live and Let Live*.

As we practice loving acceptance of others without judgment, we allow them to think and believe what, and how, they want. We are no longer the judge or jury for anyone but ourselves. This simple exercise protects our precious gift of serenity and helps those around us to maintain theirs.

TODAY'S MEDITATION
I'm grateful that when I'm able to keep the focus on me, I'm can accept what is, just for today.

"Because one believes in oneself, one doesn't try to convince others. Because one is content with oneself, one doesn't need others' approval. Because one accepts oneself, the whole world accepts him or her." — Lao Tzu

CHANGING OTHERS
OCTOBER 3

Shortly after high school I fell in love with a man who had just returned from the Vietnam War. I was happy and within weeks; we were inseparable. He was my ticket out of a troubled home.

A pattern began to emerge when we would go to his parents' homes, or to parties. I would sit, ignored, as he watched sports, kicking back and drinking beer with his friends. At these gatherings, which increased in frequency to several times a week, I was constantly ignored. Drinking made him detached, volatile, and on one occasion, I was slapped for pushing him to leave. After months of being together, I recognized he had become physically abusive. But I loved him and felt sure he would change if I just backed off.

I was sure when he got a job there would be less pressure.

If I could only get him to stay away from bars, we would be much happier.

The harder I tried, the more violent he became. Finally, he beat and raped me proclaiming, "There is plenty more where that came from."

After days off being depressed and crying uncontrollably, I said, "I'll show you. I'll kill me." I opened a bottle of aspirin and took them all. My girl-friends in the other room, rushed me to the hospital. I promised never to be with him again; and I never did, although I remained heartbroken.

It wasn't until many years later in recovery that I accepted my lack of power to change anyone. Not love, not money, nor an overwhelming need to believe, "if only...," had the power to make a difference. Change never happens unless and until the abuser decides there is a need to change. My walking away was the greatest change I could have made.

When I came to understand that truth I focused on myself and knew then, that walking away was the greatest change I could have made. Change begins and ends with me and my Higher Power who makes everything possible if it is His Will.

"You can change yourself and you can change the situation but you absolutely cannot change other people. Only they can do that." — Joanna Trollope

CONTROLLING EXPECTATIONS
OCTOBER 4

As a child I believed expectations were supposed to be met. Among those expectations was the certainty that adults must be listened to without question, children were to be seen and not heard, that Christmas meant lots of presents, and parents stayed together, forever. Over time, it became apparent that an expectation, whether good or bad, was a resentment waiting to happen as life so rarely unfolded in the manner and time I felt it should.

Now that we know better, we can do better. No longer does a satisfactory day require that our expectations be met. We are well aware that depending on unmet expectations can send us into a tailspin of morbid thinking, and paranoid reactions that sometimes follow as we wonder why others have failed us so badly.

We find success when we take life one moment at a time. Recovery helps us to learn how not to have expectations of others. When we accept a situation or person without expectation of change, our world seems harmonious and we are content.

As we become a fascinated observer of everything around us and practice loving detachment from our own thinking, we find a balance necessary to focus on what's important: our faith, our serenity, and ourselves.

TODAY'S MEDITATION
Just for this moment I focus on letting go of expectations. I will let these 24-hours unfold without any preconceived notions of what that time should look or feel like.

"Expectations were like fine pottery. The harder you held them, the more likely they were to crack." — Brandon Sanderson

Emotional Maturity
October 5

We hear it said that we see in others, either the qualities of a person we want to become, or the characteristics we dislike in ourselves.

In recovery, we learn we are as emotionally mature as the age we began our addiction. We look critically at the self we should have long ago outgrown. Maybe we are too jealous, too fearful, or too angry. Some emotional pitfalls that continue to entrap us are the Seven Deadly Sins of lust, gluttony, greed, sloth, anger, envy, and pride.

Very early in the rooms of recovery we hear that any change must begin with us. As we reconciled with our Higher Power the character defects and sins that fueled our addiction we opened our hearts to accept the love already within us.

Our Steps provide the courage to change what we know are unacceptable actions. Hurtful and child-like behaviors undermine and prevent us from being who we deserve to be. We work hard to communicate maturity and exactness as we speak from a place of love and tolerance, not self-centered fear.

Owning past mistakes, we list our emotional shortcomings, bringing them into the light. We talk to a trusted servant or sponsor and then ask ourselves, do we need these pitfalls in our life today? Do they add love and wisdom and help us get to the person we want to become?

These questions and the way we answer them are our test of emotional maturity.

TODAY'S MEDITATION

Thank you, God, for my journey in emotional maturity and for the courage to walk through unimaginable pain with grace and dignity, free of addictions.

"Maturity is the capacity to withstand ego-destroying experiences, and not lose one's perspective in the ego-building experiences." — Robert K. Greenleaf

FAITH IN THE LIGHT IN THE STORM
OCTOBER 6

Our literature says that deep within every human being, regardless of their belief, is a fundamental idea of God. We wonder how it is upon awakening we're still breathing; then realize when it is our time to die, life is not extended for one more nanosecond, regardless of man's superior technological insights.

Although never labeled a prayer, the staunch agnostic or atheist has murmured the wish for something beyond human ability to bring safety, peace, physical or mental salvation. In our darkest, most desperate hours many of us, with or without faith, cry out in hopelessness, begging for just one life-altering miracle. We are humbled, terrified by the realization we are unable to change a situation. Concessions, heartfelt promises, and appeals are made to a force unseen for mercy. "Just this one time..."

Some have spiritual encounters so profound they confirm there is a reason to have faith in a light that glimmers even in the midst of the storm.

We have no answers, nor power to understand what is not to be understood, but we have the option to believe. A sustaining faith, one without fear, allows us to breathe in the here and now with the assurance that this is all we need to know.

TODAY'S MEDITATION

Today in gratitude, I trust a power I call God to guide me now, and in my times of greatest need.

"Faith is not simply a patience that passively suffers until the storm is past. Rather, it is a spirit that bears things - with resignations, yes, but above all, with blazing, serene hope." — Corazon Aquino

Fear of Emotional Pain
October 7

I have never been comfortable with emotional pain. I thought one of two things would happen if I allowed myself to feel emotional pain. Either I would die from the enormity of it, or I would never stop crying once I had allowed myself to start. Active addiction helped me to *not* feel the pain, to withhold my tears.

In order to overcome and heal from addictive behaviors, and to replace them with new ways of coping with emotional pain, recovery is necessary.

We can no longer shield ourselves from emotional pain, which is a component of a life lived with awareness. In addiction we numb ourselves to emotional pain, but in sobriety that is not an option.

Emotional pain is the door to emotional maturity. As we give ourselves permission to feel, we begin to understand and make sense of our pain. We determine what is necessary for our journey, and what has been a mirage all this time. Journaling and talking with friends and professionals help to diffuse the pain.

The good news is that never again do we have to face anything alone if we don't want to. As it becomes obvious to us that no one has ever died from their feelings, the fellowship and a loving sponsor can show us how to be okay with whatever we are feeling. Prayer and meditation provide a grounding stability that allows us to embrace all we are, certain we are now strong enough to feel every feeling.

Today, with choices, we come to terms with life's emotional turbulence that everyone experiences, and determine how best to respond. No longer do we fear pain but accept it as a door to walk through to enlightenment.

TODAY'S MEDITATION
I am grateful for the courage to face my pain today. Through the process of letting go, I continue to become stronger in courage.

There is no birth of consciousness without pain. — Carl Jung

HUMILITY IN ACTION
OCTOBER 8

Getting out of ourselves to help others is a big demonstration of humility in action. Humility in action is the attitude that brings us closer to our Higher Power; one of our greatest achievements of all. What a miracle it is to experience co-creation with our Higher Power through the practice of humility.

Those in recovery have a yearning to experience humility's freedom from pride and arrogance, especially after years of overblown faith in ourselves alone. As we move forward in The Steps, we are given examples of humility in action.

The principles that accompanies each of the twelve steps, demonstrates humility appropriate for that Step.

Surrender in Step One admits to powerlessness and unmanageability.

As we come to believe in Step Two, *Hope* is built upon the humility of acceptance that there could be something greater than ourselves, and we are not it.

Willingness in Step Three, moves us forward as we turn our will and life over to the care of a Higher Power, an exercise we practice many times throughout our day.

Step Four offers *courage* as we forge a fearless and moral inventory of ourselves. Courage enables us to accept all that is dark in that inventory, opening the door to see the role we played in in our hurtful interactions with people, places, and institutions.

Honesty and Integrity in Step Five, is humility in action as we share with our Higher Power and another person the exact nature of our wrongs.

Willingness is strengthened by humility, giving us the attitude necessary in Step Six to become ready to have our defects removed.

Humility comes to bear in Step Seven as we humbly pray to have these defects removed.

We practice *action* in Step Eight as we prepare a list of those people harmed and become ready to make amends. Humility makes it possible to confess the wrongs we have committed.

The first eight Steps have all relied on humility as we are now ready to move *forgiveness* of ourselves and others into our hearts and make the amends required of us in Step Nine.

Vigilance presides over the maintenance Steps of Ten, Eleven, and Twelve as we work to achieve a 24-hour reprieve against our addictions based upon the maintenance of our spiritual condition. The virtues of acceptance, attunement and service, pave our way, but it is humility that reminds us of the necessity to *trust God, clean house and help others* on this spiritual and life-changing walk.

TODAY'S MEDITATION

I realize I've been practicing humility all along as I work The Steps. I am comforted to be a part of the solution instead of the problem.

"Humility must accompany all our actions, must be with us everywhere;
for as soon as we glory in our good works they are of no further value to our
advancement in virtue. " — Augustine of Hippo

THE THREE "I"S
OCTOBER 9

For those of us in addiction, there are unnegotiable truths that prevail. The Three "I's," are among the most important; they name behaviors that, unchecked, can lead to death.

Isolate. This sets the stage for paranoia and the acceptance of all kinds of falsehoods and fears resulting in a life devoid of hope. Isolation can be the beginning of a downward spiral in where depression and delusional thinking take root. Cut off from others, we see ourselves as a victim, a loser. We prefer to disconnect from those who love us. Although we may not yet be back in active addiction, we quit going to meetings. Interaction with others comes to a halt.

Insulate, is a secondary layer to isolation. We sink into our self-imposed prison of "poor-me," and find comfort in keeping friends and family as far away as possible. Removed now from the world, we begin to believe our paranoid thoughts and become entrenched in self-pity. We protect our privacy and our misery at all costs. The outcome is obvious.

Intoxicate. Now completely withdrawn into ourselves, our thinking obliterates hope. This self-induced insanity says there is no way out of our pain. We are hopeless here, ready to surrender absolutely, a slave to our addictions. As sick perceptions cause inevitable physical and emotional pain, we are defenseless against a first drink which for many, leads to the last.

For us, to drink is to die.

TODAY'S MEDITATION
Life's terms can be too difficult to overcome alone. I must never forget recovery is a "we" program. Together, *we* stay alive, clean and sober. Alone, we invite death.

"The only reason for me to pick up a drink again would be to commit suicide--that's what alcohol is to me--a lethal weapon. . So, I stick with the winners and work The Steps to keep myself spiritually fit to deal with life on life's terms."
— Pat H.

LETTING GO

OCTOBER 10

During meditation I realize, with bittersweet reflection, the anniversary of my daughter's death is near. Like millions of others who have lost loved ones, it is now my time to let go of sorrow yet again. Still, my thoughts transport me to her. As seconds, minutes, hours, and days of our time together consume my thoughts, those memories compel emotions and as if on cue, a tsunami of tears overwhelms me. I grieve once more, even as I recognize the need to let go.

It's not the number of intervening days that soothe the emptiness and make still the cries from my raging soul. Rather, it is the space created by her absence that must now be filled with the healing balm of acceptance. Life teaches us that woven with the joys of engaging with others, is the heartache of letting go of the pain experienced in losing those we love.

Letting go of that sorrow creates an open space in our heart. So vast is that space, so surreal is the wound, we become free from the insignificance of life as there is nothing that compares with this horrific, yet redeemable feeling of loss. Memories of loved ones gone before us still hold their place, but sorrow now, becomes tempered with unconditional faith, acceptance and enduring love.

TODAY'S MEDITATION
My falling tears signify an unending ache of profound loss. Rather than turn the other way, I open my heart as tears dissolve my sorrow in the space God has created called *love without end*.

"There is a sacredness in tears. They are not the mark of weakness, but of power. They speak more eloquently than ten thousand tongues. They are the messengers of overwhelming grief, of deep contrition, and of unspeakable love."
— *Washington Irving*

LONELINESS VS. BEING ALONE
OCTOBER 11

Without even knowing, I developed a snug comfortableness in isolation, but there was always an undercurrent of fear. I knew that in isolation I was hiding from something. That something was the feeling that I never belonged. When I was with others, it was as if there was an umbrella of inadequacy that hovered over me. I was apart from others no matter where I went. So, I developed a set of messages that protected me in my isolation and I grew to feel safer alone than in a group.

I was safe because you didn't know the thoughts that kept me from you. Sure, I wanted to be accepted and loved, but was terrified of being rejected. I told myself if you knew the real me that is what you would have done. Inside, I was desperately lonely.

In learning to differentiate being alone from being lonely, we find we can be alone but not lonely, if alone is what we want to be. We concede that while loneliness causes emotional pain, recovery gives us the amazing power to change our thinking and action.

As we engage others and their needs, we cease to be a victim of loneliness. Our ability to care about something or someone other than ourselves lifts us out of that dark pit of loneliness. Prayer and meditation help to reduce the feeling of loneliness as we remember we are no longer alone. We realize in amazed honesty the Ninth Step Promise that says, "That feeling of uselessness and self-pity will slip away," has come true for us. When we choose now to be alone, we are no longer lonely, just alone.

TODAY'S MEDITATION

God, when I focus on loving thoughts and apply them with you, I am everything I need to be right this moment. With your encouragement, I help others and when I am alone it is by choice. I can be alone, but never have to feel lonely again because I have you.

"...alkies are tortured by loneliness. Even before our drinking got bad and people began to cut us off, nearly all of us suffered the feeling that we didn't quite belong." — As Bill Sees It, page 909

Never Go Back

October 12

Early in recovery life's twists and turns, what became obvious to me is that regardless of what happens in my life, I made a conscious decision that, "I can never go backward." I watch with sorrow, what happens to others when they chose to try some controlled drinking or switched to drugs. Many never make it back and, if they did, they tell how hard it is to accept their addiction and a half-hearted need to begin all over again.

I realize, wholeheartedly, that of myself, I have no power to prevent a slide back into old behaviors.

Recovery instills the humbling truth that our job is to do the next right thing in front of us. Not next week or a month from now but just for today. Work, pray, help others, clean house; these are *our* responsibilities. We rest in blissful satisfaction that there is no reason for us to go back when we do our part because we are convinced sobriety is the easier-softer way of living. We ask our Higher Power to take care of the rest of our life.

The Ninth Step Promises will continue to come true for us. Not all at once. Some come to fruition more quickly than others. But as we stay the course, thoughts, actions, motives, and answers become obvious. We remember we've been given a 24-hour reprieve based upon the maintenance of our spiritual condition. As we continue to seek His guidance and ask in prayer every day what His will is for us, more is constantly revealed.

We know too much about ourselves in recovery today to go back out. Turning around cannot be an option. We've come too far and worked too hard! Most of all, for the first time in our life, we feel certain we *deserve* what we have achieved: peace, serenity and respect from our fellows.

We help others and contribute in ways that bring us assurances of usefulness and strong self-esteem.

Most of all, we know that to use would take us right back to where our insanity began, with that first drink. Our responsibility is to think the addiction through to the other side – to the pain and degradation as we remember, that *This Too, Shall Pass*, because everything does if we let it.

"Don't go backwards, you've already been there." — *Ray Charles*

Many of us abhor the term powerlessness because it goes against everything we think we are. We're convinced we can do *anything*, fix anything, solve every problem in our path if we try harder, do better, and want to succeed badly enough. We know this must be true in every avenue of our life because we believe we control everything in our lives–except for the disease of addiction. But that sense of control is a fantasy.

We are powerless over weather, war, illness, and other people. This does not mean we are weak or a failure. If keeping the plug in the jug was all that was required, alcoholism would no longer be a concern. We believe it to be a symptom of underlying issues and behaviors that will not be stopped by sheer force, willpower, or self-knowledge. Imagine people treating cancer or diabetes without help from medical professionals, believing they can be cured by willing the disease away. Make no mistake, those of us who live in addiction have a disease.

Recovery is for people who *want* it, not for people who need it. Recovery through the twelve steps is a journey that defies everything we think we know. We are asked to embrace a position of open-mindedness and willingness, and to be humble enough to admit that we are powerlessness over our addictions. Seeking help from A.A. or other avenues are demonstrations of raw courage, resilience and strength, born out of a desperation called powerlessness. It is in this admission of powerless of going it alone, that we grasp hope and humility and seek the help we need. Many of us become desperate, near death before many we concede to our innermost selves the indisputable fact of our powerlessness.

Nothing more than our inflated perception of self keeps us defiant, stuck in the illusion we have power over the baffling pull of addictions. With each passing day, we find we have none at all.

If we did we would be God. Nothing could be further from the truth.

TODAY'S MEDITATION

Dear God, we already know addictions are a pre-meditated set-up for failure. I'm tired of failing. With you, one day at a time, I will be a success so long as I don't pick up, no matter what.

"A man is truly free, even here in this embodied state, if he knows that God is the true agent and he by himself is powerless to do anything." — Ramakrishna

PRACTICING FAITH
OCTOBER 14

Growing up, my home was fraught with hostility and overt demonstrations of anger. Faith was just a word. Although at times Faith was spoken, it could never be believed or understood. The words that had power, the ones that repeated in my psyche and played out by adults in my family became a sad mantra: life sucks, and then we die.

How then do we find a faith where there is none? We have to reach past the periphery of sight, past this world that entraps us, and move to a place that cannot be seen. The more we trust, the stronger becomes a seventh sense call faith. Recognizing that we are walking blind, we come to embrace faith as if it were tangible, as if we have no choice.

We become co-creators with an omnipotent one, as faith is ours alone to experience and define in our own way. At times we become the student, while at other times, the teacher for those on the same journey.

Many follow a religious regimen handed down by the great theologians of the ages. Others chose to develop personal rituals based upon their under-standing of faith. The choice is ours to make. Having found that personal faith, the next step is to practice this faith. We exercise faith with the same dedication we make when we work out in a gym. We prepare ourselves phys-ically and spiritually, and allow for a focused, humble and quiet period of time to pray. This time is ours: sacred and closely guarded from distractions of the day. We *will* report in for our spiritual workout.

Because this is a Higher Power of our choosing, we open our hearts, enabling miracles to transform us. We are no longer alone. At last, no matter where we go or what we do, we are assured by faith, we are being led.

TODAY'S MEDITATION

Dear God, I know miracles are the result of faith. Please use me as your channel so others may experience their own miracles through what they see in me.

"Faith is taking the first step even when you don't see the whole staircase."
— *Martin Luther King, Jr.*

RESTARTING MY DAY
OCTOBER 15

New to recovery, I remember I continually complained that each day was like the last: fearful, with a never-ending feeling that the other shoe was about to drop.

Someone asked, "Why not restart your day? Close your eyes, and with a quick prayer, ask your Higher Power to help you look at your life as being just the way it is supposed to be, right this moment."

If you are on the wrong path and the weight of the day is a burden you can barely lift, you can stop where you are and restart your day.

That pause, accompanied by a quick prayer can change our perspective and become the beginning of a new, stress-free day. Do this more than once a day if you have to. It works!

We never have to stay stuck in obsessive and destructive thoughts. We can stop, and restart our day, changing the direction of our thinking from negative to positive.

As we practice this redirection, we align ourselves with the good in the universe. We are grateful to be living examples of people who can restart their day over again for others to emulate.

TODAY'S MEDITATION

Restarting my day gives me the courage already within me to change my attitude for the better. I'm grateful to be a force that activates the courage needed to change.

"When everything seems to be going against you, remember that the airplane takes off against the wind, not with it." — Henry Ford

RELEASING JUDGMENT
OCTOBER 16

Being judgmental assumes that we see ourselves as exceptional people. We are sure we are smarter, more creative or knowledgeable when, often, we are plain ole jealous. The world has a way of letting us know we are none of the above—except jealous.

Some of us learn firsthand the pain of rejection having been left out or ignored as a child, a parent, or spouse, and so we choose to be the one doing the rejecting, making judgments as we do.

I am reminded that as we point a finger at others, three are pointing back at us. Every time I open my mouth in judgment about another, I need to end the story with, "Just like me."

No one is perfect, and we are all guilty of many of the same, or different, imperfections.

We all want validation as we are, without condemnation. The good news is that being judgmental is nothing more than habitual behavior. It becomes modified through awareness, practice, and corrective action on our part.

Judging seeks to diminish others, often to validate ourselves. When judgment of ourselves is suspended, we accept others where they are for without judgment, we are equal.

We can celebrate our freedom from passing judgment on the people who surround us when we practice Live and Let Live.

TODAY'S MEDITATION
I am reminded to keep my fingers pointing back to my heart so I might judge myself first. Then I will know what it may feel like for someone else to be judged.

"Do not judge. You don't know what storm I've asked her to walk through."
— God

THE NOT YETS
OCTOBER 17

In the sixties and seventies there was little discussion about the horrors resulting from the disease of addiction. And much like the stigma that continues to shroud mental health issues, old perceptions and beliefs about addiction persist.

The abundance of recovery meetings worldwide, together with a growing awareness that alcoholism is a disease, are instrumental to change, but ignorance is a slow-moving train loaded with old ideas.

One old idea is the notion that a *real* alcoholic has to be homeless, incarcerated, or non-functioning. Nothing could be further from the truth. Alcoholism does not discriminate. No one is exempt from the disease, although many a drunk convinces themselves they are as they lay dying of the disease. Many have had no consequences, yet their personal deterioration is enough to move them to enter recovery before their *not-yets* become a reality.

Recognizing that the pain and insanity of addictions are the same for all, regardless of their place in the world, many get off the elevator before it hits bottom. Those that seek help before the worst happens make this decision, not because their body is shutting down or because they are on the verge of suicide. They decide to seek help because they can *see* those things waiting for them if they persist.

It is only for now that those dire outcomes are our *not-yets*. How fortunate are those who do something different now, instead of later.

We can alter the course of our lives, under any condition, if we want to live.

We can stop right this moment and seek the help that's waiting for us. All we must have is the willingness to do so.

TODAY'S MEDITATION
It takes just one person to lead for others to follow. With a mustard-seed of faith, anything is possible.

"Sometimes we seek that which we are not yet ready to find." — Libba Bray

Changing our Story
October 18

Remember as a child, the hoops we would jump through to avoid getting caught skipping school, being somewhere we were instructed not to go, or hanging with those friends our parents didn't want us to be with. I changed my story more than I care to admit. I did the same thing into adulthood prior to recovery. After a while, I couldn't tell the truth from my own lies, forgetting who I said-what to.

How often have we looked back over our lives, hoping if we looked hard enough, our past would go away? That's what recovery does if we let it. It changes our perception. With maturity and acceptance, the pain and hardness of our story changes. We cannot change the past, but as we look through the eyes of forgiveness for ourselves we admit that nothing is ever as we thought it was. We equip ourselves by working The Steps to prevent repeat behaviors and learn to forgive behaviors from the past. As our Higher Power illuminates our truth of who we are today, faith finds the courage to accept and forgive that past, which then changes our story.

We accept mistakes as lessons learned because we've changed. We are no longer the person we once were. If we were to be honest we admit that, while addicted, we only *thought* we knew the truth of what transpired.

Regrets remind us of unfinished business that still seeks our attention, a signal that re-examining root causes may be necessary. We ask: Why do we need this remorse? What defects of ours do we justify keeping alive, and *why*? How will letting go benefit our highest good and, the highest good of others?

We deserve to be free on an emotional and spiritual level. The Steps point us to a passageway that leads to a forgiving and gentle existence. How we get there is through hard work that comes from asking tough questions of ourselves, while leaving the clubs we beat ourselves up with behind.

We make amends and, in the name of blessed serenity, we let it go. We don't forget harms done, but rather, we make new decisions out of love and tolerance for us and others.

We pray that, just like me, if those that offended and hurt us knew better they, too—would have done better. Embracing this path, we continue on to freedom as we change our story using the enlightenment of forgiveness.

TODAY'S MEDITATION
Dear God, it has taken me so long to understand that by looking at my life differently, I see opportunities for forgiveness. My peace and serenity are paramount.

"When you change your story that you tell about yourself, you change your life. You can start telling a better story right now." — *Sheri Kaye Hoff*

DETACHING FROM OLD BEHAVIORS
OCTOBER 19

As a new member of recovery, it became clear there would be lots of work to do at home with family members. First, there was the explaining. My extended family couldn't understand why I had to continue attending meetings; asking, "For how long?" My husband clung to his long-standing denial of the severity of my addictions, while my daughter sought emotional comfort from her dad, as I was not to be believed, regardless of what was said.

The family felt vulnerable and conflicted about my recovery; they knew how to interact with the addicted me. My new behavior, while more loving than hostile, showed signs of a new independence. Requests for teamwork were perceived as a threat from a mom who had been a one-woman caregiver, even if that caregiver did everything under the influence.

Recovery gives us the ability to detach from others' behaviors and expectations. It pulls us back from old addictive actions, as we discover and maintain our new voice, regardless of others' resistance. Detachment from old entrenched behaviors of others allows others the freedom to be who they are.

While amends may be necessary, the greatest amends we make are living amends, and like recovery, they happen one day at a time. Each day we stay the course by making our recovery, our motivations, and our Higher Power a priority. We detach from others' old behaviors and embrace new ones better suited for family intimacy and mutual responsibility, even if our family resists.

Although we practice love and tolerance, we no longer take responsibility for how others may feel or act out. After all, we are the ones who have a cherished program of recovery with solutions, and have experienced the Miracles of Recovery. As we keep the focus of *our* responsibility on us, steadiness and trust show our love for them never ceases, but the way things get done in the family have changed. Growth has a ripple effect. Once we begin demonstrating this healthy change in all of our affairs, there is no going back, giving-in, or negotiating. Our long-term self-respect and sobriety depend upon our exhibiting patience, loving exchanges and constant perseverance.

When we give others rightful authority over their own feelings and permission to be who they are, together, we mature through The Steps. Isn't that what we all want?

Independent but together, we practice the gifts of love and tolerance through loving detachment from old behaviors.

TODAY'S MEDITATION

I have such gratitude that I am now able to demonstrate my love for others without having to accept certain behaviors.

"The 'self-image' is the key to human personality and human behavior. Change the self-image and you change the personality and the behavior."
— *Maxwell Maltz*

FEAR OF CONFRONTATION
OCTOBER 20

I used to cringe when speaking to people in authority or to someone who had a degree. I never believed I was smart enough, worthy enough, to carry on a conversation with someone smarter than I was, which I felt sure was just about everyone. I feared I had nothing at all to contribute. I feared others would soon learn how ignorant I was about everything. Confrontation meant that you could see right through to my ineptness and low self-worth; I just knew you saw me as a drunk.

Recovery gives us courage to see that we are equal to anyone. We are intelligent and have tools now we didn't have before. We allow for a space-filled pause before responding to ensure that if the conversation warrants a response, it will come from a place of loving kindness. We pray, remembering we have no obligation to respond if we don't want to. Considering the question, "How important is it compared to my serenity?" gives us the time necessary to assess our motives before we speak. Sometimes a mere smile is the right response.

Confrontation is no longer a threat today. We are comforted knowing what someone else says is about them and their personal agenda. We get to determine how we want others to hear us and decide what is necessary to say out loud and what can remain unsaid. While not perfect, we are much better when we make choices grounded in acceptance and compassion for ourselves and for others.

TODAY'S MEDITATION

I'm grateful to be a work in progress, and remain forgiving of myself. I never respond with fear of confrontation when I come from a place of forgiveness and gentle tolerance.

"On the other hand, people who address the mini-conflicts head-on in order to straighten things out tend to have the great, long-lasting relationships."
— Ray Dali

IMPATIENCE
OCTOBER 21

This defect continues to be a silent snag in my psyche. Intolerance and discontent combined with an inflated ego are the defects that support impatience. Confrontation often begins because our expectations are extreme, and our demeanor is demanding. An over inflated ego and undernourished sense of self insists we barge through situations, people, and life, expecting everyone and everything to snap-to. Impatience is the outcome of our imagined importance.

In recovery, our impatience expects wisdom and serenity to dawn overnight, without considering how far we were from being there to begin with! Here we are reminded to take it easy. This may mean counting to ten and examining our motives before we engage. When we do this, we learn to let go of the stringent demands we place on others and ourselves.

As we become more tolerant and patient we learn to ask, "What would our Higher Power want us to do?" When impatience, again, threatens to overwhelm our newfound self-control, we ask ourselves, "Is it going to matter 24-hours from now?"

We ask, "How Important Is It?" which is the pause necessary to recapture our balance. Keeping expectations and the practice of refrain from blaming others helps to reduce cries of impatience.

TODAY'S MEDITATION
I'm grateful for tools of recovery that bring me back to center. My God will get me there if I remember I'm not expected to do it myself.

"Perhaps there is only one cardinal sin: impatience. Because of impatience we were driven out of Paradise, because of impatience we cannot return,"
— W. H. Auden

INCREASING CONSCIOUS CONTACT
OCTOBER 22

If we were to ask long-time members of a recovery group how they stay happy, joyous, and free, one answer would come up over and over, increased conscious contact with their Higher Power.

Early in recovery many of us recoiled hearing of the God-thing. Some remained uninterested yet still found recovery in the rooms. Most of us, however, embrace a power greater than ourselves, acknowledging that the link between recovery and our Higher Power is indisputable. Although ready to become clean and sober, the missing piece of ourselves that forced us to our knees was the lack of a conscious contact with our Higher Power.

We only thought it was us who had found our way into recovery, believing once here, our job was done. We only thought we had arrived by maintaining our recovery and working The Steps. Driven by ego, this selective thinking overruled a God-seeking, conscious-contact thinking, and so we fell short. We call it a slip, but it has another, more accurate name: E.G.O., or Edging God Out.

We spent a lifetime trying to out-maneuver and out-think a disease that has squashed hundreds of thousands before us. Off the beam and delusional, we felt sure we had fulfilled the requirements of recovery! It wasn't *our* fault if recovery didn't work. Our only fault was that we tried to go it alone.

Our Higher Power, already within us, asks only for a willingness to seek Him in prayer. Without prayer, self-will runs us in circles. This is not a human conspiracy but rather, a spiritual truth. To seek our Higher Power is to ask in prayer. Our willingness, coupled with faith, is conscious contact.

TODAY'S MEDITATION
Dear God, I am grateful that as I seek you, you provide strength, courage and direction to move me to do what's in front of me, which is the next right thing.

"In my deepest, darkest moments, what really got me through was a prayer. Sometimes my prayer was 'Help me.' Sometimes a prayer was 'Thank you.' What I've discovered is that intimate connection and communication with Higher Power will always get me through…." — Iyanla Vanzant

LEARNING TO STAND ALONE
OCTOBER 23

Prior to recovery, I had no concept of what it meant to stand alone. I had no backbone, no courage to face frustrations that any mature ten-year-old could handle. I was emotionally wounded and terrified beyond belief. Facing all my fears sober was unthinkable, unimaginable. To do so remains as vital today as it was during those first wide-eyed, fearful days of new recovery.

Sobriety is the letting go of all things unnecessary. As we prepare to answer to our Higher Power, standing alone clean and sober, we begin to drop everything that prevents us from reaching this goal. We realize our life's purpose is not dependent upon relationships with family and friends, but rather on the rising above everything human to reach what is unseen except through faith. When our intuition calls us to look at ourselves, it is our Higher Power we answer to. With our last breath, it is a God of our understanding we will seek to secure that lofty place of perfect peace, no matter what our beliefs are.

Learning to stand alone means we love others, but we rely upon *our* truth, regardless of what that looks like to those around us. Standing alone means we wait for no man or woman to define, judge, or make us whole. We are already whole, perfect in the eyes of our Higher Power.

We need other people, but lean on and trust ourselves first, knowing that we act, guided by a force greater than ourselves. A deep moral and spiritual conviction assure us that we answer to our Higher Power, regardless of how many mouths we've fed, how many people we've loved, or helped on our journey, or what state of degradation our life may be in. Standing alone, we turn toward the light.

TODAY'S MEDITATION

Dear God, I trust you are with me now as I seek to hold steady on this walk that leads to you.

"It is poor faith that needs fair weather for standing firm. That alone is true faith that stands the foulest weather." — *Mahatma Gandhi*

PROGRESS NOT PERFECTION
OCTOBER 24

I am mesmerized as I watch a parade of ants, acting as one, as they engage in the task of building tunnels of sand and dirt. What began as a tiny pile of dirt now resembles engineered highways.

I, too, have worked incessantly seeking a different kind of perfection. I thought that doing things perfectly gave me immunity against others judging me. Under the grip of addictions, I developed a gnawing self-inflicted emotional sore from trying to maintain an impossible record of perfection. By the time I reached recovery, I did not understand who I was, or who I wanted to be.

Born pure and perfect in the eyes of our Higher Power, we are destined to be imperfect as we work through life's limitations. We can breathe relief as we come to understand that perfection rests with our Higher Power. Today the mantra *Easy Does it, But Do it*, commands our attention.

As our spirit matures in faith, what was once a crushing need to prove ourselves decreases, while truth from our Higher Power's authority over everything, increases. Progress is where our serenity thrives, not perfection. Like the ants, we do the work, and leave the judgment of what we have done to our Higher Power, comforted that our steps today, are progress, not perfection.

TODAY'S MEDITATION
I'm grateful for harmonic chords of progress that resonate in my contentment. Progress is the scale that shows me I am enough.

"The essence of being human is that one does not seek perfection."
— *George Orwell*

STINKING-THINKING
OCTOBER 25

Obsessive-compulsive thinking paralyzes us and elevates fear to extreme heights. This thinking grips our heart with one hand, and our soul with the other. For those of us in addiction this irrational fear *feels* real, no less compelling than a drink or drug before us. It's called stinking-thinking.

Stinking thinking *thrives* on the idea that if we are not found out we won't lose out. Ever-vigilant, stinking-thinking takes the role of a supreme bodyguard. The first trigger to the loss of a hard-fought recovery, it preys on a deluded sense-of-self. Sometimes the imaginary committee which *is* stinking-thinking, starts its incessant chatter days or weeks before *an event*, preceded with thoughts of "Yeah, but," or an inner voice that insists, "You know you can't stop drinking anyway." Stinking thinking *thrives* on the idea that if we are not found out we won't lose out. Ever-vigilant, stinking-thinking takes the role of a supreme bodyguard. If not eradicated and replaced with positive thinking, our good intentions are sabotaged by these and other self-defeating messages. We buy the lie and resume our addictions right where we left off.

We're no longer fighting ourselves alone. Our open heart and mind provoke dominion over our thoughts as we walk together with our Higher Power. Our sacred rooms of recovery remind us we let go of fear-filled obsessive thinking by doing everything differently, one day at a time. In time, stinking-thinking loses the powerful grip it once had over us, as our spiritual consciousness becomes stronger. Still, every day is the day we must maintain focus on our sobriety or the committee returns stronger than ever.

Practice strengthens our new reality and we shift closer to that person of integrity we have always wanted to be. Slow and thoughtful, we free ourselves of the negativity that bound us to our addictions. With the hand of our Higher Power in ours, we bring stinking-thinking into the light and feel courage rise over sad, mistaken beliefs that conspire to keep us sick.

TODAY'S MEDITATION

Old beliefs of stinking thinking are slowly being replaced with logic and maturity. The journey is always worth the walk into a nurturing, healing place of love.

"You are where you are, you are what you are, by what goes into your mind. Change where you are, change what you are, by changing what goes into your mind." — Zig Zigler

LONELINESS

OCTOBER 26

I recently discovered I could live alone and not be lonely.

There was never a time I was not lonely. I was lonely in my marriage. I was lonely at family gatherings. I was empty inside, punctuated with low self-esteem, little-to-no faith, and a constant, ever-present awareness of never fitting in anywhere. I stood, alone, on the outside looking in.

Recovery proves loneliness is the hallmark of addictions. This ever-present bond of loneliness makes up the core of our addictions. The Steps allow us to see the meaning and depth of our soul-sickness and we develop a relationship with hope in the form of a Higher Power.

We understand there is a difference between being alone and being lonely, as if a piece of us was missing. Through working with others and the blanket of love our fellowship affords us, we find a self-esteem sufficient to stand alone, live alone and on most days, feel comfortable in our own skin.

TODAY'S MEDITATION
Just for today I am alone, but not lonely!

"We're born alone, we live alone, we die alone. Only through our love and friendship can we create the illusion for the moment that we're not alone."
— *Orson Welles*

Being Good Enough
October 27

How many times have we struggled to say what others wanted to hear, do what they wanted us to do, and be what we thought they wanted us to be. We lived to prove we were right where *they* wanted us to be! Contributing in every way imaginable we gave, we performed, we worked, always in the hope of being good enough.

But just what *is* good enough? Haven't we proved ourselves good enough to satisfy our employer, our loved ones, our circle of friends? How do we know? The measure used to determine what is enough is different for each person, but for those of us in addiction, the measurement always falls short. As we give, we exhaust our physical, emotional, monetary and spiritual energies hoping to satisfy an imaginary yardstick. The harder we try, the more expectations others put on us and they never stop, because *we* don't stop. We have something to prove!

All of these spell F.E.A.R., *False Evidence Appearing Real*. We become so comfortable in allowing others to determine what is enough for us that false evidence of *not* meeting others' expectations appears real. It *feels* real because we've been exhibiting this behavior for so long. But it is a manipulative guise, an emotional hook we've hung ourselves on for a long, long time. And we did so without emotional boundaries to protect ourselves.

Our Higher Power gives us the ability to decide for ourselves what is enough.

We become good enough when *we* say we are. We stop helping, doing, proving and convincing others of our worth when we have had enough of giving. As we look at motives and become honest with others, when we pull back and look inside, we intuitively acknowledge and abide by our limitations. We do what we can, not what we can't. No one knows what enough is but us.

Awareness of boundaries helps to determine what we will and will not do before we commit. We ask ourselves, "How much am I willing to do, and where do I stop? Why am I committing? Is this what I want or need to do for *me*, or am I hooked on proving something to you?"

When we gain clarity in our intentions, we become honest in our responses. Even if we make the choice to do nothing at all, we are enough.

TODAY'S MEDITATION

Dear God, thank you for those who came before me and introduced me to myself.

"Self-care is the number one solution to helping somebody else. If you are being good to yourself and your body and your psyche, then that serves other people better because you will grow strong enough to lift someone else up."
— *Mary Lambert*

FEAR OF FEAR

A group of women got together for introductions prior to embarking on a week of sharing their craft of writing. As they went around the room describing schools, family settings and dynamics, they came to one woman visibly distressed, wringing her hands in agitation. Expressions of pain and panic showed her readiness to bolt out the door, but she sat frozen in place, instead. Tears in her eyes, she told of her overwhelming fear of sharing her past with strangers.

Fear is a debilitating emotion for many of us. Filled with overwhelming fear, many of us act out emotionally as this woman did.

Fear can manifest itself as the physical response to, "fight or flight," producing PTSD-like flashbacks, panic attacks, and emotional numbness. Learning to breathe through feelings and letting them pass, allows us to replace fearful messages with messages of positive reinforcement targeted to the specific fear. Deep breathing, and/or talking with other like-minded individuals helps to facilitate the passing of these fear-assaults.

When challenged by fear, we remember that feelings are not facts. Everything passes. Our task is to be gentle and kind to ourselves. As we gather composure and become the warriors we are meant to be, we walk out the other side of fear, strong and free.

TODAY'S MEDITATION

What a gift it is to remember that everything passes. My actions today are in alignment with who I want to be. I do not carry the baggage of yesterday's fear.

Too much self-centered attitude, you see, brings, you see, isolation. Result: loneliness, fear, anger. The extreme self-centered attitude is the source of suffering." — Dalai Lama

You are A Wonderful Child of Your Higher Power

October 29

Seeing ourselves as harried, overworked, over-committed, and over-critical, we spend many of our waking hours feeling insufficient.

Sometimes we see ourselves as robots moving to a mechanical script of emotions without any genuine thought or feelings. This disconnect became habitual a long time ago. As life became more demanding, so did our self-talk.

What about our spiritual health? We must acknowledge our magnificence as spiritual beings. We were born perfect, out of a unique perfect image from a perfect Higher Power and deserve to treat ourselves with the same tenderness and attention we give to those we love.

If we do not stop to see ourselves as inspired, spiritual creatures, then we see ourselves as less than worthy, and will never silence the not-enough messages inside our heads. As we feed our undernourished psyche with strong, encouraging affirmations, we stop perpetuating this image of insufficiency and rid ourselves of those messages of low self-worth.

Our truth is, we are born wonderful and we are still wonderful. We've merely squandered the precious energy needed to sustain us, but that can change.

We are what we tell ourselves we are. Prayer, meditation, and journaling help to authenticate who we think we are. These actions serve to make real what we can't see, which is our spiritual alignment. As we come to our Higher Power with all that we are, we honor Him with a love of self and the realization we are deserving—or we wouldn't be here.

The daily reinforcement of loving, nurturing rituals give way to the emotional self-care necessary to strengthen our ability to meet emotional demands of the interactions we have throughout our day. We are worthy of putting our emotional selves first because we know now, we are children of a loving higher power.

"You are a perfect child of a divine Creator, and nothing about you is imperfect. The Creator, being perfect, does not create the imperfect. It is therefore humble— not arrogant—to accept the divine perfection of your true self..."
— *Marianne Williamson*

STAYING VIGILANT IN RECOVERY
OCTOBER 30

Many in recovery are satisfied with just getting by. They are the ones who subscribe to the thought that life has returned to "normal." This thinking is what recovery refers to as complacency. Not engaged in addictions, our disease tells us, we are better now.

Some decide one meeting a month is enough, and let go of rituals and spiritual maintenance, once a vital part of their daily routine. This is enough for them—until it's not.

Without realizing it our disease moves, pulling us over time away from our fellowship and from our meetings. The last stronghold is our turning away from our Higher Power, the foundation of recovery we once coveted for our own.

Then, one day, life swings a bat delivering a wallop that knocks us off our feet. We pick up a drink, and our world comes crashing down. We are aghast, in disbelief. How could this happen to us? Disoriented, embittered, restless and discontented, we forget who we are—a person with an incurable disease that *never* stops. Similar to cancer in remission, our disease lies dormant until we pick up that first drink or drug, and then it's back. Each time we're told by those who made it back, was worse than before, never better.

We are told to be alert, watchful. Alcoholism alone is cunning, baffling and powerful. We become complacent, less than vigilant, and we will feed our demons again. Even as we abstain, our disease is doing push-ups, never losing the power to seize our first moment of weakness and sabotage our sobriety. We forget we're afforded a mere 24-hour reprieve based upon the maintenance of our spiritual condition. Protecting our sobriety is as important as the air we breathe because without recovery, our breathing doesn't matter anyway.

TODAY'S MEDITATION
Dear God, myself, my sobriety, and you are the three most important things in my life today. Without all three I cannot stay sober.

"We are not weak if we make a proper use of those means which the God of Nature has placed in our power... the battle, sir, is not to the strong alone it is to the vigilant, the active, the brave." — Patrick Henry

WHAT IS THE NEXT RIGHT THING?
OCTOBER 31

Do the next right thing, we hear in recovery. But what does that mean?

For those of us new to recovery, it means we go to any length for our sobriety, no matter what, under any circumstances, but do it one-day-at-a-time.

For some, it can mean getting busy; for others, it means take it easy. The next right thing says we quit playing director or running the show. We *Let Go and Let God* do for us what we could not do for ourselves.

Some old-timers proclaim it means clean house, trust our Higher Power, and help others.

For those of us not familiar with recovery it could mean putting our Higher Power, our sobriety, and ourselves first in everything we think and everything we do. Asking the question, "What is the next right thing?" is always the right thing to do. Asking for help, showing up for others and service work, resting; all of these can be the next right thing.

What is the next right thing for you right now? How do we know? Because when we pray and meditate we have done all we can do. There are no mistakes in my Higher Power's world

TODAY'S MEDITATION
With you, God, I relax in the moment knowing that as I ask for help that I'm doing the next right thing.

"Sometimes it is better to lose and do the right thing
than to win and do the wrong thing." — Tony Blair

CHANGING OUR STORY
NOVEMBER 1

The greatest source of disillusionment and horror for someone with a life rooted in addictions is to have no hope whatsoever.

In recovery, we hear of those who never made it back. The stories shared tell of personal tragedies, failures unimaginable, and lives destroyed. And those stories ring true for all of us because we've been there, done that.

Many of us say, "I would die of shame if you knew the truth about me," or, "You couldn't begin to understand." Those who stay away from recovery often do so convinced that no one could be as bad as me.

Can we honestly say we remember every small detail from childhood? Are we sure *we* didn't cast the first stone? For those gutsy enough to stick around and recover, lives transform, irrespective of the stories that will be told. The facts don't change, but our reaction to our story does.

In Step Five our perceived horrors, once a tale of excruciating shame and self-condemnation, are now, nothing more than our story.

Much of what happened in our past is colored by perceptions and mixed with story-telling. The Steps illuminate a path to a love-of-self and self-for-giveness we once thought was impossible to achieve. We re-create ourselves in recovery in collaboration with our Higher Power. In so doing, we are relieved to discover that much of what happened was never about us, let alone our fault. And if it was our fault, we work on taking our power back by releasing that part of our story.

No longer are we victims of our past. We begin to drop closely held beliefs about ourselves, ones that threatened to destroy us. With new awareness we change our perspective, which in turn, changes our story.

Because of The Steps, we have changed. We surrendered, to win. Recovery through acceptance of what was continues to heal our broken hearts. What used to be a debilitating, horrific past serves now to demonstrate how grace and the Twelve Steps grants us the wisdom to change our story. The solidity of our faith makes this possible.

TODAY'S MEDITATION

Thank you, God, for forgiveness necessary to accept my imperfect self, riddled with conjectures and half-truths. I know that because of you, I am better than I ever thought I was.

"Life is a series of events and sensations. Everything else is interpretation. Much is lost in transition - and added in assumption/projection"— Rasheed Ogunlaru

Getting Out of our Comfort Zone
November 2

Familiarity of routines can bring us comfort during times of distress. The repetitions are reassuring.

In recovery we sometimes refer to living in our comfort zone as a red flag. In recovery we hear our addiction say, "Just this one time," and we believe the lie. In this comfort zone, complacency, combined with a fragile sobriety makes us vulnerable to our addictions—which to us are where we have lived our day-to-day lives.

Familiarity and complacency are the wiring that link us to the very people, places, and things we worked so hard to remove ourselves from. The likelihood exists that if we are comfortable in what we are doing and what we have always done, we are closer than we know to reactivating our disease. We might as well be walking through life with eyes closed, stumbling over rocks in our path. The rocks we fall over are justification, rationalization and indifference.

It's called doing the same thing the same way and expecting different results.

Recovery reminds us we have to change *everything*. We develop new trusted friends who are safe for us. We travel unfamiliar routes that bypass the slippery rocks that tripped us. We seek safe paths brightly lit by a new spiritual connectedness. Traveling this way, we set new boundaries and develop rituals that fortify our emotional, physical, and spiritual selves.

Sometimes it feels impossible, even overwhelming. We're not used to taking suggestions from others, nor are we comfortable calling someone we don't know for help. A warrior's courage and heightened self-esteem are our rewards for practicing these new behaviors as we face our fears and do it anyway. Every single thing we do differently, no matter how small, is a demonstration of a faith and determination we never thought possible, but one that was always within us.

Through practice and the support of others, we develop the connectedness and faith necessary to maintain our course in a direction that moves us away from the danger of destructive, addictive thinking. The place we once called our comfort zone.

TODAY'S MEDITATION

God, your presence is a daily reminder that I am not walking alone. Thank you for the courage you give me one day at a time to do life differently.

. . . .

"Only a person who is willing to lose everything will transform himself or herself. Only by moving outside our comfort zone of the past ...Now that I am desperate, I am dangerous. I am also ripe for transformation." — Kilroy J. Oldster

. . . .

SELF-CARE AND BLAMING OTHERS
NOVEMBER 3

Many of us in addiction spent years wandering in denial, blaming others for our shortcomings. Everyone and everything were the cause of our discontent, disappointment, and maladjustment to life. "If only you would stop," we cried. "If only our company operated like this." If only–if only.

We are all works in progress. We absorb a little information about ourselves each day. Self-care looks and feels different for each of us. For some it has to do with boundaries. For some it means taking responsibility for our actions and choices made with or without regard for others.

We learn that what we say is a personal opinion, a reflection of our feelings and agenda at the moment. We no longer blame others for the choices we make. Pointing fingers is no longer necessary because we know now, that what we say and do has always been our decision. Working The Steps has made us too aware and too awake to hide behind anyone or anything any longer. Our responsibility begins and ends with ourselves, our truth, our actions, and our motives.

This is how we live, by owning what is ours.

Self-care is designed for one purpose and one purpose only; to nurture, protect, and honor who we are becoming.

TODAY'S MEDITATION
Just for today, I'm reminded to keep the focus on me. As others are free to be who they are without my consent, I get to reinvent myself and become the responsible person I always knew I wanted to be.

"It's time to care; it's time to take responsibility; it's time to lead; it's time for a change; it's time to be true to our greatest self; it's time to stop blaming others."
— *Steve Maraboli*

IGNORING FEELINGS
NOVEMBER 4

Who among us, while in the stranglehold of addiction, acknowledged that our feelings even existed? Did we say to ourselves, when angry or out of control, *excuse me, but I'm feeling quite disturbed at this moment.* When jealous, did we acknowledge the fact that we were jealous and convince ourselves to react with love and kindness instead?

In addiction, feelings are what we are escaping from. Regardless of how angry, unhappy, happy, or intolerant we may act, the message screaming inside our heads is *don't feel!* Forget *about it, these emotions will go away*, or *it's not important.* This was our truth in the moment, no big deal, until it was repeated, vying for our attention again and again.

Nothing *ever* goes away. Emotions hide until they push to the surface like the slow-building pressure inside a volcano about to erupt.

Feelings still have weight and are neither inherently good nor bad. Emotions can serve as healthy reminders of unfinished business. And even when those emotions are uncomfortable, perhaps even threatening, they can serve as red flags to alert us that something is not right. To ignore our emotions is to invite self-destructive behaviors or depression.

In recovery, some of us become emotional sleuths unearthing where our feelings come from, and why we are experiencing them. The calming energy found in prayer and meditation allows for feelings to just be. As we observe ourselves, we honor these feelings for what they are: subliminal thoughts of affects and behaviors.

Once we acknowledge them for what they are, they dissolve as if delicate snowflakes as we either watch them pass or take what we need from them. We do not have to react, but we do have to feel.

TODAY'S MEDITATION
As I face feelings in the light, their control over me is diminished. How do they impact my serenity? Not at all.

"One of the most courageous decisions you'll ever make is to finally let go of what's hurting your heart and soul." — Brigitte Nicole

Trusting the Process
November 5

Have you prayed or cajoled others hoping to affect an outcome to satisfy yourself? Have you ever thought, if only I tried harder, pushed more, demanded or insisted with greater conviction it would have worked?

As we recover we become convinced that unless an outcome is pre-ordained by our Higher Power, nothing will change the outcome to suit us. Our literature speaks of, "Lack of power..." as our problem. We've been given a choice to trust a process that shows no matter how hard we work to change what is, the outcome rests elsewhere. We're not living on our time, but on a time that belongs to our Higher Power.

Although we have much control over our own choices, decision making, and self-will, we lack the final, most important piece of the puzzle: the outcome. Universal truth proclaims if the outcome of anything should be different, it would be.

As our wisdom grows, we change our perception and accept what is. We do the best we can, and trust the process that promises more will be revealed in the divine timing of our Higher Power.

TODAY'S MEDITATION

Today I remember that nothing but me is my business. Every time I think I am in control of someone or something, I am reminded of how wrong I continue to be. It's easier to just trust the process.

"You must stop asking how. Life is a step-by-step process you don't control, not a 3-step formula. Without a doubt, believe in it". — *Roxana Jones*

SPONSORSHIP
NOVEMBER 6

Maintaining sobriety can be jeopardized by the simple delusion that we don't need anyone's help, the boastful claim that says, "We can take it from here." Yet for most of us this is the wall of ignorance we hit in our addictions. Is it impossible to stay clean and sober without a sponsor? Probably not. Would maintaining sobriety be easy to do without a sponsor? Definitely not.

Sponsorship is a part of A. A.'s unity in service; and represents for some of us, our first semblance of a trusting relationship with another human being. Sponsorship is not a promise of monetary help, food, or shelter. Having worked The Steps together, the relationship has the potential to grow into a long-term friendship. For many others, the sponsor/sponsee relationship ends after working The Steps.

When choosing a sponsor a few basic considerations may be useful. Sponsorship is a pact with someone of the same sex who will keep our confidences, and who we believe can be trusted. As demonstration of their dedication to their own sobriety, sponsors will have their own sponsor. Together they form a chain of help. Sponsors attend meetings and are involved in service work. Consider choosing a sponsor who has worked The Steps and has sobriety, equal to the time it took them to finish The Steps. A potential sponsor's religion, color, faith, political or societal standing is not important. What *is* relevant is their active practice of The Steps, and a commitment to work The Steps face-to-face at agreed upon times.

Lastly, if a sponsor doesn't refer to our literature for answers, but depends upon personal opinions, we may want to think twice before committing. Why? Because answers to all our problems are found in our literature.

TODAY'S MEDITATION
I am grateful for the loving sponsors in my life who paved the way for me to succeed with detachment, patience, and tolerance.

"Your job now is to be at the place where you may be of maximum helpfulness to others; so never hesitate to go anywhere if you can be helpful." — A. A., page 102

LOVE THE YOU THAT YOU ARE
NOVEMBER 7

Sitting at a red light with my two dogs smiling behind me, I felt the calm compassion of self-love. It was sublime, intentional, and it affirmed the person I've become.

With tears running down my face, I pulled over, stopped the car, and allowed myself to absorb this healing, expression of love. Arms around myself, I hugged that little girl deep within and she hugged me back with excitement.

I realized what I was receiving was complete acceptance and unconditional love. These moments are the tangible manifestation of our goodness in this space of bliss. Some refer to it as the fourth dimension, that transcendent aura of completeness where the physical, emotional, mental, and spiritual are in concert with one another. These moments of goodness, exceed any space we've ever experienced.

In this place of complete bliss rests our playful, inquisitive and affectionately demonstrative little child inside each of us who begs for recognition and acceptance, and holds us tight. The more we encourage our inner-child to feel safe through loving self-talk and inner-work, the easier it is for us to nurture that self. It is a place of wholeness, of being complete and taken care of the way we always wanted to be as a child, but we never were.

TODAY'S MEDITATION

I will practice being gentle with *all* of me. I am deserving, and worthy of my love of self. As I open myself to return to pure bliss, I freely share my authentic self with others.

"This is what the author, John Bradshaw, meant by 'reclaiming our inner child'. In recovery, we can begin to nurture our inner child and connect deeply with our heart and spirit." — Christopher Dines

RESENTMENTS

NOVEMBER 8

Growing up, I was consumed with resentments. Imagining someone said something wrong or did something I didn't like was enough for me to take personal offense. I perceived my world and its people were all out to get me. I felt burnt up, resentful; trusting no one.

Not until I became honest with myself did I see that the noose of anger I used to hurt others was strangling me. My suspicious magnifying mind churned up thoughts that said I could never measure up, while at the same time, the delusions of egocentric and grandiose thinking kept me sick. I was sure that the real solution was to somehow get others to change so I could live in peace. Surely, they would see things my way.

Today, because of recovery, we avoid retaliatory assumptions by reviewing *our* motives. Instead of yielding to mistaken beliefs, letting uncontrolled reactions and schemes of angry revenge dictate a response, we examine our resentments through the eyes of loving detachment. The fact is, **we— don't— know** what someone else's truth is. The word, *maybe* becomes the compromise needed to free us from our judgment. The truth is, whenever I am dis-contented, there is something wrong with me and my attitude.

If our Higher Power was standing in front of us, what would we do? We hold the resentments up our Higher Power and ask that they be taken from us to set us free.

Recovery gives us a way to quiet the demanding childlike cries of an over-inflated, ever-present ego, one which is perpetually crouched in fear.

TODAY'S MEDITATION
God, I know I cannot afford to hold on to resentments any longer. If I turn to you, will you take these from me?

"As smoking is to the lungs, so is resentment to the soul; even one puff is bad for you." — Elizabeth Gilbert

PROBLEM SOLVING
NOVEMBER 9

We hear in recovery that for some of us, it can take five years to get walking-around sense for our brain to recover from our fanatical drinking. I remember the feeling of pure excitement the first time I reconciled bills while merging and calculating funds. This was the start of taking control of my life.

Problem solving for normal people comes without effort. They take a step back and detach from everything but the facts. Must the problem be addressed right this minute? What is the impact if the problem were to be left unattended? To ourselves? To others?

A wise approach to any problem asserts that we take our time to think and pray before we decide. A trusted friend suggests we allow forty-eight hours with prayer and meditation before taking any action.

Characteristics of successful problem solvers includes clear thinking regardless of the conflict and a willingness to compromise. These problem solvers understand they won't have answers to everything and if their assessment is incorrect, they begin again. Problem solvers lean on available facts and have a knack for exploring all options by dissecting the big picture.

How effective are you at tackling difficult situations? The fact is, we can all be keen problem solvers when we set our emotions aside and become ready and willing to focus on what's in front of us. We use contemplation, prayer, and thoughtful detachment from everything except the facts. When we pause, we will hear what we need and feel a special pride in the process without taking ourselves too seriously. We appreciate the return of walking-around sense that comes with our sobriety.

TODAY'S MEDITATION

Thank you, God, for the power of discernment, patience, and the ability to base my decisions on the facts, not my emotions.

"We cannot solve our problems with the same thinking
we used when we created them." — *Albert Einstein.*

PRIDE

NOVEMBER 10

Pride is the cultivation, preservation, or exalting of self. It is a protecting and building up of ourselves in our own eyes and the hope our bloated sense of self-worth will raise us in the eyes of others. Pride is an excessive, narcissistic belief in one's superiority. As if sanctioned by the Devil, pride refuses to be small before our Higher Power and balks at connection with others unless to confirm the prideful person's superiority.

For those new in recovery, pride helps prop up our diminished sense of adequacy. Pride validates defects instead of admitting them. We arrive in recovery having never been willing to admit when we were wrong, let alone ask for forgiveness. Instead, we felt extreme shame or embarrassment when our pride was questioned, which only made our pride more vocal. We were the first to feel shortchanged, even hurt if we were overlooked. With arrogance, pride asks, "Excuse me, but, what about me?"

There is no room in recovery for pride. Pride puts itself on a pedestal and then looks down on everyone. Pride would push our Higher Power out of the way if it could. Pride can only be overcome by humility. Only then does pride get down from the cross and accept a power greater than itself. Awareness, a connection with those around us, and a grateful heart can be the beginnings of an exchange of pride, for humility, an attribute to be practiced daily.

TODAY'S MEDITATION
Dear God, please direct my thinking so that, with humility instead of pride, I may be more useful to my fellows and to you.

"As long as you are proud you cannot know God. A proud man is always looking down on things and people and of course, as long as you are looking down you cannot see something that is above you." — C. S. Lewis

When was the last time you thought about what you deserve? What did it mean to you? Did you equate it with something you weren't getting that you felt you deserved? Did you feel someone was cheating you out of something you deserved?

The definition of *deserve* is worthiness, or the act of being worthy. So, instead of thinking about how someone else is cheating you, we can look within and ask, when was the last time *you* felt worthy?

Rarely do we honor words or actions long enough to notice our self-worth. Our worth, however, is waiting for us to name it, claim it, and move it into our consciousness, holding it there in that place of knowing.

We are not perfect; our Higher Power is not done with us yet. Each of us breathe the same air in the same shared moment. We are all given the same daylight and the same chance to become our best selves. Think about it. This shared wealth of gifts proves we must be as deserving as the next person, or we wouldn't *be* here.

One way to ensure we are deserving is to make a declaration that we are, and to do it every day until, through practice and humility, that affirmation becomes us.

Recognizing that a higher goodness is being transformed within us, we invite our Higher Power to walk with us daily. Those who know their self-worth, see the miracles and beauty already within them. They already know they are deserving of goodness and grace.

Our truth depends upon our authentic self and speaks with confidence, changing our thoughts from ones of self-loathing and fear, to a self-proclaimed vision that we are a warrior of deserving goodness, no more or no less than the next.

"You yourself, as much as anybody in the entire universe, deserve your love and affection" — *Gautama Buddha*

STAIRWAY TO SERENITY
NOVEMBER 12

Outdoors in quiet meditation, I feel my heart beat in a steady rhythm, attuned to natures canopy of sounds around me. The birds break the silence of early morning. They do not observe their tone, their pitch, their chirp or the beauty of their voice, but we do. These are their gifts to us. We are connected in spirit as one, to the life that breathes through us all.

In this oneness, I am a channel of a Higher Power that orchestrates all in this complete, ever-encompassing cycle of life. As thoughts quiet, I close my eyes and walk an imagined stairway to serenity. With each step I release material desires. Superficial and mortal wounds suffered to body and soul slowly disappear as I reach the next step of the stairway. Each step becomes lighter, bringing me closer to the tranquility I seek. I am lifted in spirit, imbued with a penetrating faith and comfort that manifests in these moments of perfect acceptance.

As I revel in the peace that radiates from the sunlight of the Spirit, I am infused with an excitement and trusted assurance. Although fleeting, my faith is recreated. With practice and a willing surrender, I seek this meditative and humble state of serenity again and again.

TODAY'S MEDITATION
Just for today I surrender resistance and seek a calming peace as I walk up that stairway to serenity.

"Be calm. God awaits you at the door." — *Gabriel García Márquez*

DETACHING WITH LOVE
NOVEMBER 13

There are days when I find myself sucked into that whirling vortex of others' frustrations and unhappiness. I am ready to jump in and save them from their own pain. How easily I forget that I am powerless over anyone but me. I am not experiencing these emotional rifts. They are.

When this happens, we have to work hard to remember that the behaviors and feelings of others belong to them, not us. Whatever someone else tells us they feel is not our signal to fix or ease their discomfort. The idea we are responsible for trying to change another's behavior, or feelings, what they choose to do or not do, how they feel, or don't feel, can be a dangerous belief. Each person has their own Higher Power, and we are not it. We are separate adults responsible for ourselves only.

Today, when a loved one acts out emotionally, we are reminded to focus on what is in front of us to do since their behavior mirrors something affecting *them*, not us. Unless we were asked, we maintain our autonomy without intervening. Saving ourselves first is the first rule of caregiving. By encouraging the independence of others to address their own issues as they choose, we detach from their behaviors because we love them.

Is this not how we want to be treated? We don't want to be fixed.

The route to mutual acceptance and responsibility becomes cloudy when we interfere and assume we have answers to someone else's problems. We take comfort, grateful to remember that we are agents of change for *our* own recovery and take responsibility for our reactions to life. Anything else is between the other person and their Higher Power.

TODAY'S MEDITATION
Just for today I will work on remembering where I begin and end.

"To be able to enjoy fully the many good things the world has to offer, we must be detached from them. To be detached does not mean to be indifferent or uninterested. It means to be non-possessive. Life is a gift to be grateful for and not a property to cling to..." — Henri J.M. Nouwen

FEAR OF TOMORROW
NOVEMBER 14

It wasn't so long ago I was petrified of everything. The less hope I had, the more fear paralyzed me. I remember asking my husband, "Why dream? Dreams never came true." The degree of my fear, so deep and troubling, reflected a low self-worth and a lack of trust. Shame kept me captive. At times I was so hopeless. I thought I would never live to see tomorrow.

The Steps gave me the ability to see how futile it is to fear something that hasn't happened yet. Tomorrow is not here. Fear of tomorrow is the reminder we're taking today for granted. It's only today I can manage because that's where my feet are. Breathing becomes easier, and I find relief knowing I'm right where I'm supposed to be, in my here and now. In these moments, this is *all* there is.

I claim responsibility for the moments, and hours leading up to my 24-hours. If I am graced with yet another 24-hours, then and only then will I decide about that day. In these 24-hour increments, life stays manageable, efficient, and safe for me to think about. The only power and control I have is right here. The Steps and faith renewed each day remind me that my Higher Power is responsible for my tomorrow, so I *Let Go and Let God* today.

TODAY'S MEDITATION
When I stay in today, living one day at a time, there is no fear. There is only acceptance and faith.

"If you want to conquer the anxiety of life, live in the moment, live in the breath."
— *Amit Ray*

LOVING OURSELVES
NOVEMBER 15

A woman at work spent years caring for others. So focused was she on those who needed her, she neglected her own needs for years on end. She came to recovery in tears, drained and exhausted, her own life in shambles.

We forget our troubles can be mountainous, often difficult to navigate even on a good day. Without reserves of energy, an abundance of faith, food, and water, we fall down the rabbit hole, too drained and exhausted to pull ourselves out again.

We must put the focus of our energies where it belongs most, on ourselves. How do we show a love of self? How do we honor ourselves first and foremost? Where have we fallen short of nurturing our own needs, choosing instead to give everything we are to others until our inner resources dry up?

We can't give away what we don't have. Before we help others, we must know how much sustenance we need to maintain our own health and well-being. My friend couldn't maintain her emotional and mental weight or project goodness to others because she had no reserves. She was over-extended and exhausted.

We may have to revisit the gym in our minds, to practice habits of a love of self, and develop boundaries between what we can and cannot afford to do. Each day is the day we get to show ourselves forgiveness, respect, and love. We do this first, then pass it on to others.

TODAY'S MEDITATION
Affirmations, daily prayers, and practicing spiritual principles for my own growth and healing are the springboard I use to launch myself out into the world with others.

"If you aren't good at loving yourself, you will have a difficult time loving anyone, since you'll resent the time and energy you give another person that you aren't even giving to yourself." — Barbara De Angelis

WORDS CAN'T HURT ME

I grew up believing the world was against me. I contrived ways to keep others away so I wouldn't be hurt.

Recovery allows us to see our chief defects are often fear and anger. Exaggerated false beliefs, a sense of inferiority and low self-worth keep us stuck. In recovery we learn to make choices based on fact instead of feeding paranoid perceptions of what we "think" others imagine us to be. We learn to honor the mantra, "No one can hurt us without our permission." This and other examples of power that exists within each of us, helps to make real the fact that words can't hurt us any longer.

Detaching from toxic people and old, mistaken beliefs, requires continual practice. There were times when someone verbally stepped on our toes, and we took it personally, often when we didn't need to. We retaliated, often when we didn't need to. It is only when we *agree* with the words of others, when we see the truth in these words that we accept it. Otherwise, we let the words go without taking offense.

As we become grounded in our truth, we feel new strength in the conviction that our self-worth is non-negotiable. None of us does any of this perfectly. Just for today, we embrace our authentic self without fear or threat. We ignore unkind words, unless our intuition tells us to look closer.

TODAY'S MEDITATION

By myself, I can do nothing. Faith, combined with a steadfast focus on me is the rich soil for growth of new ideals and behaviors. The words of others cannot shake the faith I have in me.

"Pain can be endured and defeated only if it is embraced.
Denied or feared, it grows." — Dean Koontz

SOFTENING THE GRACE OF SELF-FORGIVENESS
NOVEMBER 17

Oftentimes as we age, we go through all kinds of gyrations to soften facial lines that appear, seemingly overnight. Our reflections show us the stress in our life's journey as we seek to minimize those obvious signs of age. As we wonder which combination of creams will do the trick we ask ourselves, what combination of words will help us soften a similar hardness into self-forgiveness?

Sometimes, as we stare into that mirror, soothing words of compassion surface of their own accord. Feeling love expand deep inside, we wrap our arms around us in a loving embrace. We deserve all things good because suddenly, we are sure we're doing the best that we can.

In front of that bathroom mirror, we lean over to kiss that person looking back and recite, "My best is good enough." We complete this tender ritual of self-actualization by allowing our arms embrace our shoulders and accept all we are: wrinkles, lines, beauty and warts with the gentle, softening grace of forgiveness. We walk now, engulfed in the glow of an inner-elegance known as self-compassion, and we feel it as we've become energized, secure in all that we are.

We begin this ritual of self-forgiveness again as we tell ourselves we are perfect, right here, right now. We are enough. Equipped with an abundance of grace, we are now ready to pass on what was so freely given to us.

TODAY'S MEDITATION
Thank you, God, for letting me know that where I am in my moment, is where I am supposed to be.

"Grace isn't just forgiveness, it is forgiveness fueled by surrender."
— *Amy E. Spiegel*

During the day, it is so easy to forget my list of reminders, preferring to go to a movie or visit with friends, straying without awareness that I am off track.

And so, it is with messages of recovery. Daily reminders are the rituals we hold onto and depend upon. They are our lifeline. They help keep us on the beam, walking in the sunlight of the Spirit. They encourage us to do the next right thing. Instead of letting our mind dissolve into thoughts of darkness following a maze of fear-producing turns, our daily reminders keep us attuned to our higher purpose for living.

Morning rituals provide the space in our mind necessary to regroup, rethink, and re-center ourselves on what is important. Remembering to pause when agitated or doubtful throughout the day is vital. Without this intentional hesitation, life set on auto-pilot can create drastic results without notice. The Tenth Step encourages a review of our day by silently reflecting what we can do to repair our standing with others.

Sometimes we get flustered. This simplistic ritual of daily reminders, while automatic for normal folks, is a process many of us have to work at remembering. It requires a discipline that encourages us to do it, regardless of how we feel about it.

As I remember how grateful I am for simple rituals and daily reminders, I become humble knowing that I need them for my recovery, as they require my personal attention with a focus on my actions.

What are some of the daily rituals that you use to start or end your day?

TODAY'S MEDITATION

Daily reminders encourage me to stay the course, be in the solution, and practice living for the greatest good of everyone.

"Rituals keep us from forgetting what must not be forgotten and keep us rooted in a past from which we must not be disconnected." — *Tony Campolo*

DETACHING WITH FORGIVENESS
NOVEMBER 19

How many days, months, years, have we abused others, holding the gavel of judgment over everyone but ourselves?

It was effortless to be judge and jury when it came to judging others; a prosecution necessary to stop us from looking at ourselves. "This was all *your* fault!" we said to them. Consumed with self-righteous indignation and grandiosity, we could not admit that we dug our hole a little deeper each time we focused on the shortcoming of others. That hole constricted us ever-tighter in a grip of shame and guilt because we knew we were in the wrong when we did it.

Recovery through The Steps allows us to climb out of the hole of denial we dug for ourselves for all those years. Each time we point fingers at others, we stop to remind ourselves that it was *us* who first needed forgiveness. It never was about the other person. Forgiveness was the answer all along. Each time we forgive ourselves for shades of our old behaviors, we detach from them and discover a personal triumph for having done so. We seek out opportunities to make amends as each negative thought reminds us—we are the problem.

Self-forgiveness frees us from the accusations we made of others and opens our heart to compassion. We do this with our Higher Power as we begin the process of detachment and forgiveness in prayer. Detaching with forgiveness from old behaviors is one of the kindest acts we offer ourselves. In so doing, we find that as we set the gavel down, we stop judging ourselves and others.

TODAY'S MEDITATION
Thank you, God, for allowing me to see it was me I crippled all those years, with the hammer of superiority. Detaching with forgiveness is life-changing.

"The greater the sin you forgive them of, the greater the measure of the Spirit that will come to you." — R.T. Kendall

BEING GENTLE WITH OURSELVES
NOVEMBER 20

I never knew how to be gentle with myself. I only knew how to be critical. I put myself down every chance I got. I used terrible words against myself in punishment and realized in those moments; I heard them as if I were still a kid being criticized by an adult. Years later, in recovery I shared a part of my story about being a recipient of hurtful words and how I wished I would have been beaten instead. In telling my story, I heard the hurt in my own voice.

Many others, just like me, harbor twisted self-images. We believe we became what we heard we were growing up, regardless of the truth. We are *not* those words we still use against ourselves today. We accepted them as truth because they were told to us by a trusted adult and we reinforced the lies, using those words against us long after we had grown up. Our actions followed our irrational beliefs.

Through the life-saving, life-giving Steps, the fellowship and trusted servants, we learn to be responsible to ourselves and to speak our truth. We do not pass on the same treatment we received as children. We treat a young child with the same kindness and respect we now offer to that child within us. We stop repeating irrational beliefs. Instead, we substitute images and self-talk we can live up to as we recreate ourselves into a person of integrity and honor that we *want* to become.

Ask if seeking a dear friend, we trust we will find a love of self we never knew, waiting for us. We continue on until we do. No longer do we shrink from what we've needed to find all along, the true love we must have of ourselves. We courageously lift one foot and then the other, out of the sludge of shameful lies that kept us hurt and diminished. We practice this until we believe it, until we become transformed and radiate our authentic selves to ourselves and to others which, for most of us, is a lifetime. Being gentle with ourselves, like our sobriety, is now our priority.

TODAY'S MEDITATION

As I look at that little child that is me in the mirror, I lean over and honor her with a kiss. I renew my commitment to no longer use words against me as I deserve affirming love.

"When I am centered on love I don't need to be better than you. I don't need to be rich. I don't even need to be extraordinary. When I am centered on love, who I am and where I am at is enough." — Renae A. Sauter

GETTING OUT OF OUR WAY
NOVEMBER 21

I used to stumble over myself, getting in my own way at every possible turn, all the while convincing others I knew what was best for them. I knew what you should do and when you should do it. I had answers I didn't even know I had! All you had to do was to ask me.

Recovery shows we are not all that we think we are and, to our dismay, have *no* answers for anyone else. Our ego screams, "Of course we do!" but it is an illusion. If we were honest, the confusion we've caused others when we intervene becomes obvious now. We've pushed them out of the way in an attempt to take the spotlight or do for them what *we* thought they needed, while those we *helped* turned away.

Awareness gives us tools to begin the leveling of pride which starts when The Steps work in our lives. Being able to see the confusion we created for others, was the beginning of a personal transformation of our own self-centered pride into humility. As we make a place for our Higher Power to live within us, we begin to talk less and listen more. We accept that we are not unique, just an equal among millions of equals. While we may hold the keys to our lives and sit in the drivers' seat, we let our Higher Power be the navigator on our journey. What a miracle it is to trust enough to get out of our own way!

When we become right-sized and allow others to be who they are without contradiction, we get out of our *own* way. We stay small, which is right where we belong.

TODAY'S MEDITATION
Just for today God, I will remember you are in charge, and give thanks that it is no longer me.

"Get out of your own way. Often we're our own worst enemy when working towards our goals." — Robert Kiyosaki

HOW HAVE WE HURT OTHERS?
NOVEMBER 22

The aftermath of one of our drinking fiascos is often punctuated by the realization that, while under the influence we caused serious harm to others. We
engaged in deceitful actions and said things that, once sober, were difficult to
take back and, even more painful to face.

Harms of indifference are one example of how we hurt others. In our emotional and physical unavailability, we are immune to the pain we cause. The
harm is a result of our underlying selfishness and self-centeredness, often a
central theme in our homes, and the source of exasperation and heartbreak
for family members. The more we try to minimize broken promises, cover
our lies through overspending, commit acts of omission and overindulgence,
the sicker we become as we strive to regain the trust of others. Without
recovery, we are doomed to do the same things expecting different results.

Those who loved us were betrayed because we couldn't stop addictive behaviors, no matter how hard we tried. We never meant to hurt anyone. Sensing
we were already judged, we engaged our addictions with a fury to numb our
self-loathing. Denial was the veil that had to be lifted before we could see the
real truth about our harms.

Sobriety through recovery and restitution may or may not be enough to elicit
forgiveness in others. If it does, it is a miracle beyond measure. Regardless
of the outcome, we stay clean and sober, even if we are not forgiven, and we
continue to walk the walk of blessed recovery.

TODAY'S MEDITATION
My sobriety is not contingent upon forgiveness from others. It is through hon-
esty with myself and my God that I earn respect and regain the same from those
I love, in your time, God.

"The truth is, unless you let go, unless you forgive yourself,
unless you forgive the situation, unless you realize that the situation is over,
you cannot move forward."— Steve Maraboli

GRATITUDE

NOVEMBER 23

A gentleness not recognized comes over me and I feel grateful.

I close my eyes long enough to bring that feeling to my heart. As my eyes open, it feels as if the world before me is magically transformed.

Gratitude embraces me and I am at peace with the grace of what it feels like to breathe in and exhale blissful rest in the now. In this moment, I am aware of being as small as a blade of grass as I grow, flourish, and reach toward the sunlight of the Spirit drawing a little closer each day. This feeling is unlike any other. All encompassing, it is the anchor that holds me in profound humility like soil to a rooted blade of grass.

Blissfully, I am transformed, wrapped in a profound knowing, cradled in the arms of an all-encompassing grace.

Oh, the magnificence of gratitude!

TODAY'S MEDITATION
Dear God, gratitude takes the lead and I follow, with thanks for all you've given me.

"As we express our gratitude, we must never forget that the highest appreciation is not to utter words but to live by them." — John F. Kennedy

HAVING OUR NEEDS MET
NOVEMBER 24

Living with the disease of alcoholism, it was normal to blame others for our unmet needs. We blamed employers, spouses, and children when our needs weren't being met in the manner and time we thought they should be. As long as we indulged, we believed the burden of taking care of us belonged to the other guy. We saw no need to become self-reliant, and so we stayed the ever-stunted victim.

There are many ways to address the issue of having our needs met. Some of us do this passively, allowing others to tell us what we need. Others become angry, demanding our rights with complete disregard of anything or anyone else. Then there are those who are calm, yet assertive, believing that to be in charge of one's life is to ask for what we need. Being assertive nurtures self-esteem, encourages compromise, and reduces anxiety, whether we get what we want or not. We already know the difference between what we want and what is necessary for our security, safety, and self-respect

Recovery readies us to have our needs met by the actions *we* take. It encourages us to care for and accept responsibility for ourselves. Our newfound sense of self-reliance is powerful proof of our growing emotional maturity. As we develop honest assessments of what we need by searching within, our needs become fulfilled through collaborative action with our Higher Power and our own intuition.

We deserve to have our needs met either by ourselves, or through asking directly and lovingly for the help of others.

TODAY'S MEDITATION
I remember that as a work in progress I will not always prevail; but if I don't ask, I won't receive.

"What we call happiness in the strictest sense comes from the (preferably sudden) satisfaction of needs which have been dammed up to a high degree."
— Sigmund Freud

MINDFUL ABUNDANCE
NOVEMBER 25

As I put pen to paper in thoughtful prayer, I create a spiritual portal in my mind that opens my heart to receive an abundance of love and faith. My capacity to receive the love of my Higher Power grows as bliss and contentment begin to wash over me in a gentle flow.

This is an energy that illuminates my psyche. It is a fulfillment. The vibration of energy travels from my head to my heart where it expands, filling me with gratitude for the effortlessness of my breath. The simplicity of existence, like a soft, moving cloud, engulfs me as joy radiates outward from my heart, my limbs, through my skin.

This mindful abundance of life brings a blessed joy. While still in peaceful contemplation, I rest, content in this moment that where I breathe is enough. Here, a peaceful mind and spirit reverberates an awareness that abundance is—the blessing of less.

In this moment there is nothing I need as I sit in mindful abundance in the presence of my Higher Power. This completeness of my day is my spiritual experience.

TODAY'S MEDITATION

With a deep breath, I inhale all that is given to me in the moment with quiet gratitude.

"Realize the past no longer holds you captive. It can only continue to hurt you if you hold on to it. Let the past go. A simply abundant world awaits."
— *Sarah Ban Breathnach*

BEING OF SERVICE
NOVEMBER 26

Very early one morning the telephone rang. As a member of a recovery hotline, it was my week to receive calls. On the other end of the line was a soft, feeble voice, someone reaching out for help.

Being of service, any kind of service, is the reminder of why I am alive. Examples abound in the big book of *Alcoholics Anonymous* that reminds us our most important purpose, besides maintaining sobriety, is to help others. When I'm helping you, I forget the problems looming over me. The simple act of talking to another connects me to the rest of my world, much like a lightning rod discharging a jolt of electricity, rendering it harmless.

It is not a coincidence that service is not only our Twelfth Step but it is also one of our three treasured legacies. Without service to others, there can be little recovery. Over seventy-five years ago, one alcoholic talking to another became the backbone of service and our fellowship. As a result, *Alcoholics Anonymous* was born.

Even now, this scene is repeated day-after-day, hour-after-hour, for it is through helping others that *we* stay sober. Each time our voice proclaims hope to another, each time we share our experience, our strength, our hope with resolve, we are graced beyond measure.

We work the twelfth step and intercede to help another sick and suffering person who is just like me.

TODAY'S MEDITATION
Recovery is the miracle that happens because I have come to believe in my own worth which in turn encourages me to help others. Today I am a gentler, kinder person because of helping others.

"The best way to find yourself, is to lose yourself in service to others."
— *Mahatma Ghandi*

THIRTEENTH-STEPPING
NOVEMBER 27

There are times when men or women in recovery take more than a passing interest in a newcomer. A seemingly innocent offer is made to meet after a meeting over coffee to talk. A newcomer in recovery is easily influenced, often without boundaries, scared, and desperately wanting to be a part-of.

There are some people in the rooms with their own agenda that does not necessarily include sobriety. Some prey on the newcomer. Thirteenth-stepping, or intentionally circling a newcomer, can be an emotionally charged encounter. Such encounters in our sacred rooms hold no reward for the newcomer, whose sole purpose should be to focus on themselves and their newfound sobriety without intimidation or manipulation by anyone.

Distraction by a thirteenth-stepper can nudge the newcomer out the door. In this confusion, they may drink or drug again—too afraid to return. This is one of the reasons some sponsors remind us that men stay with men and women stay with women.

Each of us has a right to feel safe in recovery, and, if threatened, to feel comfortable enough to tell someone who can help.

We are committed to a single purpose: to stay clean and sober, and to help others achieve sobriety.

TODAY'S MEDITATION

Dear God, please open the newcomer's eyes to protect the fragility of their newfound sobriety. Help them to recognize and avoid interference from those whose agenda does not coincide with our singleness of purpose.

"Once I stopped focusing on the guys and started focusing on The Steps and my own recovery, everything changed." — Anonymous

MIND MY OWN BUSINESS
NOVEMBER 28

A private investigator has a bumper sticker that says, "Your Business is My Business." On a personal level, some of us were delusional enough to believe that is true of us as well.

But when your business is your business, and my business is mine, everyone wins. When we stay out of the business of others, including immediate family members, when we live without having a need-to-know about anything outside of ourselves, we have a better chance of living in the peace we long for. No longer do we need to gossip or hold unnecessary opinions. Minding our business means we've stepped down from the bench of judgment over anyone's inventory but our own.

Sponsors lovingly remind us that we are a full-time job.

When we ask, "What is not our business?" our sponsor replies, "Everything but you!"

Our business begins and ends with ourselves and the actions and reactions we are responsible for each day to maintain the highest level of serenity.

TODAY'S MEDITATION
With your help, God, I will keep my magnifying mind where it belongs and not look for attention by taking another's inventory.

"Justice means minding one's own business
and not meddling with other men's concerns." — Plato

WHO WE ARE TODAY
NOVEMBER 29

In looking over our lives we reflect on careers, passions lost, and people once loved who have slipped away, out of view. Sometimes, we resurrect them in our minds, imagining what life would be like today were they still with us. We're told it is okay to look back so long as we don't stare. Through assimilation, we carry them with us, and bring the best of our yesterday's, into who we are today.

Maybe we always wanted to be more like that special someone no longer a part of this world. We can take those attributes or mannerisms that made them who they were and incorporate them into our own life. Imagine the satisfaction that comes from carrying more than just a memory of that person with us and sharing their best traits today. Did they have a unique knack of doing or saying something silly, always at the right moment? Were they likely to perform a random act of kindness, give a special hug, a handshake or communicate something remarkable? Did they have an abundance of love and kindness? We become who we are today because of those who have gone before us.

While it's not the same as their being with us, they are here in spirit, present through us as we call on them. We become a conduit of their goodness, fulfilling part of who they were. In this way, they live in, and through us.

We are reflections of the intellect, talent, and grace of others, passed on to us through our Higher Power. We can incorporate the attributes of those who left before us into who we are and then pass them on.

Who we are today is proof that no one is gone if the best of who they were lives on in us today.

TODAY'S MEDITATION

Dear God, thank you for allowing me to see the goodness within each of us. I'm grateful we are all connected, in some way, and that the good in those gone before us can live on in me.

"All things appear and disappear because of the concurrence of causes and conditions. Nothing ever exists entirely alone; everything is in relation to everything else." — Buddha

FRUSTRATION
NOVEMBER 30

One definition of frustration is falling short of maintaining desired results. Many times in my life I have failed to maintain results. No matter what the situation, the outcome was always a sliding back into old destructive habits. I became discontented, and discontent quickly became frustration.

Repeated disappointment goes hand-in-hand with being a victim. This line of reasoning feeds into negative talk that starts with, "What is the matter with me?" Typically, this signals that something more is going on with us. After all everyone suffers disappointments it's not like we are being singled out. The inability to cope with life's disappointments, expectations and fears can be a problem.

When experiencing frustration, a different approach is helpful. Giving ourselves healthy and empowering messages works. We ask for patience and tolerance, even if it is just enough to quell the frustration. There is no room for perfection in recovery. Asking ourselves, *How Important is it?* helps to put frustration in perspective. A little self-compassion comforts us when things don't go our way.

TODAY'S MEDITATION
Help me, God, to focus on outcomes I want to achieve and let go of frustration. Right here, right now, I am doing the best that I can.

"Our fatigue is often caused not by work, but by worry, frustration and resentment." — Dale Carnegie

GIVING IT AWAY

DECEMBER 1

Giving it away in recovery means we have changed. We've changed enough to put another's well-being before our own. We've gone out of our way to share with others proof that if we could change, then anyone can. We lead by example. By seeking to incorporate the principles of recovery in all of our affairs, we allow others to see a spiritual connectedness, a faith beyond measure that moves before us and enables us to stay clean and sober.

Through a giving heart, we become the change that inspires others to want what *we* have as we give of ourselves away. Without this selfless, loving act of sharing what we have, our gifts wither and we return to an isolated, self-centered existence.

Our giving is not showy. We are not saying, *look at me! See how good I am?* Giving it away is a silent demonstration of selflessness. Whether we call a newcomer, extend our hand in conversation, or share our story, opportunities for giving what was so freely given to us are all around in and out of recovery.

Abundance creates more abundance. When we give ours away, our wealth only increases.

TODAY'S MEDITATION
Thank you, God, for positioning me as a change-agent for others. In recovery we *are* the example of change that can lift up the sick and suffering.

"...we can seldom keep the precious gift of sobriety unless we give it away."
— *12 Steps and 12 Traditions, page 151*

NEW YEAR PREPARATIONS
DECEMBER 2

We often imagine setting new goals beginning with the New Year. We vow time and again to come closer to an ideal we've set for ourselves, but still fall short. Maybe we lacked determination. Although we thought the goals were what we wanted, we became overwhelmed, defeated, or just changed our minds.

This year, we commit to the Big Five. These are five goals considered important but attainable. They aren't expensive, or grandiose. We began small and kept them within reach of our personal best. It could be we promise to read a book a month or take a new class. Maybe we make a pact to begin a hobby or habit we've always thought about. We may decide to perform one random act of kindness each month for someone we don't even know. What matters is the *energy* that precedes our actions as we pursue and move closer to our goals.

Reaching these dreams is one way the universe acknowledges the significance of our efforts. It makes bigger dreams a reality, because we've already proven to ourselves and our Higher Power that we deserve to carry them out, and we do!

We deserve to dream and receive gifts that lie ahead, sight unseen, just by accomplishing them. Happy New Year dreaming and achieving!

TODAY'S MEDITATION
If I *see* my dream, then it is already within me to make it my reality. I'm so grateful for the sight of faith.

"Cutting out drama... Healthy mind and body choices...
Intent followed by action... Keeping real friends and letting go of the pretends...
Livin' clean for Twenty Seventeen!" — Steve Maraboli

HOLIDAY GIVING

DECEMBER 3

Before recovery, holidays were often stressful. We worked overtime and over-did everything. There were too many people to please, too many parties, too many gifts to buy, and too much money to spend, even when there was none. Then came the baking, cooking, and our own exaggerated expectations. Holidays became our permission to perform beyond the everyday norm and revel in our achievements. Look what we've done! Our payoff became more insanity, and less grandiose accolades than we thought were deserved. We told ourselves we were unappreciated, overworked, and exhausted from giv-ing and doing. We were resentful!

Recovery teaches that, not only do we seek balance in *all* things, but that we can satisfy our need to celebrate the holidays by giving of our time to those less fortunate. It doesn't bloat our ego, nor is it as flamboyant as walking in with an armload of gifts, but the rewards are genuine.

A loving sponsee was distressed at the thought of being alone over the hol-idays. Her child had moved away, and she cried, not knowing what to do. Someone suggested she buy fresh bouquets and visit those also alone in the hospital or nursing home. She recounted her personal satisfaction going room-to-room, leaving a flower and a piece of her heart as she gave of herself to a series of strangers.

When we give without expectations, it helps others while stimulating endor-phins within our bodies, and we feel fulfilled. We become connected to others on a spiritual level instead of a material level. As we give for the simple pleasure of giving, we lead with our highest, intuitive selves. The pressure of giving enough, spending enough, and being enough is no longer a concern. What fulfills us is the act of rising above ourselves to experience our spiri-tual connectedness to others, and becoming a part-of, through the unselfish giving of our time.

This selfless giving is the essence of living in abundance.

TODAY'S MEDITATION
Please use me, God, to be a channel for your peace and an example for others.

"If you want to feel the truest spirit of Christmas, go out and find someone sadder than you, lonelier than you, poorer than you … The best Christmases always require the gift of self." — Toni Sorenson

LET THERE BE PEACE ON EARTH...
DECEMBER 4

In remembering this beautiful tribute, the words that linger are, "And let it begin with me." This timeless classic reminds us of the power we hold to affect change. If we want peace and freedom, we are responsible for making it happen.

No longer are we like leaves being swept away by another's opinions or suggestions. How we interpret our world and feel about those in it belongs to each of us. As we accept our truths, we realize our need to live an authentic life in a manner pleasing to our Higher Power. Assessing our day becomes easy as we look to what is important for our hard-fought peace and serenity. Our prayers for discernment of His will, and for the power to carry His will out, becomes routine for us.

We only thought our happiness came from making others smile, or as we exchanged pain for satisfaction, but our energy was being misdirected. Everything we think and do must begin with us. Until we go deep inside to find our truth, we cannot change our inner "peace on earth."

Change must begin with me.

TODAY'S MEDITATION
It feels wonderful to know that regardless of others' reactions or fleeting feelings that they are not facts and require no response from me unless I choose to do so. I will be who I am by letting my life begin with me.

*"Let there be peace on earth and let it begin with me.
There is nothing to do but be."*— Stephen Levine

AWFULIZING
DECEMBER 5

Awfulizing sets into motion a chain of self-fulfilling thoughts, feelings and actions. Expectations that things can get worse cause our thinking to predict and sometimes actualize our own failure.

Some call awfulizing making a mountain out of a molehill. We go there when we want to make a point. Drama. It is a game we play to engage others in a myriad of fearful, negative scenarios. We become stressed and exaggerate the worst outcome of what *could* happen, *may* happen, *might* happen, or has a good chance of happening. But, rarely, does it ever happen.

How do we stop awfulizing?

Recovery offers options for us to consider. We take a deep breath in and then breathe out the excitement created by awfulizing. "It" hasn't happened yet. We assure ourselves our thinking must be outside our 24-hours which is where we live, and we **STOP**-right where we are. With intention, we look down at our feet and remind ourselves we are right here. We know in these moments, we are content, and life is unfolding as it should. We say the simple prayer, *Higher Power, please help me* and change our thinking. We get into action.

Awfulizing is the mistaken belief that life could not get any worse and we are powerless. Awfulizing expresses the *enormity* of our helplessness: a ruse, an attention-getting reaction used as an excuse to engage in fear-based behaviors. It is old behavior. If we sit immersed in the thrill of our "what if's" long enough, we drive ourselves to drink!

What we fail to remember is that we hold more control than we recognize. Recognition is awareness and awareness is a premeditated, thoughtful response. It means when we pay attention to our awfulizing, we take control of these fear-based falsehoods and apply *positive* energy through empowerment. We are in charge of our emotions. We change direction, change perspective and create a loving space for our reality that exists where we breathe because this is the only time we have to stop the madness of awfulizing.

"I think and think for months and years. Ninety-nine times, the conclusion is false. The hundredth time I am right." — *Albert Einstein*

LET IT BEGIN WITH ME
DECEMBER 6

In the sister program of Al-Anon, a typical part of their closing ritual says, *"Let it Begin with Me."*

The mantra of the three-C's carries a message meant for all of us: (a) I didn't cause it; (b) I can't cure it; and, (c) I can't control it. That leaves me the only person I have the power to change. I cannot control what my husband wears, what he says or the image he portrays to others, even though before Al-Anon, I spent years trying.

Recovery teaches that we keep the focus of change on ourselves, our thoughts, and our reactions. The change we seek is progress, not perfection. Al-Anon tells us to be gentle with ourselves, as we practice these principles. The less we harp on our spouses, our parents, and others, while letting change begin with me the easier our lives become to manage.

Accepting that we are the only ones who we can change without creating a personal disaster, keeps this thinking simple. We quit trying to control the actions of anyone as we sought the outcomes we thought were best for them.

When we place more importance on our peace and serenity, our lives change. Together with those we no longer seek to control, we find mutual respect and a common peace as we mind our own business.

We remember that whenever we are engaged with others, we pause, breathe, and, *"Let It Begin with Me."*

TODAY'S MEDITATION
Today, I find satisfaction in setting a course for myself which others may emulate, but only if they choose to. I let peace begin with me.

"If you will change, everything will change for you. Don't wait for things to change. Change doesn't start out there, change starts within.... All change starts with you." — Jim Rohn

AN ATTITUDE OF GRATITUDE
DECEMBER 7

The opportunity to look at the world through grateful eyes is there at all times, but the ability to do so is, for many, a learned process.

In the first step in this attitude adjustment we come to understand that just because we may feel like a martyr, or like we deserve to be angry and upset, we need not include others in our disappointments.

Part of our payoff for stinking-thinking is sharing our woes with others, so they could appreciate and feel sorry for us, too. We call this, "Pour Me—Pour Me a Drink, behavior." As we become clean and sober, we realize that initial change, which is keeping pain to ourselves, is too much work. And so, we move to the next step which is letting the pain go.

While addicted we were sure if we felt something, we had to embrace it. When we were happy, we became over-the-top happy; and, when we were sad or disappointed like an actor, we reveled in playing the part to the hilt. In sobriety we discover that we have power over our feelings.

As we become responsible and aware of thoughts, behaviors, and appropriateness of our response, we see the enormous power within ourselves to change our perspective and feel better by putting the grievance down and turning toward the light.

It is only in hindsight we realize what has happened. We have become grateful.

TODAY'S MEDITATION
Thank you, God, for every breath I take. I thank you for allowing me to find gratitude in the moment.

"When a person doesn't have gratitude, something is missing in his or her humanity. A person can almost be defined by his or her attitude into gratitude."
— Elie Wiesel

RELEASING OTHERS
TO BE WHO THEY ARE
DECEMBER 8

One side-effect of addiction was holding my family so tight there was no room for them to be who they wanted to be. They were consumed with dodging the landmines of my expectations, my fear, and the guilt I induced when they did not meet my incessant demands. I was a master controller.

My husband lived for a short six months around my fifth year of sobriety. For the first time I became the wife and loving helpmate he had always wanted. I gave my husband and daughter to our Higher Power, recognizing at last it was not me who controlled their lives. I stopped dictating, acting as if I knew what was best for them, because I didn't. With acceptance and lots of practice I let them go to be who and how they wanted to be as I said the Third Step Prayer.

Sometimes life-altering events have to happen before we reconstruct and put into practice new life lessons. Peace and bliss come through acceptance. By embracing our authenticity, we allow our Higher Power to do its job. As we continue to trust the process of recovery, we become right-sized, putting our attention where it belongs, back on us.

TODAY'S MEDITATION

Dear God, I see so clearly the harmony and love that flows from allowing others their right to be who they are without interference from me.

"The individual has always had to struggle to keep from being overwhelmed by the tribe. If you try it, you will be lonely often, and sometimes frightened. But no price is too high to pay for the privilege of owning yourself."— *Friedrich Nietzsche*

MAKING DECISIONS
DECEMBER 9

The song, *Should I Stay or Should I Go,* reminds me of my typical style of decision making, which meant making no decision at all. I was scared of offering an answer, afraid I would make the wrong choice. I never trusted myself. "What if I'm wrong?" was my slogan. I couldn't bear the thought of being judged. Trapped, stuck, and alone, I was incapable of forward motion.

A friend suggested I hang a picture of myself as a child in the bathroom. Each morning and night I leaned over and kissed that little girl, assuring her of my protection. I embraced my goodness and let go of the mistaken beliefs that had held me hostage for so long. The more I trust myself, the easier it is to make sound decisions. I leaned on my *God gut,* that intuitive part of me, and heard that the only mistake I could make was to make no decision at all. The change was modest at first. Progress began in making little, inconsequential decisions.

The miracle of recovery is proof we are not walking our journey alone. Today we can be thankful that our decision will be the right decision because our Higher Power is working with us in prayer. There are no mistakes.

TODAY'S MEDITATION
I am free to assert myself and make decisions. When I invoke my God, my motives and answers become clear.

"Don't entrust your future on others' hands. Rather make decisions by yourself with the help of God's guidance. Hold your beliefs so tight and never let go of them!" — *Hark Herald Sarmiento*

TRUST IN TIMING
DECEMBER 10

I've learned that when my life doesn't work out the way I think it should, it's because it's not my turn to receive whatever it is I think I need. This universal truth helps me to keep my yearnings in perspective.

When the student is ready, the teacher appears. When our heart is open and we gain sufficient emotional and spiritual maturity to grasp what's about to unfold, we are ready to accept and receive whatever comes. Although the outcome may not be what we want, faith shows it is always what we need. This unveiling is evidence of the will of our Higher Power, and it can be trusted.

Instead of suffering stress and worry, we bend like a willow tree, accepting the lesson that this is how it should be. In our Higher Power's perfect timing, we trust we are not alone. We trust the unspoken timing of a force greater than ourselves, and we rejoice in the promise that when it's our time to know, more will be revealed.

TODAY'S MEDITATION

Burdens are lifted from me when I relinquish my need to know. There are no coincidences in God's world, only perfect timing.

"I've learned over the years to appreciate God's timing, and you can't rush things; it's gonna happen exactly when it's supposed to." — Sevyn Streeter

A GRATEFUL HEART

DECEMBER 11

An old-timer in recovery often talked about the need to have a grateful heart. He told us how his ability to see life through an attitude of gratitude protected him from life's more challenging situations. He assured us there was nothing in life that could make it worthwhile to restart his addictions, then he told us how he kept that promise. "Our job," he said, "Is to find gratitude in everything."

Sometime later this beloved and respected member in recovery contracted cancer. Even though he could hardly remain awake and upright after his chemo regimen, he made his meetings, continuing to show others what love and acceptance looked like, and how to face, even the darkest times with an attitude of gratitude.

Today we remember this humble, gentle man and pass on his example of acceptance, his attitude of gratitude.

TODAY'S MEDITATION
I'm so grateful that as I keep coming back, I have the opportunity to learn how to live life from others who came before me. With their example I practice an attitude of gratitude.

"The best and most beautiful things in the world cannot be seen or even touched – they must be felt with the heart." — Helen Keller

TO THINE OWN SELF BE TRUE
DECEMBER 12

My experience has been that lessons do not come into our awareness until we are prepared to accept that lesson as our truth. Living through the eyes of addiction, I never considered the mantra, *to thine own self be true*. How could I be true to myself when I stood for nothing at all, except for my singleness of purpose at the time: my next drink or drug?

Years later in recovery I was told to remove my necklace containing my daughters' ashes while at work. Because of my non-compliance, I lost that job. I would have never learned the lesson that few truths are non-negotiable had I removed that necklace. As I remained steadfast, I saw I had been true to myself, *regardless* of the consequences.

After that firing, facing financial insecurity, I trusted Higher Power that I would be taken care of.

Job or no job, I am assured in prayer and in faith I am in charge of my reactions to situations. I remember there are no mistakes in Higher Power's world and have faith another door will open for me when it is my turn.

Integrity is the confidence that comes from not compromising what is important: being true to self, regardless of what happens. Today I stand in faith with Higher Power.

What are your truths?

TODAY'S MEDITATION
Today, I remain true to my sobriety, myself and my God. These three are non-negotiable.

"Rather than love, than money, than fame, give me truth."
— *Henry David Thoreau,*

GRATITUDES, BACK-TO-BASICS
DECEMBER 13

I am fortunate to have lived two lives: the life I suffered before sobriety, and the life I am living today in recovery.

Writing gratitudes is often the first thing suggested in early recovery and with good reason. Gratitudes have the power to transform how we feel about our world and ourselves. As we write, we see and we feel just how dark and hopeless our life was when we looked for but could not find gratitude. Hidden deep beneath years of self-loathing, shame, and self-pity is the essence of who we *still* are, but have only seen glimpses of: a curious child filled with love, compassion, and goodness. Our job is to resurrect this lost part of us ourselves from the depths of our consciousness.

We retrieve all we are as we put pen to paper and list what we are grateful for. As we write them, many of us experience an actual shift in thinking. This is our miracle of hope. We start small and keep gratitudes simple as we notice in awe, the magnificence that comes from the freedom of our arms moving, and, too, the freedom of hands and fingers as they glide over paper. As we close our eyes, we smell and feel our world, observing new gratitudes one-by-one, as the miracle of faith often begins here. We follow where the spirit leads and with each sentence, our gratitudes increase.

We are grateful because by now we're convinced if we spot it, then it's already within us. Our job is to name it, claim it as our truth, and feel the power transferred from our fingers, on to the paper, then back to our psyche.

Keeping it simple is the ritual of learning to maintain the focus on us, our breath and every spiritual gift we own. With practice, we see how much worse our life could be as we feel gratitudes reach high above our past, above our negativity, and above our hopelessness. The air is light, weightless, as our gratitudes transform us, one line at a time.

Gratitudes are the acknowledgements we make to the universe that all is well.

TODAY'S MEDITATION

I am forever grateful for the miracles and transformations that become available to me through the courage of faith, hope, and gratitude.

"Be thankful for what you have; you'll end up having more. If you concentrate on what you don't have, you will never, ever have enough."— *Oprah Winfrey*

THE BEGINNINGS OF SELF-CARE
DECEMBER 14

For as long as I remember, I assumed self-care meant selfishness, so I worked to become the best people-pleaser I could. I thought constant acts of selflessness fulfilled a primal role called care-taking and did it all without complaining.

In recovery I came to see that by honoring myself with the same consideration I gave others, my reward was that I became less a gladiator for those around me and more a champion for myself, because I saw that I deserved it.

We are such works in progress.

As I walk baby steps on this journey of self-care, I see opportunities to nurture myself all around me. As I put myself, my Higher Power, and my recovery above all else, these are the inward signs of a love of self, necessary to become efficient, balanced, and better able to discern what my self-care needs are. In this manner I am prepared to assist others in ways they cannot do for themselves. When I practice self-care, everyone wins.

TODAY'S MEDITATION
Thank you, God, for reminding me of my worthiness to indulge in self-care.

"Affirmations are our mental vitamins, providing the supplementary positive thoughts we need to balance the barrage of negative events and thoughts we experience daily." — Tia Walker

IT'S NOT SUPPOSED TO BE
DECEMBER 15

In a recent conversation with a friend who had lost his wife and other loved ones, we talked about his missed opportunities to say goodbye. The only thing I knew to say was, "If it was supposed to be different, it would have been."

This is a mantra that offers us a free pass to forgiveness. We have no way out otherwise, except to berate ourselves, and to pay for situations we deem should have never happened.

In truth, we have no idea what the course of events should or should not have been, but remorse resonates deep as we ask, "What happened? What should happen next? Can't anyone see this but me?" We think we need a reason, an answer, some justification or logic. We hope beyond hope that knowledge will soothe our anguish, but our questions echo in an empty room.

The easier, softer way in recovery never changes. We accept what is. To do otherwise is to invite self-flagellation that implodes misery over the past that cannot be changed. As we futilely imagine other outcomes, our Higher Power screams back, "Don't *you* get it? This isn't about you!" This is how I've worked since the beginning of time."

If a situation was supposed to be different, it would be. The dots would have connected, the desired outcome would have happened without force, duress or angst. Everything would have fallen in place meeting *everyone's* expectations. But it didn't.

We have a choice today to accept what is, or to struggle. We know how to struggle; it is an inherent part of our makeup. What we find so difficult to do is to accept and surrender to what is. The choice is still ours. We can let go of our preconceived notions and feel comforted that our Higher Power has everything under His control. Or we can rail against what-is, while our Higher Power *continues* to call the shots. Because only He can.

TODAY'S MEDITATION
A wise sponsor once said to me, "You don't have to like it, you just have to accept it!"

"Understanding is the first step to acceptance, and only with acceptance can there be recovery." — J.K. Rowling

DENIAL
DECEMBER 16

If someone were to ask you if you were in denial, what would you say? How would you know? Could you recognize it? Denial speaks to us so persuasively, it seems as if it is telling the truth.

The voice of denial says, "My life would be so much better if only *you* would….." Denial always lays the blame on someone else. I spent what seemed a lifetime denying my part in my troubled marriage, or anything else others would identify as my responsibility, working hard to deflect any hint of wrong-doing. I became a perpetual liar and soon was known as someone who couldn't be trusted or depended upon, for anything.

It took my walking into the rooms of *Alcoholics Anonymous* to quiet the voice of denial. It took asking for help. It took a surrender, with an openness I never knew I possessed, to sit and listen to the other guy. Writing gratitudes and recognizing how they made me feel, was the start of breaking down the denials that masked my fear.

We have to get honest and look at things we can do to change our denial, our inaction, into acceptance of what is, followed by action aimed at fixing what we can. How can we open doors of positive, healthy and reassuring change in our life otherwise?

TODAY'S MEDITATION
Today I am free to share with others. My secrets have been set free.

"You will find peace not by trying to escape your problems, but by confronting them courageously. You will find peace not in denial, but in victory"
— J. Donald Walters

GRATITUDE IN SOBRIETY
DECEMBER 17

As I sit and begin my morning ritual of prayer and meditation, I prepare myself to receive whatever the universe needs me to hear. I light a candle that signifies the light and thoughts I hope to receive from Higher Power. This ritual helps me convey the magnitude of intention and gratefulness that, for so long, was crowded out by deep despair and sadness.

In recovery, we substitute gratitude for grief, self-pity, and negative emotions. Success in recovery depends on our ability to change our thinking in all things. As we practice rituals of positivity, we feel a profound shift in our outlook. We may not have a job, enough money, or a place to live, but those in recovery with us offer reassurance and hope that, together, we can survive anything clean and sober no matter the obstacle. And we do.

As we look at our blessings, feelings of self-worth and hope increase. This ritual of gratitude practiced each day encourages our excitement for life. As we embrace the solution instead of the problem, we become conscious of a sustaining grace that could only come from our Higher Power who walks before us. In these moments of gratitude, we realize we are loved unconditionally.

TODAY'S MEDITATION
Thank you, God, for the grace that grounds me to my world. Just for today, I will continue to keep my thinking small so I will never exclude yours.

"Walk as if you are kissing the Earth with your feet." — *Thich Nhat Hanh*

EXPECTATIONS OF OURSELVES
DECEMBER 18

Growing up in our family disease of alcoholism and emotional turmoil meant expecting the sky to fall as I tried to be perfect and dodge accusations of wrongdoing. Predicting ever-changing expectations required telepathy. I sensed I never measured up, falling short of some imaginary expectation of others, a disappointment to everyone. I became a perpetual people-pleaser with an inferiority complex. It was a prime set-up for failure.

Recovery offers miracles of self-discovery. The Steps prove we only need to meet expectations of ourselves. We examine our motives. What are *our* expectations? What is important? What is it *we* need? How will this work for *our* greater good?

By learning to be true to ourselves, the word **no** becomes the road to a secure self-esteem regardless of anyone's acceptance but our own unless it enhances our highest-self. Recovery promotes a trust of our loving, nurturing, inner-interpreter, whose purpose is to guide us through these and other questions of what we expect from the rest of our day. When we trust our Higher Power, clean house, and help others, our reliance upon our voice grows stronger.

TODAY'S MEDITATION
Dear God, thank you for giving me courage to remember that expectations of myself are the ones I must scrutinize.

"I'm not in this world to live up to your expectations and you're not in this world to live up to mine." — Bruce Lee

I AM NOT ALONE
DECEMBER 19

I knew I was different from my friends, family and work associates. Never content or comfortable in any situation, I saw myself as odd-man-out: out of relationships and communication skills, standing outside the periphery of life. I didn't fit in anywhere, and always felt alone, damaged and unacceptable to others. Drugs and alcohol provided me with the same merrymaking I saw in others.

One day though, everything quit working. Fear and shame of being me returned, and I experienced a crevasse of loneliness never imagined.

Recovery offered a way out of the sick world I had created, and I accepted. The fellowship availed itself, and with the constant hand of a Higher Power, I never had to be alone again if I didn't want to be.

I am learning how to replace that dark hole in my chest with my Higher Power and the fellowship. On most days although alone, I am not lonely.

TODAY'S MEDITATION

Dear God, thank you for being ever close to me. You are proof that, just like me, anyone can have this miraculous gift of sobriety without ever having to be alone again.

"I think this is what we all want to hear: that we are not alone
in hitting the bottom, and that it is possible to come out of that
place courageous, beautiful, and strong."— Anna White

LEARNING TO LEAVE UNWORTHINESS

DECEMBER 20

I've heard it said that life is forever trying to love us. Addiction is the embodiment of the perpetual tug-of-war we engage in with our ego that says we are unworthy of sobriety. For years I drenched myself in old beliefs of unworthiness. So convinced was I of never amounting to anything, I remained a mental midget, an under-achiever long into adulthood preferring to perfect a role called "not good enough."

For some of us, the courage to look within is often born out of one last hope to rid ourselves of emotional pain. As thoughts work against us, we begin an intense and personal dialog with our inner child. The power of The Steps and inner-work continues to shed layers of unworthiness. In the place of unworthiness grows a newfound conviction of positive self-worth. We retrieve our power of self-worth and allow fears and mistaken beliefs to disappear. As we honor and embrace that little child deep within, our ego becomes balanced. We become a competent reflection of the person we've always wanted to be.

I know because it worked for me, it will also work for you!

TODAY'S MEDITATION

The gift of courage in sobriety has given me a choice to see that I am worthy of so much today. I embrace and hold tight with love, the little child that is me.

"I am willing to release the need to be unworthy. I am worthy of the very best in life, and I now lovingly allow myself to accept it" — Louise L. Hay

ACCEPTANCE OF WHAT IS
DECEMBER 21

I grew up in recovery when the aura of my home group was sacred, and mutual respect and hope ranked high for individual healing. Sometimes energy in the rooms changes because people change. People we know come and go while others are there for the wrong reasons. They may be court ordered. Some expect a quick fix to save their marriage, their job, and threats of a divorce because of DUI's.

Sometimes egos remain "at large" and never get out of the way. Some people are disruptive and the focus of the meeting gets lost. There are those that can be down-right rude.

This is when we need to practice acceptance of what is. We are mindful that *our* disturbance is the result of a lack of acceptance. We do not tolerate a person, place or thing, and admit that some fact in our life is unacceptable to us. Without acceptance of what is right then, we become disturbed. The disturbance is always about us and our expectation of what should or should not be happening. It's not about a meeting gone off course or someone's ego taking over, although it could be. When we are disturbed, *it is about us* and our lack of tolerance and acceptance, since we are affected. In these moments we have no compassion for others, which means—we have none for ourselves.

We know how to get up and walk out. To do so means we've learned nothing at all. Old behaviors run rampant and we have missed the lesson of looking within. How do we accept an intolerable, bothersome situation? Will changing my perspective help? More that can be imagined. We pray for that person and remember that just like them—we are sick too. We show acceptance, and practice love and tolerance through acceptance of what is.

TODAY'S MEDITATION
My serenity depends that I remember when in our rooms, I am charged with being an example of others see what emotional maturity looks like. In quiet prayer, I accept what is, take what I need, and leave the rest.

"My philosophy is it's none of my business what people say of me and think of me. I am what I am, and I do what I do. I expect nothing and accept everything. And it makes life so much easier." — Anthony Hopkins

Embracing the Sunlight of the Spirit
December 22

Sitting on my porch, I watch the day begin. The warming rays of the sun opens wide the leaves on the trees that shimmer in radiant hues of colors. Reflections dance in greens and gold.

As heat from the sun caresses and warms my face, I am engulfed in the radiance of the day. In an instant, I'm reminded of the beautiful, breathing soul that is me.

In unspoken prayer, I embrace the sunlight.

The brilliance of the sun ignites the universe before me. Transfixed, I rise with my spirit to meet it, overwhelmed in gratitude. I am connected to a oneness that is my world.

TODAY'S MEDITATION

Thank you, God, for the magnificence that is you. I am at peace, so blissfully grateful to be alive.

"I want God to play in my bloodstream the way sunlight amuses itself on the water." — Elizabeth Gilbert

GIFT GIVING
DECEMBER 23

Gifts were one way some of us manipulated others while in active addiction. It was a way of staying in good graces with friends and family. We did nothing to earn their respect, their trust, or love, other than purchase something. It was a sad substitute for what they wanted, which was us. Addictions though, worked hard at keeping us away. Holidays were even more stressful as our egos engaged in an exaggerated game of extravagance.

Over time in recovery, messages of balance, motives, and intent become a normal part of our thinking. We look at actions daily and substitute precious time for frivolous gifts. As we examine motives for gift-giving, we see a compromise such as giving a treat where everyone can be engaged. Maybe the act of honoring someone special with a homemade meal with imagination would be worth as much or more than dousing them with quick afterthoughts of no significance.

With more creativity and less pomp, we discovered we could give of ourselves. Gift giving takes on new meaning and provides an abundance of appreciation as we give from the heart, with precious time and, most of all, with love. The saying, "Money Can't Buy Love," is true. It cannot be a substitute for what our families need and want the most of all, our sober presence and support.

TODAY'S MEDITATION
Thinking of doing for others for the sheer act of doing is my gift to me. I see value and necessity of giving with intention, but always, from the heart.

"The greatest gift one can give is thanksgiving. In giving gifts, we give what we can spare, but in giving thanks we give ourselves." — David Steindl-Rast

Knowing What We Need
December 24

There wasn't a day when I didn't have a handle on what it was I thought I needed. Whether the need was food shopping, planning events, work considerations or forecasting, I had the answers to everything; I thought.

Recovery brought me to humble submission. Imagine my shock as I read a passage from one of our stories where a doctor conceded he did not understand what was good or bad for him. He turned his will and his life over to the care of a God as he understood God. This story, taken from "And Acceptance Is the Answer," in The Big Book of *Alcoholics Anonymous* stopped me in my tracks. How could I know with certainty what was good for me, let alone my loved ones, or anyone else?

In recovery we find that what we think we know is often nothing more than an illusion, an opinion. The fact is, we have no evidence of power nor of what we need in five minutes, an hour or a week from now, let alone what anyone else may need. Time is fluid and elusive as people and situations change in an instant.

The lesson is, if we don't know what is good for us, then we might as well keep our thoughts and opinions to ourselves.

TODAY'S MEDITATION

Dear God, thank you for the reminder that the more I *think* I know, the less I know.

"I know that I am intelligent, because I know that I know nothing." — *Socrates*

PREPARING FOR THE NEW YEAR
DECEMBER 25

The closer I get to the end of the year, my personal pain and trepidation rise over lost opportunities. I so desperately want the shame of my addictions to stop but don't know how to begin. I resolve next time, it will be different.

Today is the day to change our thinking beyond what we ever imagined possible. It begins when we walk into the rooms of recovery. With nothing more than a change in our perspective, we change our thinking and our actions soon follow. It is that simple. We don't *have* to wait for the New Year, the next holiday, the next excuse to stop our addictions. Today is all that there is so, right here, right now, why not do something different?

This moment could be our last alive. Making a change is nothing more than the risk we take as we get out of bed. Haven't we been in fear long enough? Haven't we given in, changed our minds, taken a step back and retreated just like we've always done? Imagine instead, making a brave move to grow through change. We don't have to be all-or-nothing people. We change with slow deliberation one moment at a time.

It starts with a decision to succeed. Today, we own our power because our actions prove sobriety and serenity are the most exciting changes ever before us. It's the beginning of purposeful planning of our hard-earned freedom. What a great New Year of possibilities this can be!

TODAY'S MEDITATION
Dear God, with your grace and my preparation for the New Year, I expect success.

"We spend January 1st walking through our lives, room by room, drawing up a list of work to be done, cracks to be patched. Maybe this year, to balance the list, we ought to walk through the rooms of our lives...not looking for flaws, but for potential." — Ellen Goodman

SELF-FORGIVENESS
DECEMBER 26

So much time passes before many of us can glue together pieces of our shattered souls. In my dysfunctional home to survive I sought the mask, the right persona, to protect me. I thought this mask would shield me from a barrage of questions and accusations. Instead I felt isolated, hopeless, and trapped.

Most of us with addictions know they want freedom from the terror and bondage of self that holds them paralyzed in fear but have no hint where to begin. Working each Step with a sponsor brings relief and a healing forgiveness. Like the withered leaves that give way one-by-one to new growth, our hearts begin a transformation of letting go of the hurts and false beliefs that kept us strangled emotionally. The glimpse of self-forgiveness through exploration in our Fourth Step and the light our sponsors uncover in the Fifth Step, prove to be a start to a forgiveness of self that is life changing.

We saw drugs and alcohol mask a multitude of pain. Forgiveness, combined with a commitment to loving ourselves, our recovery, and our God, allows for light to expose our soul so truth will, forever, set us free.

TODAY'S MEDITATION

Each day as I look at myself, I'm reminded of my obligation to me, and the consistent need for self-forgiveness.

"Self-forgiveness comes when we realize that if God has forgiven us, we needn't remain angry with ourselves, needn't hate ourselves any longer. God will use it all for good." —Robert Morgan

OWNING OUR POWER
DECEMBER 27

Life is a roller coaster. Someone is angry and we take it to heart. A wonderful event happens, and it fills us with complete joy. In recovery, we learn the secret of our capacity for positivity and resilience no matter what comes. No longer do we move as a weeping willow tree, bending, swaying with each blow of the wind. Our tenacity and courage come from within.

Awareness gives us the courage to replace outdated messages and lies with positive and powerful affirmations. This intuition requires an intensive fact-finding exploration within and a sincere readiness to trust and work with our own Higher Power. With this awareness, we focus on forgiveness of ourselves and others in every area of our life.

Owning our power over our own happiness is a sign of a growing independence. With maturity, we grow along spiritual lines. With practice self-forgiveness becomes automatic. So does letting go. We embark on this path to freedom and quit fighting everyone and everything. As we continue in practice toward a love-of-self and gentleness with that little child within us, our capacity to heal the gaping wound that once defined us becomes stronger. By forgiving ourselves, we have made space deep within, with enough freedom to forgive others.

TODAY'S MEDITATION

Dear God, as I close my eyes, I face myself with quiet acceptance, grateful for your sovereign watch over me.

"God's grace is amazing! We're saved by grace - God's undeserved favor - and we live by grace, which is also God's power in our lives to do what we could never do in our own strength...." — Joyce Meyer

DIVINE INTERVENTION
DECEMBER 28

There was no *one moment* when my spiritual and intuitive transformation took place, but before recovery, I lived a life warped by delusions of grandeur as though on a stage all my own under a spotlight. I was sure my disproportionate ego wanted me to believe I was more alive and did everything better under the influence.

Then I picked up a pen and wrote what I felt down.

Through the power of journaling, a connection of mind, body, and spirit took hold. Although I couldn't articulate, or bring to light, gentleness in my words when speaking, I discovered a softer way to express myself on paper. Putting pen to the page allowed me to touch the heart of truth. With my words captured before me, I couldn't look away, deny, or manipulate who I was any longer. This was the beginning of my Divine Intervention.

A conceptual shift about who I was, and what my drug of choice did for me began when thoughts were transferred to paper. It was the start of an honesty with myself and allowed for a deeper faith to grow.

With that newfound faith, I felt the touch of a warm healing hand, and it began with the simple act of admitting to myself, in black and white, all that the insanity of my addictions had cost me, and where I now found myself.

TODAY'S MEDITATION
Today I align myself with the power of positive energy. Gentle awakenings reveal themselves as I walk this journey, pen in hand, and do the work one day at a time.

"Faith is an oasis in the heart which will never be reached by the caravan of thinking." — *Khalil Gibran*

PERFECT PEACE
DECEMBER 29

As I sit in quiet contemplation, I allow my Spirit and thoughts to drift at random without constraint. With eyes closed, I attune myself to the ebb and flow of my breath, transported to a place of perfect peace and calm.

Comforted, I am right where I'm supposed to be, doing what I need for spiritual healing.

I am aligned with our Higher Power, my heart and soul open to receive all I need.

As I seek to remain teachable, thoughts flow like water in a channel, coursing, turning. Before they go around the next bend, I bring them back to center, taking what I need and leaving the rest.

On my spiritual journey I become a fascinated observer.

My aura is the lantern that lights blissful awareness. I am here now, centered, grateful for this perfect peace and calm.

TODAY'S MEDITATION
I relax in these moments of profound enlightenment, grateful for your lead, God, as you are forever with me.

"You may assuredly find perfect peace, if you are resolved to do that which your Lord has plainly required, and content that He should indeed require no more of you — than to do justice, to love, mercy, and to walk humbly with Him."
— John Ruskin

LET IT BEGIN WITH ME
DECEMBER 30

Many Al-Anon Family Group Meetings close with the phrase, *Let it Begin with Me*. At first, I took this mantra as my own, falling into the familiar stance of victim. "Here we go again," I'd think. "It's all *my* fault."

But *Let it Begin With Me* doesn't mean more self-sacrifice, more guilt. This mantra is at the core of an awareness and acceptance that holds the power for change. No longer do we manipulate or use those around us. We conserve energy for changing what we can inside ourselves and let our Higher Power take care of everyone else.

Let it Begin with Me is the welcoming entrance to a life we could not have imagined when we thought we carried the world on our shoulders.

Freedom to become the person we have always wanted to be, while detaching from the unhealthy behaviors of others, slowly becomes our new reality. This concept is the guiding principle behind the wonderful life-altering steps we practice. Accepting this truth, we take responsibility for ourselves and our lives continue to change as we practice *Live and Let Live*.

Now we know where we begin and end.

TODAY'S MEDITATION

Dear God, I'm grateful to be a representative for all that you exemplify, and recognize that I am the only person I can change.

"Change your opinions, keep to your principles;
change your leaves, keep intact your roots." — *Victor Hugo*

A YEAR IN REVIEW
DECEMBER 31

As the new year fast approaches, I sit in quiet contemplation, remembering the highlights of yet another year gone by. It seems the harder I try to grasp where I've been these last 365-days the less I remember.

I've heard it said that to know where we're going, we have to remember where we've been. It helps to institute a ritual of writing intentions as we approach the New Year. This list includes ten to fifteen achievable goals listed in order of significance, on or near the opening page of a journal that begins with the New Year.

The day before New Year's Eve, we look at our list from the beginning of the present year and check off goals achieved. This becomes our year in review. We determine whether we need to carry forward those items not checked off from the year before, or create a new list of goals and intentions. This exercise lets us see what we've done, where we've been and provides a road-map to help us accomplish what we have identified as our goals for the year ahead. As we look at those lingering goals and examine new ones we ask, "Is it achievable?" Our goals should not set us up for failure. They should be within reach.

As we choose these goals we frame the life we desire and consider the direction we must take to get there. Looking back over the year past, we see where our intentions shifted and new goals surfaced.

Sometimes, everything on our list will change and at other times, everything is achieved. But writing the list is a good way to begin the journey that is a new year while looking back at the goals from the previous year keeps us honest. Enjoy your journey. With intention we can make our dreams and miracles come true!

TODAY'S MEDITATION

It is exciting to review where I've been. This pause to reflect over my year allows me to change my course and develop a new direction for my life, with purpose, while celebrating goals achieved.

"Write it on your heart that every day is the best day in the year."
— *Ralph Waldo Emerson*

ACKNOWLEDGEMENTS

Heartfelt thanks to my mother, Esther Latz; Delores Gurr, my first counselor; and my aunt Rena B., who loved me when I couldn't love myself. To my dearest mentor and friend, Juliet C.; to Scott M., treasured counselor; Kakie P.; Jo S.; Kathy S.; Carla H. Special thanks to the first woman I ever trusted and worked The Steps with on-line in 1999, Marlee L., now deceased.

To wonderful beta readers Annette K., Carla H., Ed V., Ewart F., Kevin K., Linda R., Richard D., Sharon S., Scott M., Terry C., and Veronica S., who gave so freely of their time and energy. Special thanks for her expertise go to my editor, Adrian Fogelin, author of *Crossing Jordan* and numerous other Young Adult works; and to Gina Edwards from AroundtheWriterstable.com, for her patience and depth of insight so freely given. I thank you both.

To the village of writers, authors, consultants and editors I've been privileged to learn from: to Lyla Ellzey's Critique Group and my awe-inspiring *Sisters of the Sentences* who coached, counseled, loved and believed in me. Because of all of you, *Miracles of Recovery* is a reality. To Rhett DeVane, award winning author of *Parade of Horribles*, and several other books, for suggesting the title, *Miracles of Recovery*.

Each contribution helped to produce what I hope will touch the hearts of my readers in some small way.

Always and forever daughter,

Laura Kristen

December 2, 1986 – August 6, 2013

Next Steps

1. Get your FREE REPORT, *Eight Steps to a Powerful Change in Perspective. Stop negative thinking and change your life* at www.HarrietHunter.org. You'll also receive a complimentary subscription to my newsletter, which covers topics like fear, faith, trusting the process and a lot more!

2. Like my Page at: Facebook.com at: www.Facebook.com/recoveredru to get more tips, strategies and inspiration to live a more inspired life!

3. Please take a quick moment and give me a review of this book in Amazon. Your review is so important and will help to guide me further in my writing endeavors. Thank you.

ABOUT THE AUTHOR

When she's not writing, Harriet spends time blogging and helps others in AA via on-line support groups and in meetings. She loves playing with her two dogs, golfing, cooking and taking care of her home and property. Harriet also developed and facilitates a six-week journaling class entitled, "*Journaling With a Purpose.*"

Harriet belongs to the Tallahassee Writers Association, Florida Writers Association, Florida Association of Poets and Authors, and writing critique groups. She is working on Book II.

Testimonials

Miracles of Recovery is a must read for every person early or seasoned in recovery. The heart-wrenching and heart-warming stories will stay with you throughout the day as you meditate on the lessons learned from others' journeys."

Melanie Barton Bragg, LCSW Ed. D; author of
*Quicksand: Marion's Memories, a story of emergence from
a dysfunctional marriage to a sexually addicted minister."*

After reading *Miracles of Recovery,* I found it to be one of the best summations of all the wonderful and spiritual sharing that I have heard around the rooms of recovery over my eleven years of sobriety. This is a joyous book and should become a part of the A. A. approved literature as well for daily reading for those in and not in the rooms or recovery. **Miracles of Recovery** is a fine spiritual book that can benefit and inspire anyone, especially those that may be currently struggling with the myriad of causes and conditions of life on life's terms."

Will Evans; Author of, *The Hydrologic Balance of Lakes:
Physical and Mathematical Fundamentals*

Miracles of Recovery is a compilation of alluring musings that can only be inspired by grace. If you are among the many that begin their days with a quiet time of prayer and meditation, I suggest that you invite these inspired messages into your repertoire. For me, this book serves as the conveyor of many spiritual blessings and has prompted me to gently and humbly self-critique in order to flourish and thrive in my life of recovery."

Jane Dwyer Lee, MSW, LCSW

"Harriet's daily meditations are filled with truth and compassion that comes from personal experience. This work reads like the author is right there with you, providing insight and encouragement and, above all else, hope."

Cassie Dandridge Selleck; Author of, *The Pecan Man* and
What Matters in Mayhew; www.CassieDandridgeSelleck.com

This is a program that works if you work for it. Harriet tells you how in a personal day- to-day journal I have found very useful. As she says, take what you need and leave the rest. I encourage you to explore what she says and see how it can apply to your life. It does get better.

James McMichael, Ph.D.; Author of 1997 Best Book for Business,
The Spiritual Style of Management: Who Is Running This Show Anyway,
Co-author of *Spirituality in the Workplace.*

NOTES:

Each reference from *Alcoholics Anonymous* World Services, New York is used with permission. They are listed here. Each quote was taken from the first 164 pages, Third Edition., Thirty-eighty Printing, 1990.

1. *Alcoholics Anonymous; Third Edition, Chapter 5 in How it Works*: "Half measures availed us nothing..."
2. "Amazing Grace," written by John Newton, Lyricist, 1808
3. "Assets", noted in AA's 12 Steps and 12 Traditions, Forty-Fourth printing, 2007
4. *Alcoholics Anonymous*; "Spirit of the Universe"
5. *Alcoholics Anonymous.* "Great Reality"
6. Alcoholics Anonymous, Chapter 5 in How it Works: "Half measures availed us nothing."
7. *Alcoholics Anonymous*, "Yes, there is a long reconstruction period ahead."
8. Alcoholics Anonymous, Chapter 5 in How it Works, "Some of us have tried to hold on to our old ideas and the result was nil until we let go absolutely."
9. Alcoholics Anonymous: "...pause, when agitated or doubtful..."
10. *Let it Begin with Me*; by Jill Johnson and Sy Miller, first introduced in California in 1955
11. Alcoholics Anonymous with regard to "Instructions for Living"
12. Alcoholics Anonymous, with regard to service work; "Our real purpose..."
13. *Alcoholics Anonymous*, "Faith Without works is dead."
14. *Alcoholics Anonymous*, "And acceptance is the answer..."
15. *Alcoholics Anonymous*, "We are going to know a new freedom and new happiness."
16. The Serenity Prayer, early 1930s by Reinhold Niebuhr, "...the courage to know the difference."
17. "To Thine Own Self be True," coined by William Shakespeare. In Act 1, Scene III of *Hamlet*
18. *Dr. Wayne Dyer, "Getting in the Gap", Hay House, Inc., publisher; 2014. "puts us in that space where we return to our Higher Power."*
19. *Margaret Mitchell, "Gone with the Wind," Published 1936, "As God Is my Witness, I'll never be hungry again."*

20. *"Should I Stay or Should I go" by the Clash; released in 1982 on the album, "Combat Rock"*
21. *Alcoholics Anonymous*, Third Edition published 1990, "we step on the toes of others…"
22. *Alcoholics Anonymous*, Third Edition published 1990, "we step on the toes of others…"
23. *Alcoholics Anonymous*, Third Edition published 1990, "a daily reprieve contingent on the maintenance of our spiritual condition.
24. *Alcoholics Anonymous*, Third Edition published 1990, "…sometimes quickly, sometimes slowly."
25. *"Let There be Peace on Earth";* written by Jill Jackson and Sy Miller in 1955,
26. *Should I stay or Should I Go*, written by The Clash.
27. The 12-Steps of Alcoholics Anonymous https://www.aa.org/assets/en_US/smf-121_en.pdf used with permission of AA's General Service Office.

Index

D

E

F

P

R

S

W

Y

31765131R00271

Made in the USA
Columbia, SC
03 November 2018